World Faith in Action

World Faith in Action

The Unified Missionary Enterprise
of Protestant Christianity

EDITED BY

CHARLES TUDOR LEBER

THE BOBBS-MERRILL COMPANY, INC.

Publishers

INDIANAPOLIS · NEW YORK

266U
L492

117134

Contents

Introduction

This book comes out of a sense of great need—the need for more adequate information and for stronger and more compelling conviction as to what the Church is doing and is able to do in such a world as ours.

Here are some of the questions people are asking: Is the Church winning or losing ground? Does the Church have any actual knowledge of, or relevance to, what is going on in the world? Will Communism succeed in wiping Christianity off the face of the earth? Isn't there a way the churches may unite to defeat Communism? Hasn't the overseas work of the Church merely been "pouring money down a rathole"? In this era of power politics and economic revolution, of what good are the Church and religion, anyhow? Can any religion stand up under the modern scientific discoveries? If there are about 700,000,000 Christians in the world, where are they and what are they doing? Isn't one religion just as good as another? Hasn't the atomic bomb become the determining factor in history and in most minds superseded Almighty God? Hadn't we better admit that today the Christian has been "left, with all his unrivaled powers of expression, rather vague about what to express"?[1]

One must neither condemn nor evade these questions. They must be answered, if we are to have a free and better world. They rise out of the mind strain and heartache of both Christians and non-Christians torn by two world wars, totalitarian slavery and unbelievable destruction. They come from minds tormented by pain, frustration and disillusionment. People are tired, hurt and afraid —even the strongest.

We believe the answers to these questions are in the great factual story of "world faith in action"—the Christian faith at work throughout the world.

[1] Evelyn Waugh, *Helena* (Little, Brown and Co., 1950), p. 113.

7

Christianity is not the only faith doing business over the earth today. The faiths of Communism, Fascism, Islam, Buddhism and other modern and ancient religions are very much alive. They offer their answers, too. Indeed they are contending desperately for the searching mind of modern man. Christianity must be willing to meet all needs and claims. It isn't a question of argument. It's too late for that. It's a matter of life or death. Therefore, we formulate no academic treatise. Our emphasis is strongly on the side of urgent action.

Implicit within the story told in these chapters is the meaning of Christian faith. We have not attempted to state an explicit, comprehensive definition of our faith, fundamental and necessary as that may be. We give, rather, "the reason for the faith that is in us" in terms of its impact on life and by documenting the results of its individual and collective expression. The testing formula today is inherent in: "By their fruits ye shall know them." Nevertheless, that there may be clear understanding, we heartily identify ourselves with an international group of Christians who, threatened by the catastrophe of war, in answer to the question "What is the Church's faith, in its special meaning for our time?" replied:

"We live by faith in God, the Father of our Lord Jesus Christ.
"Above all and in all and through all is the holy will, the creative purpose, of the Most High. The world is His and He made it. The confusions of history are in the grasp of His manifold wisdom. He overrules and works through the purposes of men, bringing to nought their stubborn and rebellious lust for power but building their fidelity into the structure of His reign upon earth.
"Man is the child of God, made in His image. God has designed him for life in fellowship with Himself, and with his brothers in the family of God on earth. Yet in the mystery of the freedom which God has given him, man chooses to walk other paths, to seek other ends. He defies his Father's will. He seeks to be a law unto himself. This is the deepest cause of the evil and misery of his life. Alienated from God, he seeks his salvation where it cannot be found. Impotent to save himself, he stands ever in need of conversion, of forgiveness, of regeneration.
"Who then shall save? God saves, through Jesus Christ our Lord. 'God so loved the world that He gave His only begotten Son that whosoever believeth on Him should not perish but have

everlasting life.' This is the heart of the Christian Gospel, the Gospel which we proclaim." [2]

Above and beneath, within and completely surrounding all that is written in this book is personal, living and eternal Christian faith.

On the basis of this faith, we who contribute to this book have come together as members of the ecumenical fellowship to present the world Christian case. In our writing we have not been able to withdraw from the "heat and burden of the day," nor have we desired to do so, even temporarily. Rather, we have recorded timely and dynamic evidence of the Christian movement while actively participating in its global strategy.

We have limited the story, almost completely, to the increasing purpose and current affairs of the Protestant Church. Able men have filled many shelves with the perspective of Christian history. Further, we leave to those far better qualified to write what the non-Protestant churches are doing. They, too, have much that should be told of present faith, heroism and devotion. We have made no attempt to tell the whole story, nor could we. But we do believe the most significant contemporary facts and determinative trends are here. Of course the Christian story is still in the making. The chapters that will be written later may well be the most thrilling and hopeful of all.

With accent on action, even the proceeds from this book will contribute to the task in which we are united. Except for minimum payments, the royalties will be given, equally divided, to the International Missionary Council and the World Council of Churches.

Friends and associates in many lands have been of invaluable help in the preparation of these pages. They are too numerous to name. Each one will know, nevertheless, how grateful we are. We must mention, however, Miss Mary A. Nesbitt for her invaluable assistance in the editing of the manuscripts and Mrs. Robert E. Washington for handling so efficiently the stenographic task. Most of all we are indebted to Mr. Julius Birge, of The Bobbs-Merrill Company, Inc., for his initiative, counsel and friendly encouragement.

[2] *The Madras Series* (International Missionary Council, 1939), I, 174.

Justice William O. Douglas once met with a misfortune which almost cost him his life. He was restrained for a long period by a severe physical disability. Describing his emergence, he wrote: "At last I felt released, free to walk the trails and climb the peaks and to brush aside fear." [3] These words express what we dare hope, in spiritual terms, this book may mean to many now held captive by the sickness of our time.

C.T.L.

Brightwaters
New York

[3] Douglas, *Of Men and Mountains* (Harper & Brothers, 1950), p. 108.

World Faith in Action

What Too Many People Don't Know

1

By CHARLES TUDOR LEBER

THE Iranian plane suddenly veered to the left, dipped perilously and sharply leveled again. The nerve-racking roaring of the engines and the shuddering of the fuselage never let up for an instant. I glanced out of the window. Proud, towering Mount Demavend was now on our right. No doubt we had turned about and were flying back toward Teheran. Looking around the interior of the old weather-beaten crate, stripped of everything but its twenty leather-covered seats, I saw that none of the passengers was much concerned. There were only five of us. The two Iranian passengers were reading. Both of my fellow Americans were sleeping. I settled back, relaxed, and soon would have been asleep too, except that abruptly the cockpit door opened and a tall, stout girl pushed sideways into the cabin. She was bulging out of a blue, frayed uniform. Her faded blue cap rested like an overturned china bowl on a bushy mass of brown tangled hair. She reminded me of the "conductorettes" during the first World War on the old trolley cars in Baltimore. This stalwart lass was our stewardess. Later I learned that she was a refugee from Poland.

Before the cockpit door was closed I caught a glimpse of the heavy-set French pilot on a high-back seat behind the controls. A big cigar stuck out of his mouth. He, too, was much overweight. He wore a plain blue uniform and a visored cap. He looked for all the world like a prison guard. Two other men, in European clothes, were in the cockpit also, a copilot and a radio operator, both Persian.

The stewardess, with a pleasant smile, spoke in Persian to the two Iranians on her right and then in English to the three Americans at her left. She confirmed what already we had surmised. We were going back to Teheran. "Engine trouble," she added. We

13

hoped for the best—and it happened. We came down with surprising smoothness and safety. We were right where we had started from an hour before. Stepping down the steep, narrow metal ladder which hung on the doorsill of the unpainted Douglas C-3, I noticed that the wide barren airport was just about empty. Only one other Iranian air liner, a BOAC ship and an Air France Douglas C-6 stood unattended near by.

Two Iranians in overalls began yelling something in Persian to the stewardess as she disembarked. The pilot climbed down, still with the cigar, and then the shouting grew louder and more furious. The stewardess beckoned to the bewildered passengers, huddled together by the plane. We followed toward the airport building. Then an Iranian air-line official appeared as from nowhere and ordered us to follow him. This we did. In a moment or two we were climbing aboard the other Iranian plane. The heated argument, in which the official, the pilot, the ground crew and the hostess joined, rose to a terrible clamor. The official won out. We stayed on the Iranian plane. It was a duplicate of the former, but it did a better job. The engines burst into a tumult. The plane and we trembled. We were hurled along the hard dirt runway. Up we lifted. We set our course toward Meshed, 600 miles away. And this time we didn't turn back.

The terrain between Teheran and Meshed is rugged and treacherous. Sharp crags and steep crevices cut crazily through the vast barren, brown, mountainous heaps of dead earth. Now and then one could barely see small strings of tiny objects penciled on a pass —caravans of pilgrims. Meshed, now on the edge of the horizon, appeared fantastically unreal as we flew across the last mountain range and came upon the wasteland border plain 7,000 feet below. The ship was behaving beautifully. We seemed to be hanging motionless in mid-air. The mountains receded. An ocean-wide expanse of sand was far beneath us. We looked down and watched the immense spread of flattened wilderness slowly roll by. Alone, isolated, surrounded by unending desert, the city of Meshed now became quite visible. Flat roofs of muddy-yellow houses set rigidly in rows, with darker yellow ribbonlike streets between, were interrupted frequently by the smooth, mounded tops of mosques. Minarets pierced upward. Meshed is one of the eight provincial capital cities of Iran, the farthest eastward, just over 100 miles from Afghanistan and not more than 50 miles south of the U.S.S.R. border. Meshed is a holy city. For some Moslems it is more holy than Mecca. It is a city crowded with pilgrims, especially at "Ashura."

It was at the height of this celebration that we arrived in Meshed. The streets were filled with seekers after Allah. The magnificent golden Imam Riza Shrine and the adjoining Mosque of Gohar Shad had drawn thousands from all over the Moslem world. The broad pavements around the sacred buildings were covered with the prostrate bodies of men and women, young and old, that they might be cleansed from their sins and find the assurance of the Eternal. We dared to go nearer than we should to the holy places. An Englishman had been stabbed to death not long before because he had approached a sacred doorway. We meant no disrespect. Cautiously we walked past the high-arched, mosaic-bordered entrances to the shrine and the mosque, awed by the throng of worshipers pressing all about us. Evening came, the city was quiet. Amid the long shadows we walked through the narrow cobblestone streets between forbidding high mud walls cut away, here and there, by native shops with open fronts blocked carelessly with expensive Persian and cheap American merchandise. Shopkeepers sprawled lazily on packing cases in the entrance ways smoking their kalians. We entered a brick-walled compound at the edge of the city enclosing a small Christian chapel. A capacity congregation of Iranians and a few Americans had gathered to receive us. Together we worshiped God.

But this was not the end of our pilgrimage. A borrowed car took us beyond Meshed out on the desert to an oasis. There we found a concentration of misery uncomparable to any other suffering. It was a leper colony. The lepers were sunning themselves at the gateway. They followed us, hobbling and crawling, as we walked hesitantly past rows of dilapidated shacks, their dwelling places. A small park of trees and grass was in the center of the compound. Out of a miraclelike spring a stream of water flowed through the oasis consolingly.

An American Christian physician was our guide. He had come to the colony on his semiweekly visit from his mission hospital in Meshed. He led us into a little frame building where the worst cases were. I drew back cowardly. Except that shame prevented me, I would have turned away. The ward contained undistinguishable forms. One could not tell whether a man, a woman or an animal lay huddled on each bed. Suddenly a cry from one of the beds startled us. A strange, unearthly cry it was—not of pain. It had an exulting sound.

"What in God's name is that?" I asked.

"It is a poor, blind leper," my interpreter replied. "He has recognized the voice of the Christian doctor. In Persian, he has cried out, 'Thank God! You have come!' "

Thus we found the Church, the Ecumenical Church, in a far-distant, almost unknown frontier city and, also, on a desert oasis near the border of Afghanistan. . . .

An idiot child, perhaps ten or twelve years of age, lay stark naked on the station platform. Her frail body was covered with a crust of dust. She moaned and twitched and sighed. I almost stumbled over her. It was eleven o'clock at night, in Ludhiana, a frontier town in northern India, not far from the Pakistan border.

A train was standing at the station. I hurried toward an open compartment, threw in my bags and bedding roll and turned, wondering what could be done for the girl. I watched policemen, soldiers, merchants and travelers pass by, some even stepping over the tragic little form. Most seemed to be accustomed to such things. Perhaps some felt as helpless as I did.

The business of life went on heedlessly. Hindu hawkers, carrying their wares or pushing them in unkempt carts, kept repeating and repeating their insistent, shrill and haunting cries. Emaciated baggage coolies shuffled along overladen with luggage. Lame and deformed beggars in filthy rags besieged the train. Railroad laborers loitered sullenly and dismally. A family of Britishers sauntered across the platform. Train guards stood by indifferently. The hysterical chatter and excited shouting in the packed "third-class" rose in a mad crescendo as the piercing engine whistle blew violently. The station bell clanged. The train crept away.

Looking back from the compartment window, I saw a young American in khaki shorts kneel by the Indian girl. I recognized the young man. He was a Christian missionary. I do not know what he was able to do. At least he cared. I hope he was able to comfort her. Perhaps he took her away where others healed her. If he did not, I know that soon God, in His ultimate mercy, did. For it was clear that Eternity could not be very far away.

It was my third visit to India. I know it is a truism that this chaotic nation is a land of contrasts. One sees astounding beauty and vast wealth. One marvels at political, cultural and spiritual achievement. But the curse of paganisms, old and new, like a swollen, ugly stream flooding everywhere, depressed me as never before. The poverty and suffering in both cities and villages are unbelievable. Professional beggars and the neglected poor crowd the streets, follow you pitifully, surround you at the stations, reach in through automobile and train windows with pleading hands. These tell of India's (and the world's) basic problem—the tragedy of humanity. God's humanity. And in its midst is the Church, many times on its knees. . . .

One winter's day a traveling companion and I landed at the airport in Budapest, three years after the Communists had taken over Hungary and had made the whole country a vast concentration camp. The plane was two hours late. A Hungarian Protestant minister met us. We drove to a large, historic church on the central city square. The sanctuary was crowded. The people were singing hymns. As we walked down the center aisle, it looked as though a religious convention of some sort was in session. It turned out to be a reception which the Hungarian Protestant pastors and church members had prepared for us. They had come to bid us welcome as representatives of the World Church. We were the first Protestant ministers from America to enter Hungary since the Communists had taken over. The speeches were deeply moving. We responded haltingly, endeavoring to interpret the unbroken and steadfast fellowship of world Christians. The following Sunday, in that same church, to a congregation which filled every corner, with people standing at the rear, along the walls and even down the center aisle, I preached beside a Protestant bishop, from his high pulpit, on Christian freedom. In Budapest, under Communist domination, we found the Christian Church, determined, unconquerable, ecumenical. . . .

What shall we say to these things? Are these but isolated incidents impressive because of human interest, unrelated and irrelevant to our contemporary problems? Or is there something here very basic and comprehensive, offering a way out of the present world chaos? What is the Church? Where is the Church? And what and where is *ecumenical?* Let us see.

In the first place, *ecumenical* is one of the most intriguing and poignant of words. It is, of course, much more than a word. Weighted with history, it is discovery, achievement and adventure. Many people don't know the word. And if they do, the majority are unaware of its range, power and possibilities. To those who do know, however, the ecumenical not only means "the great new fact of our time," it is hope in the face of despair, it is worldwide unity in the midst of division, it is purpose and order where chaos confuses, it is fundamental to peace.

The word *ecumenical* means, literally, "pertaining to the inhabited world," from the Greek *oikoumenikos:* from *oikein,* "to inhabit" and *oikos,* "house, dwelling"; denoting, according to *Webster's New International Dictionary,* "general; world-wide . . . *Eccl.,* pertaining to, representing . . . the whole church; as, an ecumenical council." *Ecumenical Bishop* is the title assumed by the Patriarch of Constantinople and is sometimes used by the Pope of Rome. The most common usage in history is that applied to the ecumenical church councils, of which there have been twenty, beginning with the First Nicene in 325 and continuing to the Vatican Council in 1867-1870 which decreed papal infallibility. John Henry Cardinal Newman, early in the nineteenth century, wrote: "Those writers who in every nation go by the name of Classics . . . have (so far) a catholic and ecumenical character, that what they express is common to the whole race of man and they alone are able to express it." In 1900 a Protestant missionary conference was designated "ecumenical." At the Hague in 1919, in the discussions at a meeting of Protestant churchmen from thirteen countries, planning for a world conference of churches, *ecumenical* appeared also. In both of these latter cases, and no doubt on other occasions during this period, *ecumenical* was used as indicating merely *interdenominational* and *international.*

The deeper and more dynamic use of the word prevalent today began to be planted in the mind of Protestantism in an address delivered by John Alexander Mackay, then a missionary to Latin America and now president of Princeton Theological Seminary and chairman of the International Missionary Council, at the annual meeting of the Foreign Missions Conference of North America at Atlantic City, New Jersey, in 1928. Dr. Mackay had been attracted by the definition of *ecumenical* in the secular sense which Count Hermann Keyserling, the German philosopher, had developed in the early twenties. Keyserling had interpreted *ecumenical,* as world-wideness, affirming that the world was an "ecumenical organism" in which any major stimulus applied anywhere would be felt everywhere. He further pointed out that we were in an era of world history in which, for the first time, all men were neighbors and contemporaries. By translating this concept into spiritual terms Dr. Mackay captured it for world Protestantism.

It was not until 1937, however, that the word really took hold in its present and widely accepted connotation. In the Conference on Church, Community and State held in Oxford in that year, Dr. Mackay, as chairman of the Commission on the Universal Church and the World of Nations, actually introduced the word *ecumenical* in the place of and to signify as much as but much *more* than *international* or *universal.* To the secular term *ecumenical,* meaning purely "pertaining to the inhabited world," he added a spiritual principle of unity, namely, Jesus Christ and the Christian Church. What culture was as a principle of unity in the "inhabited world" of the Greeks and law in the "inhabited world" of the Romans, Christ and the Church became in the "inhabited world" of our time. The "ecumenical" was clearly distinguished from the "international."

The "international" problem was set forth as a movement from the circumference to the center in search of a principle of unity. The "ecumenical" problem was presented as a movement from the center already found, which is Christ, in search of the implications of the unity in Him for the Church and for the world to the uttermost circumference of both. A later development in the interpretation of *ecumenical* is the Science of Ecumenics, a chair in

which was founded in Princeton Theological Seminary in 1938;
Ecumenics meaning "the science of the church universal conceived
as a world missionary community, its nature, functions, relations
and strategy."

After the Oxford conference it did not take long for the new
interpretation of *ecumenical* to catch the imagination of Protestant
churchmen. It did so quickly in America, more gradually in
Europe. With surprising rapidity it achieved universal and repeated use in religious publications, in sermons, lectures and addresses, and also in the secular press. The idea has not grown in a
vacuum. It has become vibrant with life and very real within
the experience of many men of various occupations, classes, nations
and races. This applies as well to countless thousands who have
never heard of the word or would not be able to spell or pronounce it, much less understand its meaning or grasp its implications and relationships. For they, too, though unknowingly, are
sustained and influenced daily by its fellowship and power.

Consider, then, certain significant facts of ecumenicity, not
only basic in their relevance to the crucial issues of the present
world situation, but essential to individual destiny—facts which
too many people don't know.

After two thousand years of praying, centuries of believing, forty
years of specific preparation and ten years of special planning, at
10:35 A.M. on August 23, 1948, in the Concertgebouw at Amsterdam the World Council of Churches was born. With the Archbishop of Canterbury, Geoffrey Francis Fisher, in the chair,
upon motion by Marc Boegner of France, chairman of the Provisional Committee of the World Council of Churches in the
Process of Formation, the 351 delegates from 147 churches of 44
countries, surrounded by alternates and visitors from as many or
more churches and lands, rose to vote unanimously:

That the First Assembly of the World Council of Churches be
declared to be and is hereby constituted, in accordance with the
constitution drafted at Utrecht in 1938 and approved by the
churches; that the Assembly consist of those persons who have
been appointed as the official delegates of the churches adhering
to the Council; and that the formation of the World Council of
Churches be declared to be and hereby is completed.

The major genius in the achievement of the World Council of Churches was and is its general secretary, Willem Adolf Visser 't Hooft. Prophet that he is, he foretold what would happen at Amsterdam when, some months before the First Assembly, he issued the following statement:

The emergence of a new historical development is never a smooth process—least of all in church history. Amsterdam will be the meeting place of churches most of which have lived in isolation from each other. They differ from each other in all the ways in which institutions having grown up in different cultures and situations differ. But they differ also in important points of faith, of church order, of their attitude to the world.

They will only slowly learn to enter into a truly creative discussion with each other. And the critical observer at Amsterdam will, therefore, not find it difficult to discover evidence of very real disharmony. But the great thing about Amsterdam is that none of these barriers to fellowship will be final. For these churches will not be meeting alone. They will meet under the eyes of the one Lord to whom they all owe allegiance and whom they acknowledge "as God and Saviour."

They may, therefore, hope that in spite of their formidable differences, in spite of the great confusion resulting from the divided state of Christendom, they will discover unity behind the disunity and will receive from the Head of the Church their common marching orders.

No word of hindsight could be clearer than this word of foresight. Dr. Visser 't Hooft epitomized correctly the *fact, discipline, power* and *hope* of the World Council of Churches.

The *fact*. I believe it was the late Archbishop of Canterbury, William Temple, who said: "The ecumenical fellowship is the great new fact of our time." There were long years of pioneering, courage, faith and fortitude behind that which emerged at Amsterdam when the major communions of the world (excepting the Russian Orthodox and the Roman Catholic) met together as "one body in Christ"; an irrefutable fact, the possibility of which had been so often refuted.

Who will ever forget the opening service of worship in historic and majestic Nieuwe Kerk (where two weeks later Queen Juliana was crowned), crowded beyond capacity with throngs standing in the streets outside, when, to triumphant music, the colorful procession of Christian leaders from 44 nations—black, brown, yellow, white—marched in unity? The opening addresses by the veteran Christian statesman, John R. Mott, and a brilliant younger church leader, Daniel Thambyrajah Niles of Ceylon, had a quality and significance far greater than the human.

Who will ever forget the daily meetings of the Assembly in plenary session, both business and inspirational, where the plans and programs of the ecumenical movement took stronger and bolder form? Who will not remain ever thankful for being part of one or more of the sections and committees where ideas and convictions growing out of such varied backgrounds were freely exchanged? With related documents two years in preparation, in which more than 200 theologians and lay leaders had participated under the chairmanship of Dr. Henry P. Van Dusen, the groups worked on statements for adoption by the Assembly on "The Universal Church in God's Design," "God's Design and Men's Witness," "The Church and International Disorder," all contributing to the general theme of the Assembly: "Man's Disorder and God's Design" (which Karl Barth in his address insisted should be: "God's Design and Man's Disorder").

The publications of the World Council were prepared as study and source material for global Christian strategy for many years among many nations. The findings of the First Assembly were committed to the officers, commissions and departments of the continuing World Council. There are commissions covering such areas as Faith and Order; Evangelism; Life and Work of Women in the Church; the History of the Ecumenical Movement; Churches on International Affairs; and departments of Study; Youth; Interchurch Aid and Service to Refugees; and Finance and Business. *Time* magazine found it "newsworthy" to report: "The Assembly was living proof that Christians could work and plan together."

The *discipline*. The First Assembly of the World Council of Churches could not deny history or erase human nature. Christians have differed and do disagree and will look out from the "one foundation" through different windows. The traditions and conditions out of which the delegates came brought about continuing differences as to theological concepts, ecclesiastical systems and social and international issues and patterns. However, in no debate or discussion was there sharpness, bitterness or unkindness. The determination to respect one another in admitted differences was a spiritual discipline which offered an example for the whole world—churches, classes, races and nations. The daily experience of facing frankly one another's strong differences, trying to resolve as many of them as possible and practicing Christian forbearance at all times pointed toward even greater world Christian unity—and peace.

A phrase often heard at Amsterdam was "the glory and shame of the Church." The evidence of this was recognized as we faced the history and present confusion of the Church in its dealing with war, politics, race, economic disorder and the divisions of ecclesiastical structures. Approaching Holy Communion, we were reminded that there is, as yet, no ecumenical theology. Therefore, there was, to our shame, no ecumenical celebration of Holy Communion. Four major Communion services were held: one according to the Reformed rite, one according to the Anglican, one the Lutheran and one the Eastern Orthodox. Yet the rigid lines of ecclesiastical divisions were broken and crossed by Christian personal commitment to the central fact of Christ's all-inclusive love. It gave confidence to hear that all the Communions were open to everyone. Furthermore, to take the largest of the services—the Reformed, which filled the massive sanctuary of Nieuwe Kerk—the presence of a large number of churchmen of different confessional groups of many nations (including conspicuously archbishops and bishops representing other traditions) contributed impressively toward making that meaningful service a strong international, interracial and interdenominational testimony to the holy discipline of God's love. Somehow the very shame of the weakness revealed by this division of the Church in its experience of Holy Communion led one to see "the glory of the Church": "And I, if I be lifted up from the earth, will draw all men unto me."

The *power*. Personality is power. The fellowship of persons of many nations and races so varied and far apart in customs, traditions and conditions was not merely a formal thing in conference and public meetings. The greatest value in the fellowship was the intimate contacts one had day by day. At Amsterdam it was possible to exchange ideas and concerns in small, informal groups and in personal conversations with such personalities as Báez Camargo of Mexico, John Baillie of Scotland, Karl Barth and Emil Brunner of Switzerland, Josef Bergraav of Norway, Marc Boegner of France, Sara Chakko of India, Themistocles Chrysostomos of Greece, Peter Kwei Dagadn of Africa, Hassan Dehgani of Iran, Leonardo Dia y Granada of the Philippines, Karl Friedrich Otto Dibelius and Martin Niemoeller of Germany, Joseph Hromadka and Josef Krenek of Czechoslovakia, Kontonzis of Turkey, Michio Kozaki of Japan, Stephen Charles Neill of England, Jens Norregaard of Denmark, Laszlo Istvan Pap of Hungary, Amir Sjahriffoeddin of Indonesia, Jan Szeruda of Poland and Wu Yi-fang of China, to mention but a few of the many and not to mention here the numerous representatives from the U.S.A. To come to know such as these in Christian fellowship brought one to realize that organization and policies might falter but that in the wide and strong spiritual companionship of world Christians, which is the greatest achievement of the institution of the World Council, there is power. As we heard at the Amsterdam meeting, "We have a unity we cannot define, but for which we thank God. Our practice is ahead of our theory."

And there is the *hope*. This Assembly of the World Council was only the *first*. Greater days are ahead. Now with a Central Committee of Ninety acting ad interim in directing and co-ordinating the plans and strategy which emerged at Amsterdam, and with the commissions and departments functioning and an enlarged secretariat at strategic world posts under the continuing leadership of Dr. Visser 't Hooft in Geneva, one thinks with great confidence of the basic structure and leadership of the Ecumenical Church.

The delegates at Amsterdam, however, did not base their hope in the new world organization itself. Worship dominated all the sessions. When the horizontal relationships were clouded, the vertical relationship was clear. For years the World Council fellowship will be drawing on the worship hours at Amsterdam. We mention but one :

One morning a young American Negro woman led the Assembly in worship. She was the wife of a brilliant young African physician of Sierra Leone named John Mussellman Karefa-Smart, whom she had met at a youth conference at Oslo. Quietly she guided us in prayer, in Bible reading, in spiritual meditation, in song and in silence. This was the heart of our praying:

O God, the Inspirer of our common worship and the Reward of all our seeking, visit, we pray thee, this assembly and each of us with thy indwelling spirit; unite us in fellowship with thy worshipers in all lands; and grant that our thoughts and words and the unspoken longings of our hearts may be acceptable in thy sight and may be offered in the name of our Master, Jesus Christ. Amen.

This was the spirit of our song:

> God of grace and God of glory,
> On thy people pour thy power;
> Crown thine ancient Church's story;
> Bring her bud to glorious flower.
> Grant us wisdom,
> Grant us courage,
> For the facing of this hour.
>
> Cure thy children's warring madness,
> Bend our pride to thy control;
> Shame our wanton, selfish gladness,
> Rich in things and poor in soul.
> Grant us wisdom,
> Grant us courage
> Lest we miss thy kingdom's goal.

In such prayer and song are the fact, the discipline, the power and the hope of the ecumenical fellowship.

The World Council of Churches is the latest manifestation of Christian churches in united action. It should be recognized that the World Council was preceded by the International Missionary Council, with which it is now in close association. The letterhead of the former reads: "The World Council of Churches, in association with the International Missionary Council." The letter-head of the latter reads : "The International Missionary Council, in association with the World Council of Churches."

The International Missionary Council was officially organized in 1920. However, it traces its origin to the World Missionary Conference held in Edinburgh in 1910. The Conference formed a Continuation Committee, which was able to carry forward a number of its functions even during the years of the first World War. It was almost immediately after the war that the permanent organization of a representative international council was possible. In 1928 a world meeting of the Council was held in Jerusalem, bringing together a larger number of representatives of the so-called younger churches than any previous Church gathering. In 1938 the Council held another world meeting in Madras. At this meeting the representatives of the older and the younger churches were equal, reflecting the principles on which the International Missionary Council was organized.

When one considers the range and outreach of the national organizations of the International Missionary Council and realizes that through related National Councils research and service are being undertaken in such fields as evangelism, Christian education, social welfare, world literacy and Christian literature, and that there is the continual study and projection of a united world strategy, one realizes the strength and possibilities in the present working together of the churches.

To appreciate the scope one should take time to read and let his imagination play on this list of the areas of the world in which there are effective national organizations of the International Missionary Council: Australia, Belgium, Brazil, Burma, Ceylon, China, Congo, Denmark, Finland, France, Germany, Great Britain, India and Pakistan, Indonesia, Japan, Korea, Latin America, Malaya, Mexico, Near East, Netherlands, New Zealand, Norway, Philippine Islands, Puerto Rico, River Plate, South Africa, Sweden, Switzerland, Thailand, United States and Canada. And other national Christian conferences and committees, not yet constituents of the International Missionary Council, are in Angola, Antigua, Barbados, Chile, Cuba, Equatorial Africa, Ethiopia, Gold Coast, Honduras, Jamaica, Kenya, Madagascar, Nigeria, Northern Rhodesia, Nyasaland, Peru, Portugal, East Africa, Sierra Leone, Southern Rhodesia, Tanganyika, Trinidad and Tobago.

The structure of Christian unity now has been well established. Through the combined efforts of the World Council of Churches and the International Missionary Council, the ecumenical movement is being continually strengthened. In this the long-cultivated and far-reaching interests and activities of American churches abroad have had a major influence. There are the growing "family" relationships of the churches of the same communion in the United States and Europe, interchangings of fellowship and, in some instances, of support. For many years there has been an annual general exchange of preachers between the United States and England. American-supported nonmissionary schools in the Near East and various countries in Europe have had many American teachers recruited by the churches. In Asia, Europe, North Africa and Latin America a staff of secular workers, supported by a number of American church bodies, has been doing work related to refugees and relief, including service to prisoners of war. Some Americans have been ministers to English-speaking churches in Europe, Latin America and Asia.

And there are the ecumenical conferences. For more than twenty-five years a movement has existed to bring various branches of the Church into closer fellowship around some major aspect of the Church's life. This has resulted not only in world gatherings, such as the meetings of the International Missionary Council at Madras in 1938, at Whitby in 1947 and at Oegstgeest in 1948 and the World Council of Churches Assembly at Amsterdam, but also such regional conferences as those in Buenos Aires in 1949 and in Bangkok in 1950, the latter held jointly under the International Missionary Council and the World Council of Churches.

Furthermore, in standing joint commissions of the International Missionary Council and the World Council of Churches, representatives from many lands have come together for consultation and united planning. Outstanding is the Commission of the Churches on International Affairs, which has had considerable influence in interpreting the mind of the World Church to the United Nations by consultation and memoranda. In addition undertakings in church unity have been launched and developed. Strong bonds forged in these ecumenical conferences and joint commissions hold firm in a world of division and conflict.

And there is, of course, the missionary movement. The churches of Europe, Britain and the United States have been engaged in sending missionaries to so-called non-Christian lands and by that process have trained and formed permanent relationships with many who have become responsible and trusted leaders in their own countries. The American churches have been accustomed to contribute a considerable fund annually for religious, educational, social and relief work abroad. In 1925 American churches were giving approximately $14,000,000 a year for overseas mission work. During the depression period this declined very materially, but at the outbreak of World War II such support was in excess to $20,000,000 per year. Further than that, between the close of World War I and the outbreak of World War II the churches of the United States sent Europe, largely for the relief of suffering, $55,000,000. Since World War II nearly $89,500,000 and 185,000,000 pounds of material aid have been sent from American church sources for relief efforts in Asia and Europe. American missionary personnel has had experience and knowledge of indigenous customs and social issues which fit them for a constructive part in relief and rehabilitation projects. Many types of social and educational agencies have sent Americans to participate in such service, but in this work the missionaries of the Church have predominated. There are some 15,000 missionaries from North America alone in Africa, Asia, Latin America and other parts of the world.[1]

Consider, also, the bare statistical facts of the ecumenical movement today. These, also, too many people don't know.

It is estimated that the population of the world was 2,057 million in 1933. Of this number it is estimated by *Whitaker* (1948 edition, p. 463) that 692,400,000 were Christians. This Christian total was subdivided as follows :—

[1] Charles T. Leber, *The Church Must Win!* (Fleming H. Revell Company, 1944), pp. 53-57.

Roman Catholics	331,500,000
Orthodox	144,000,000
Protestant Churches	206,907,000
Copts	10,000,000

These figures are disputed by some; the *Catholic Directory* for 1948 estimates the Catholic population of the world at 398,277,000. Another estimate of the Orthodox and Coptic population of the world is 172,000,000 (F. D. Bacon: *Eastern Pilgrimage*).

The figures claimed by some of the larger Protestant churches are as follows :—

Lutherans: 90,000,000—baptized community.

Presbyterians and Reformed: 21,628,577+: baptized. (Communicants: 10,714,368+).

Methodists: 11,666,646 members (approx. 23 million community.)

Baptists: 13,500,000 communicant members (approx. 25 million community).

Anglicans: 9,000,000 communicants (community: 20-25 millions).

Congregationalists: 2,495,000 communicants (community: approx. 5 millions).

These figures, the more global they become, the less reliable they are for statistical purposes, though they probably represent roughly the proportions between Christians and non-Christians and between the churches themselves.[2]

At this point we may do well to realize that in this day of the conqueror and the conquered the ecumenical movement is unconquerable. Take a look back over the ages, and though you will find the movement of the Christian Church to be one of progression and retrogression, in the over-all, "His Truth is marching on." Among others, but more completely than anyone else, Kenneth Scott Latourette has proved this vividly and comprehensively in his seven monumental volumes on *A History of the Expansion of Christianity*. Concerning recent years, this is the record:

Christianity was more widely influential in the post-1914 decades than ever before. In no state or large segment of mankind was it dominant. In some sections of what had been Christen-

[2] Kenneth G. Grubb and E. J. Bingle, eds., *World Christian Handbook* (World Dominion Press, 1949), p. 240.

dom it appeared to be waning. However, if mankind was surveyed as a whole, Christianity was clearly a growing factor in human affairs. For this the evidences were many. Among them were the efforts to regulate and eliminate war, most of them having Christian origins even though latterly espoused by many who were not aware of their beginnings; movements for the betterment of Negroes in the United States and Africa; much of the emancipation of women; contributions to the stirrings among the depressed millions of India with their demand for better living conditions; much of the leadership which was helping to guide the Chinese people through their bewildering revolution; a large part of the medical, nursing, and public health service of the world; and many of the efforts to relieve and prevent famine. Some of the non-Christian religions and systems of thought which were governing hundreds of millions were in debt to Christianity. Hinduism and in several countries Buddhism were being modified by it. Certain phases of socialism and Russian Communism could be traced in part to it. Democracy, widely spread in spite of the reaction against it in some quarters, had the Christian faith in its rootage. In practically every land, moreover, were men and women of outstanding nobility of character who were what they were mainly because Jesus of Nazareth once walked the hills of Galilee and Judea. Never before had there been so many such in as many different peoples. Here in an age of storm was a power which, usually unnoticed and unappreciated by those whose self-appointed function it was to interpret the day-by-day passage of events, was quietly at work, transforming individuals and societies, and more widely potent than ever before.[3]

It is exceedingly disillusioning and disconcerting to discover how many people believe that modern forces of might and destruction can overcome and destroy the Church. I was in Asia for a while during the second World War. After my return to America, many told me they were convinced the Japanese military would overpower and eradicate the Church wherever the invading armies marched. Pastors and laity were certain that the Christian mission would be forced "to fold up" and the Christian Church in Japan, China, Korea, the Philippines, Thailand and Burma would be no more. Needless to say, these fears were groundless. Minorities though the church groups were and are, they emerged

---

[3] *Advance Through Storm*, Vol. VII of *A History of the Expansion of Christianity* (Harper & Brothers, 1945), pp. 414-415.

from the conflict tried and tested and physically demolished and weary, but alive and active in worship, education, evangelism and social welfare.

And now come the fears as to the ability of the Church to weather the storms of totalitarian oppression in Europe, Latin America and Asia today and tomorrow. It is true that two totalitarianisms are making it extremely perilous for the Church to carry on in these areas. First, there is Communism, fundamentally anti-Christian and striving to encircle the Church with prohibitions of every kind. In addition to political action, one read in the year of enlightenment known as A.D. 1950 the following:

The U.S.S.R.'s League of Militant Godless was disbanded in 1941 to boost wartime morale, and possibly to please the other nations of the Grand Alliance. But the fact marked no real change in Russia's rulers; religion was still a menace. Last week the Soviet Society for Political and Scientific Research, by way of the Leningrad radio, announced a new, all-out campaign against the "medieval Christian outlook." The drive, to be conducted on "an entirely scientific basis," will involve a large number of propagandists armed with antireligious films and some 20 million pamphlets. Trumpeted the society's chairman: "The struggle against the Gospel and Christian legend must be conducted ruthlessly and with all the means at the disposal of Communism." [4]

Yet and nevertheless, in all Communist-dominated countries in Europe and Asia the Church continues valiantly in its worship and evangelism and, as difficult as it may be, in education and social welfare. In Hungary and Czechoslovakia, in Korea and China the Church is demonstrating surprising vitality. It is reported that more people are attending the services than before the Communists appeared on the scene.

A rather surprising and hopeful newsletter came out of China, written by Henry D. Jones, formerly head of a religious community house in Detroit. Mr. Jones, for the past two years, has been developing a Christian social-action program under the Protestant churches in China. He wrote from Shanghai just after Christmas 1949:

[4] *Time,* September 11, 1950.

Some impression seems to have got into the United States that Christianity is being stamped out of "Communist" China. I do not know about everywhere, but let me give you a picture as I have seen it this Christmas in Shanghai. For me it began on Friday night, December 16, with a Christmas Carol Service, in which the thirteen choirs joined together under the auspices of the Women's Church Federation of Shanghai. The following Sunday afternoon in a Baptist church there was another choir-music festival, sponsored by the Shanghai Federation of Churches, and so it began with Christmas music in the 145 Protestant churches and 27 Roman Catholic churches of this city. It was Christmas music; it was Christmas pageants and parties, culminating in sometimes lovely, sometimes emotionally evangelical services of the Christmas Morn.

But not only the churches and Christian homes celebrated Christmas. In government-owned factories, hospitals, banks, employees joined together for a festival of good will. All members of the families in many of these large establishments joined together for the one big fellowship of the year, the Christmas fellowship. I have no idea how many of these government institutions actually celebrated Christmas, but I know that many did.

. . . Now it is Christmas week, and the event of the week in all Shanghai seems to be the presentation of Handel's *Messiah* in a large Methodist church. There are over eighty voices in this fine choir. The church is packed to its capacity of 1,500 twice during the week. As I stood in the lobby during the first evening while people poured into the church, I recognized missionaries, choir members and church members from many of the city churches, men and women in the uniform of government services. Yes, and I knew many music lovers, not church members, who came. One professor friend of mine, a leader among the left-wing anti-imperialist group, I was surprised to see come into the church. I had never expected to see him in any church, but the lovely music of the *Messiah* drew him.

What the future may hold, one does not know. But there must be something in this God knows better than we do.

Then there is the other major foe, very much the same basically as Communism in its dealing with the so-called masses, though very few people recognize the fundamental similarity of the methods of the two totalitarianisms. We refer to the Fascist State, too often under Roman Catholic political control. This is evidenced particularly in Portugal and Spain, as well as in certain countries of Latin America.

Mark you, we have written "the Fascist State, too often under Roman Catholic political control," and not the Roman Catholic Church. We have every respect for the true Roman Catholic Church as a religious institution. Moreover, one has good Roman Catholic friends who, like a number of Roman Catholic writers, make strong assertions against political Catholicism. But in view of the dangers involved, which too many people don't know, it is essential that we face the fact that both Communism and the Fascist State suppress the freedom of the individual, use unfair propaganda, depend on force to gain their ends, persecute minorities and, in practice if not in theory, deify the State. There is much evidence frequently documented and readily seen in Fascist countries that the free, vital and live Christian Church has become a persecuted minority. The references here to the Christian Church apply to either *Protestant* or *Catholic,* if it is free, vital and evangelistic. Neither name guarantees that a church is always Christian.

Later chapters will deal more fully with these totalitarianisms, particularly in Europe, Asia and Latin America. At this point, by way of illustration, to emphasize sharply and hopefully the invincible spirit of the ecumenical, let us look briefly at Spain.

It is no secret that in 1950 another courageous and dignified message regarding religious liberty was sent to General Franco by the Spanish Protestants. Four times since 1939 such an approach has been made to the dictator. Until recently no reply was received. The silence was significant. What shall a man say who has been reported to have said already, "Better 10,000 Communists in Spain than 1,000 Protestants"? Now, finally, the Protestant churches have received an answer. Franco's head of the civil cabinet has sent them a copy, two years old, of a ministerial circular about them, addressed to the governors of the provinces, but now published for the first time:

Article 6 of the Fuero de los Españoles, having stated in the first paragraph that the Catholic Religion is that of the Spanish State, adds in the second: No one shall be molested for his religious beliefs or in his private worship. No public ceremonies or demonstrations other than those of the Catholic Church shall be allowed.

It is necessary to make clear without the shadow of a doubt the differences existing between private worship for the confession and respect for their conscience on the one hand, and abuses and infringements which are attempted under cover of this tolerance on the other.

1. Private worship by non-Catholic religions is recognized.

2. By "private worship" is to be understood either strictly private worship or a service within premises reserved for the practice of the religion in question.

3. Such worship must in no case be outwardly or publicly visible, firstly because it would no longer be private, which is the only form under which it is admissible, and secondly because only the ceremonies and demonstrations of the Roman Catholic Religion are allowed.

4. In consequence, it is likewise illegal to practice any work of proselytism or propaganda for non-Catholic religions, whatever the method used, as for instance the foundation of schools for instruction, donations having the appearance of charity, holiday camps, etc., for these of necessity mean an unauthorized outward demonstration.

5. This being so, you will devote the utmost zeal to the close supervision of the activities of the religious confessions mentioned, dealing as quickly as possible with all infringements, and informing me without delay of transgressions noted and measures imposed.

What comment need we here? Perhaps, at the moment, the following observation, written on a recent journey through Spain, 'is sufficient.

Escorial is a charming village some 30 miles west of Madrid, 3,432 feet above the sea on the southwest slopes of the Sierra de Guadarrama. On its outskirts is situated one of the most remarkable buildings in Europe, known by the same name as the village, comprising at once a convent, a church, a palace and a mausoleum. This historic edifice owes its existence to a vow made by Philip II of Spain (1556-1598) shortly after the battle of St. Quentin, in which his forces succeeded in routing the army of France. Macaulay in one of his essays estimates that, during several years, the power of Philip II over Europe was greater than even that of Napoleon.

In Escorial the Spanish Evangelical Church now owns an antique, much-repaired villa. An ancient wall encloses the old residence, the ruins of a chapel and a lovely garden. The villa was once owned by Philip II. Here he lived fourteen years. Here he planned and directed much of the Inquisition. In the study, still intact, where Philip once dreamed and labored, today a Protestant pastor works and prays. The villa is now a Protestant center for conferences, training institutes and youth camps and is quite active. (As a matter of fact the Spanish Evangelical Church reports more people in attendance at Protestant services and more young men preparing for the Protestant ministry than before the rule of Franco.)

As you enter the villa from the dusty street, through a gateway that opens on the garden, if you look closely you may see an inscription, dimmed by the years, on the overhead arch. Philip put it there, so we are told. Translated from the Latin it reads, "After all fatalities, I shall arise." Somewhere else it was once written: "Truth, crushed to earth, shall rise again." [5]

To return to our major thesis: Too many people don't know the true nature of the world Christian Church; its history; its ever-enlarging fellowship; its program and strategy; its power, endurance and invincibility; its ecumenical reality. Why?

Statisticians tell us that more than 94 per cent of the homes in the United States have radios and that two thirds of the people in these homes listen to radio newscasts regularly. The pollsters tell us also that 80 per cent of the people read a daily or weekly newspaper and that about 50 per cent read magazines. Data have been gathered to show that "more than one half of the American people belong to organized religious bodies and attend their services; fifteen million persons belong to trade unions; five million to veterans' organizations; several million more to women's clubs and other fraternal or group societies." [6] All of which means that a relatively large percentage of the people in the U.S.A. is exposed to what is going on in the world. In America communication is no problem.

---

[5] William Cullen Bryant, "The Battle Field."
[6] Erwin D. Canham, "Americans and the War of Ideas," in John W. Chase, ed., *Years of the Modern* (Longmans, Green and Company, 1949), p. 236.

But we do have a problem of information. What do people hear? What do they read? What do they know? You may answer these questions yourself by picking up this morning's newspaper and glancing at the headlines. Or at home this evening, turn on the radio and listen to any one of the news broadcasts. How much "good news" have you read or heard within recent months? It is the old, old story that "bad news" supersedes "good news." "Bad news" dominates the headlines which most people read and remember. "Good news" is not often published in the press. If it is, it is all but buried toward the end of a dispatch. Most people don't read that far.

Dr. Visser 't Hooft tells us that on a recent visit to the United States he had luncheon with one of the outstanding Christian laymen in America, a man of intelligence and means who is well versed in world affairs. But this man had no idea that there were any churches in existence behind the Iron Curtain. He was amazed to hear Dr. Visser 't Hooft say that he had just come from there and had found vigorous Christian church life. And this American layman is not alone.

The *Ecumenical Press Service,* distributed from Geneva regularly and widely over the world and issued jointly by the World Council of Churches, the International Missionary Council, the World's Alliance of Young Men's Christian Associations, the World's Student Christian Federation, the World Council of Christian Education and the United Bible Societies, to mention but one of many world publications carrying Christian world news, is available to newspapers, libraries, churches, all religious groups and any organization or person who wants to subscribe. This press service is filled with ecumenical facts. It is not because we are without the means of knowing that so many people don't know.

There are not many people, in or out of the Church, who know that there is a Christian Church in every country in the world except four. And very few people know what these countries are. Test yourself. Which four? Are they of the following: Poland, Thailand, Russia, Korea, Japan, Burma, Pakistan, Czechoslovakia, Germany, Bulgaria, Ecuador?

You may be surprised to learn that in practically every instance where I have asked a church forum the question, "In what countries is there no Christian Church today?", the answer has been: "Russia, Germany and Japan." As a matter of fact, the only countries in the world which do not have an indigenous Christian Church are Afghanistan, Tibet, Outer Mongolia and Nepal. I emphasize "indigenous" because there is an English-speaking Christian Church in Kabul, Afghanistan, made up, primarily, of the American and British government, business and educational residents.

Two things are all too obvious. First, the media of information which reach most of us either totally ignore or give diminutive space to the "good news" of good things, especially in the realm of religion. Second, the force of propaganda is more powerful than the average person realizes. Psychological warfare satiates the human mind with evil about an evil enemy. To think of a faithful Christian Church in Japan during the war was almost impossible for the average American, when we were hating all things Japanese so completely that we changed the name of the cherry trees in Washington. A member of a board of foreign missions told me in 1944 that as a merchant he would never again buy a Japanese-made product as long as he lived. How could most people do other than believe that the Church was being destroyed in Germany when most wartime news about religion in Germany told primarily of the terror of Nazi religious persecution and that churches were being bombed. How can the fear-ridden mind of the average American know that approximately one half of the Russian people are Christians and that both Orthodox and non-Orthodox churches are functioning better than one would reasonably expect under the existing totalitarianism? It is difficult, very difficult, with the pressures upon us to "prove all things," to "hold fast that which is good."

How unfortunate it is for the state of the Church and the peace of the world that comparatively few know the life, work, indestructibility and possibilities of the World Christian Church! How tragic it is that, seeking individual and collective security in such times as these, a relatively small number knows what it means to be a world Christian—the thrill and accomplishment of mission, the possession, release and redemption of unconquerable spiritual power, the sense of belonging to one another and to God!

Traveling through Europe during the spring of 1950, I called one day on a German Protestant pastor in Berlin. As I entered his study, he walked toward me, smiling, with the first fingers of his two hands clasped together, held before him and reaching out toward me. His friendly eyes seemed to ask if I knew what this gesture meant. For a moment I hesitated, and then it dawned on me what my German friend was reminding me of and why he was making this reminder his initial greeting.

Three years before on a visit to Berlin I spent a winter evening with forty German pastors in the manse of the American Church. The American pastor and his wife, for the first time since the war, were able to entertain a group of German clergy in their home. That year Germany was a sad and suffering place. The crushing burdens and tragic loneliness of defeat were very real. Asked to give a brief address, I spoke on the invincibility of the world Christian fellowship and, by way of conclusion, related this experience:

Early in 1942, shortly after "Pearl Harbor," I landed by plane in the Cameroons, West Africa. On a certain Sunday I was invited to preach, through an interpreter, in a Bulu Christian church. A tremendous congregation of over 4,000 people was packed into a large thatch-roofed church building, 'way back inland in a jungle clearing. The situation was a rather frightening one, because of the vast congregation of Africans so strange to me, and I to them, and also because of the primitive confusion of the crowd. I had been speaking in other countries on World Christianity. I felt sure that this assemblage of half-clothed Africans deep in the bush would know nothing of the ecumenical movement. So I changed my accustomed emphasis and gave a brief devotional talk with a few personal illustrations. How wrong I was in the analysis of my audience!

When the preaching service was over, the congregation remained for a prayer meeting. A tall, dark Bulu arose in the rear and prayed passionately. "What is he praying about?" I asked my interpreter. After a moment the answer came: "He is praying for the Christians in China, in Japan, in Germany, in Russia, in America; praying that they will be true in their hour of testing and that in the trials of faith the African Christians will be courageous and faithful too."

From the first row a Bulu stepped toward the platform. His eyes were smiling. His face was radiant. He spoke to me in Bulu. Before me he held his hands with each first finger clasped tightly over the other. What was he saying? What did his gesture mean? I asked my interpreter to explain. "This Bulu Christian" was his reply "is saying both by his words and especially by that sign that Christians around the world are as links in a chain, pulled by divisive and evil forces which are attempting to divide and destroy, but the spirit and power of Christ in His World Church holds and will hold the Christians of the world together." In the heart of Africa I found the heart of ecumenicity.

This story I told the forty German pastors in Berlin five years afterward. Three years later they had remembered. At least one of them had. He remembered because in his loneliness a friend had come and had emphasized the enduring fellowship of Christians. He had remembered so vividly that his greeting to a Christian friend from afar was not a personal handshake, but an ecumenical handclasp.

Ecumenical is more than a word!

The Strength of the Nation

By Roswell P. Barnes

"What are the chances for a job in the Church? After nine years with the government, working with all sorts of citizens' groups, I'm discouraged. Most of the people think that all we need is more bombs and planes and ships to make us secure in the world, and higher income with lower taxes to make us comfortable at home.

"But a few thoughtful men are getting worried about the country. They talk about it in private. They're troubled about the spirit of the people. They see there's something wrong that can't be corrected with more bombs or television sets. They don't know just what it is; but they know it's a matter of basic principles and morals and discipline.

"I think it's the job of the churches to take the lead in clearing this up. If they don't, who will? Government can't do it. I don't see anybody else doing it. Most groups are only looking out for their own interests. But I've been watching what some of you in the churches are doing, especially in the Federal Council. You seem to see what's happening and what's needed. It gives me some hope. But unless you do a better job, we're lost."

That is the most accurate reconstruction I can give from memory of the introductory remarks of a man who came into my office some months ago for a conference arranged on his own initiative.

There have been others like him. One was a high-ranking officer in the navy. He was worried about the extent of promiscuity among the personnel of the armed forces. I remember one sentence that he repeated several times: "Our American mores are breaking down." He explained that he hadn't gone to church for twenty years but had recently gone several times because he was scared about what was happening among the people.

One of the interesting things about these men was that the majority did not regard themselves as churchmen. If they had, they probably would have gone to their own pastors. They came to me because they had become acquainted with me through my work with government agencies in Washington as I represented the interests of the constituency of the Federal Council of Churches. Or they had read statements of the Federal Council in the press or elsewhere.

It is obvious that many thoughtful people outside the churches as well as inside are beginning to realize that physical power, scientific ingenuity and cleverness are not enough. The power of the nation must rest on something deeper and more fundamental.

Some of the various aspects of power have become clearly discernible in the Korean conflict. Hanson W. Baldwin, the military analyst of the New York *Times,* wrote in the issue of August 21, 1950, that "at home and abroad we forget too often the things of the spirit in our dependence upon the materialism of physical force." He quoted the familiar statement of Napoleon—"There are only two powers in the world: the sword and the spirit. In the long run the sword is always defeated by the spirit."

Whether we become involved in general war or continue in the recurrent crises of the "cold-hot" war, Mr. Baldwin insisted, we cannot achieve our purposes by military might alone. "We must, therefore, emphasize in our world-wide campaign the power of the spirit, the political ideal of democracy, the moral ideal of Western civilization, the economic ideal of equal opportunity."

Mr. Baldwin and the others about whom I have been writing are seeing deeper than the superficial and obvious aspects of power. They speak of morals, ideals and spirit. So far, so good. But what do they mean by those words? I will not be so presumptuous as to claim that I know what these persons mean, at least those with whom I have not talked. But I do know they are not all talking about the same things.

Some are thinking of ethical standards, of ideals that they associate with the history of American democracy and of the importance of psychology in influencing people. They are at a deeper level than materialism. They are "getting warm" in the search for the explanation of our disorder and the real secret of power.

Others are thinking of the basic principles from which ethical standards have grown, of the faith on which American democracy was founded and of the importance of loyalty to God as a factor in the conduct of people. They have come to understanding; they have found the secret. They are as far beyond the secular idealists in insight as the secular idealists are beyond the materialists.

The real power of the nation derives from these most basic factors. America is a Samson among the nations in physical prowess. Like Samson, she is in grave danger of pride in and reliance on the dramatic evidences of her strength, forgetting her original purpose and commitment to God. If and when the time comes when we regard the inscription "In God We Trust" as merely a symbol of a quaint, naïve faith that may have been useful for our fathers but is unnecessary or unacceptable to our "enlightened" generation, then we shall see what becomes of our strength.

It is not enough to give attention to the ideals of democracy. We must go back to the faith and commitments from which our democracy arose.

When we consider the magnitude of America's responsibility in the world today and the responsibility of the churches with regard to America's power, we begin to comprehend the significance of the churches' role in the national life. It is not surprising that thoughtful men are looking more carefully at the churches and some of them go to the churches.

We turn, then, to a consideration of some of the points at which the churches are arresting attention by what they are doing, the ways in which they contribute to the spiritual and moral power of the nation.

In the first place, they are helping many men and women to understand the nature of their own personal problems and leading them to a faith in God that gives them resources for living which they have not found—and, of course, cannot find—elsewhere.

This is not the place to define the content of that faith but rather to report what the churches are doing to help men find it.

Men come to the churches either out of frustration and dissatisfaction with their own personal lives or out of bewilderment and apprehension about the world. In the minds of many the two factors are mingled and often undefined. Some come because of what they see the churches doing; others because of what they think the churches ought to be doing.

Fully recognizing and deploring the failures or inadequacies of the churches, let us look at a few facts about what they are and what they are doing.

More than half the people of the nation are affiliated with some church or synagogue. Membership for some is little more than a conventional gesture. For others it is the absorbing focus of most of their life interests. For many millions the Church is an indispensable aid in finding the power and peace of God, the chief teacher of the meaning of life, the most trusted guide toward understanding the world, the most reliable authority on matters of conduct and the most effective channel through which to serve the world and to try to solve its problems.

There is no way of measuring and tabulating the number of contacts the pastors of our churches have with people in the normal course of the week. The services at the church are only part of the story. Consultations on all sorts of personal and family matters continue through the week in the pastor's study or in homes. The Church follows people wherever they go, carrying the ministry of religion to them—through chaplains in hospitals, prisons and other institutions, and into danger with the armed forces. There were 134 deaths among the Protestant chaplains in the U.S. forces during the two World Wars.

Baptisms, weddings and funerals bring the influence of the pastor to people at the times when joys and sorrows, hopes and fears are most poignant. He becomes in the minds of his people the representative of those forces which brighten their joys and relieve their sorrows.

Many people who seldom attend church services and may not even be members turn to the Church in connection with a wedding or funeral. This may indicate, for some, little more than a concession to convention; but even so, it is a recognition of the hold that religion has through tradition. Moreover, in most of these cases, the people on the fringes of the Church are more comfortable if God is recognized on an occasion when thoughts turn to the meaning of life and of human relationships.

Secularism is a menace. We should be troubled about the degree to which it prevails among our people. Nevertheless, we would misinterpret our situation if we did not take into account the facts that prove the hold religion has on millions who are not usually included in the tabulations of the strength of the churches.

Nor should we underestimate the influence of the Church through preaching. No amount of skepticism or of cynicism as to why people go to church can disregard the fact that in some 200,000 Protestant churches many millions listen to the interpretation of life in terms of God. Add to preaching in the churches the reports and articles on religion in the secular press and the radio programs sponsored by the churches. The total number of religious impacts in the course of the week is tremendous.

So there is a kind of power exerted by the churches directly and indirectly through its influence upon people in their personal lives and problems. It conditions behavior. It induces loyalty and respect.

The second point at which the churches are arresting attention is their work on social problems. It was this interest that brought to my office the man quoted at the beginning of the chapter. He had been impressed by what the Federal Council of Churches had been saying and doing.

It should be emphasized that when we discuss the work of the Federal Council of Churches we are discussing a program which has now become part of the program of the National Council of the Churches of Christ in the United States of America. It is not the work of an independent and separate organization, but of a delegated, representative body which is effective in so far as its twenty-nine constituent national communions are effective. We are really talking about the co-ordinated efforts of the preponderant groups of the American Protestant and Eastern Orthodox churches.

This is a power which derives from the whole corporate life of the churches and has its effect on public opinion, public policy and the actions of the nation. The basic and most important influence of the churches in public affairs is indirect, through the influence and action of its constituency. This requires the development of a larger number of men and women who as employers and employees, officers of government and voters, writers, businessmen, housewives, parents—whatever their station or responsibility—understand and practice the law of God as revealed in Christ. That is the basic function and responsibility of the churches.

But the churches themselves also have a responsibility to represent the religious and moral conscience of the nation, both to the public generally and to the centers of secular power, including government. In our country there is assumed to be a core of Christian conviction at the center of social life. The churches are expected to define it and state it as a point of reference in the light of which national policy should be judged.

There are various appropriate procedures by which the churches bring Christian influence to bear directly on government. One is the direct contact with officers of government. Occasionally the churches send small delegations, usually three persons, to the President to present to him and to amplify and explain the positions of the churches on matters of national policy. The conferences are as a rule more like pastoral calls than professional consultations. General concerns are expressed. The President is reminded that the churches are praying for him. The church representatives indicate to him those aspects of his policy and program that have the general moral support of the church constituency. Occasionally they present criticism of some aspects of national policy or make suggestions with regard to modifications. Seldom are suggestions offered about technical details, and then only on matters in which the churches have special concern, knowledge and competence, as, for example, in matters affecting religious liberty and human rights.

These approaches to the head of the state are made primarily on the assumption that in the midst of pressures from various interest groups the voice of the churches should be heard, giving assurance of moral support and speaking for the broad interests of humanity. Such visits have been appreciated and have not been without effect.

Similar approaches are made occasionally to cabinet officers and Members of Congress.

On some matters the churches have a special concern growing out of their own history or their own experience in intimate dealings with people. On such matters they speak more specifically. On matters of religious liberty and the related questions of separation of church and state, the churches take positions with respect to legislation and administrative policy. I have appeared before congressional committees dealing with problems of foreign relief and liquor advertising. These are matters on which the Church has a basis for testimony. We have extensive programs for the aid of people in war-stricken areas. We have contacts with the churches there. We know the needs, and the channels for responsible distribution of supplies. The churches have other special insights. Pastors see the consequences in human lives of the artificial stimulation of beverage-alcohol consumption by the advertising that attempts to make the use of liquor socially desirable, especially among youth.

The churches also make a contribution to public policy by providing a favorable moral climate for official deliberations. For example, at the time of the San Francisco Conference when the United Nations came into being, special prayers of intercession were offered in churches across the United States and in a number of other countries. A mass meeting of the churches was held in the Oakland Municipal Auditorium, giving tangible evidence to the convening delegates of the deep concern of Christian groups. Some of the delegates spoke of the effect these prayers had on them.

Before the opening of the General Assembly of the United Nations on September 19, 1950, leaders of Protestant, Jewish and Roman Catholic groups requested Ambassador Austin, chief of the United States delegation, to invite all God-fearing people to join in prayer for the Assembly at the moment of its period of silence for meditation and prayer. The ambassador complied with the suggestion and issued his appeal through the press and in his own radio address.

In addition to this influence, the churches are represented by a consultant to the United Nations who interprets the concerns of the churches to the delegates. At the opening of the September 1950 meeting of the General Assembly, letters were addressed to the members of the United States delegation informing them of the position of the Federal Council of Churches on certain agenda items which are of special concern to the churches. Delegates read the letters and commented favorably on the views expressed in them.

Men and women from all walks of life participate in formulating the policies and programs through which the churches bring their influence to bear on international relations, economic life, race relations, social welfare, foreign relief and rehabilitation, and the general moral and religious tone of the nation.

In the field of international affairs the churches have enlisted the efforts of a considerable number of outstanding Christian laymen who have had wide experience in the practical aspects of diplomacy and foreign affairs.

Ambassadors, professors of international relations, Members of Congress, journalists, businessmen, labor leaders and government employees mingle with foreign missionaries of experience in many parts of the world, pastors, theologians and church executives. Together they analyze the disorder of the world and the issues of American foreign policy, define the guiding Christian principles that apply, and make recommendations to the people of the churches for their study and action. Practical problems are brought into direct confrontation with principles in such a way as to clarify the immediate relevance of the churches' message and at the same time to point out the inadequacy of purely secular solutions.

When men and women from these various vocations thus cooperate in the church as churchmen they accomplish what they usually fail to accomplish in other associations. In most of their public and professional work they represent particular interest groups. In those circumstances they tend to follow a Democratic or Republican "line," or to speak from the point of view of business or labor. But when they meet together in a church conference, they come as delegates from their churches and are not accountable to the groups with which they are associated in making their living. They meet as Christian comrades, drawn together by their common loyalty to Christ, committed to the same basic faith in God and relying, together, on His guidance.

Having pointed to the wide variation of significance that may be attributed to church membership, it is still important to take statistics into consideration in estimating the power of the churches. Church membership has some meaning to almost all whose names are on a church roll. To many it is a matter of very grave importance.

According to the analysis of the *Christian Herald,* which has been keeping careful tabulations for many years, the percentage of the total population of the United States included in church rolls has increased from 39.6 per cent in 1919 to 54.2 per cent in 1949. The increase has been steadily mounting by ten-year periods. In 1929 it was 42.7 per cent, and in 1939, 49 per cent. These figures include Protestant, Roman Catholic, Jewish and others.

The distribution among the various faiths is a difficult statistical problem, because Roman Catholic reports include all baptized persons from infants up, whereas Protestants—with the exception of Episcopalians and some Lutherans—include only adults or children at least 13 years old. The Protestant statistical strength is approximately double that of the Roman Catholic. Together they account for 92 per cent of the total church membership. The Jews have six per cent and others two per cent. Christian Scientists are not included because they do not report membership statistics. Protestant membership has been increasing proportionately a little more rapidly than Roman Catholic.

In 1949 there were 275,265 congregations. This represented an increase of 6,592 over the 1948 report, and of these only 207 were Roman Catholic, bringing the total for that faith to 15,112.

The multiplicity and great variety of Protestant denominations sometimes create an erroneous impression of disorder. There are 222 denominations whose reports are considered in computing statistics. However, the 12 largest account for 77 per cent of the total Protestant membership of 48,674,823. The 31 largest, each with more than 200,000 members, account for 95 per cent of the total.

In estimating the extent of Protestant influence in America, we should not regard the 48,000,000 of church members, plus perhaps 10,000,000 of children, as a bloc within the total population that indicates the full measure of Protestant strength. America is Protestant in religious tradition. In so far as there is a religious influence in the nation, it is predominantly Protestant. There are many millions of American citizens who are not on the rolls of the Protestant churches who nevertheless recognize the importance of the spiritual and moral influences which they associate with the Protestant churches. They acknowledge the contribution of those churches to their standards of behavior and judgment. They may have been conditioned by Protestant schools or colleges. Many even contribute to Protestant churches or agencies.

So, while it must be assumed that some church members do not take their membership seriously, there are many who are "outside" the Church and yet are influenced by it and who in turn channel its influence into the community. It would be very interesting if the census would record those who claim to be atheists or agnostics or definitely opposed to all churches. They would certainly not account for the 45.8 per cent of the population who are not on the church rolls.

What, then, is the Protestant strength in proportion to total population? Membership is one index. The disciplined portion of the membership which takes the Church seriously is another—the dynamic and aggressive group. The whole unnumbered portion of the population that has a general Protestant orientation and general sympathy is still another index. However the Protestant strength is estimated numerically, it is sufficient to influence the life of the nation significantly. It is in a better position than any other group to determine the spiritual climate.

In terms of institutional and financial resources the Protestant churches have the means to carry on an aggressive program. In 1949 the ten Protestant denominations with the largest incomes reported an aggregate of congregational receipts for all purposes amounting to $720,000,000. Those denominations represent two fifths of the total Protestant church membership. It is doubtful whether total Protestant receipts were two and one-half times the $720,000,000, but it is likely that they amounted to more than $1,500,000,000.

The value of church structures, parish houses, colleges, seminaries, hospitals, homes for the aged and mission properties at home and overseas has not been carefully calculated, but it is large. There are 775 two-year or four-year colleges related to Protestant churches.

But all this calculation as to the power of the churches is somehow inappropriate. It may be irrelevant if not misleading. In New Testament terms of power, statistics such as we have been using have little meaning. The church in Czarist Russia included within its constituency most of the population. It had great wealth. What was its strength? Christians in Japan or China today are a relatively insignificant percentage of the population, but their influence is not correspondingly insignificant. The influence of Christianity is not directly proportional to the number of people who call themselves Christians.

It is quite possible that our churches would be stronger with a small fraction of the present membership if that smaller number were more deeply consecrated, courageously living out the full implications of their faith in all their work and relationships. The usual measurements of power which prevail in the secular world do not apply to religion, especially to Christianity.

To gain a sound impression and understanding of what the churches are doing it is necessary to take into consideration both the quiet, normal, day-to-day influence of the individual Christian upon his neighbors, and the activities of large groups or organizations which have a mass influence. Both represent the strength of the churches. Both are important. And they are closely related.

As an example of the unspectacular influence of individuals we cite what is known as visitation evangelism. This is the work of laymen who are so convinced of the importance of their faith that they will share it with their neighbors and try to persuade them to commit themselves to Christ and the church. The laymen are trained in the church by the minister or a director. Here is an account by a minister of a conversation with one of these laymen:

"You are looking at a man who has an accusing conscience,"
said the layman.

"In what field?" inquired the minister.

"In the work we are doing just now in visitation evangelism"
was the reply. "I am an officer in the church. I teach a boys'
class. For the past thirty years I have taught generations of
boys. A mile down the road from my farm is a neighbor's house
which I have passed four times each Sunday on my way to and
from church. Last night I talked with the man for the first time
about his relation to Christ. I found him eager to discuss the
matter. He had two or three minor difficulties which we were able
to answer to his satisfaction. We talked about the steps necessary
for him to become a follower of Christ and he sincerely acknowledged his need to take those steps and his desire to do so. He made
his confession of faith in Christ. After we had prayed together
he said, 'I feel that I have failed as a father. My son has followed
me in neglecting Christ and the church. Can you come and talk
to him tomorrow night? My brother-in-law and his family down
the road—be sure to call on them.' My conscience is goading me
tonight because of the way I had failed these neighbors for so
many years."

Such individual effort and testimony is one aspect of evangelistic
advance. Along with it there are special preaching services and an
effort on the part of the churches to carry their message to the
whole community. The combined efforts of individuals and of the
churches themselves produce such results as these: the Central
Christian Church of Enid, Oklahoma, took into its membership
235 on one day. The Fairview Evangelical and Reformed Church
of Dayton, Ohio, received 335 new members during eighteen
months of intensive effort. The Mount Olivet Lutheran Church
of Minneapolis reported 661 new members received on Palm Sunday, 1950—of whom 462 were adults.

Now look at an example of the influence of the large group, the
special occasion. The occasion is the Second National Study Conference on the Church and Economic Life which met at Detroit,
February 16-19, 1950, under the auspices of the Federal Council
of Churches. There were 381 delegates from the churches, two
thirds of them laymen. These church members in their daily occupations were associated with groups which have different, and
sometimes conflicting, interests.

It is at least as difficult to keep tempers cool in a discussion of economic problems as in a discussion of politics. In fact there is usually more emotion in talk about strikes, taxes and prices than in talk about partisan political issues. Much of the heat in politics is generated by the heat of issues in economic life.

With the increasing tendency of individuals to identify themselves with large power groups which represent special interests—business, labor, profession, agriculture—it is exceedingly difficult to achieve a constructive and even-tempered discussion of important points of difference. What begins as discussion tends to degenerate into contentious argument.

What happened at the Detroit Conference? I shall recall as accurately as possible the exact words of one of the lay delegates several weeks after it ended. He is an economist with wide business and agricultural associations and an international reputation. Here is his unsolicited comment:

I never knew before what Pentecost meant. Perhaps I never thought about it much. At least I had never had an experience that called it to mind. But the Detroit Conference must have been a Pentecost.

Something happened that I hadn't expected. I assumed that we would either avoid the hot issues in the interest of peace or bog down in endless and futile debate. I know what usually happens when such men get together. But it didn't happen there. I guess it was what you theologians call the Holy Spirit that made the difference.

I can't explain it except that the power of God was there. We were aware of the fact that we were together as Christians in the fellowship of the Church. And we got somewhere, even on the hottest problems. What we agreed on was important; but even more important was the demonstration of how men ought to work together. If we could have that kind of thing happening all over the country our problems would be solved.

It was the greatest spiritual experience of my life. The power of God was there and we felt it. That's why I call it Pentecost. From now on I'm a missionary for the Federal Council and its work.

Sometimes what the churches are in their corporate life speaks louder than what they say. The equal and nonsegregated participation of Negroes in the life and work of the churches may be a more important contribution to good race relations than the best resolutions.

The Federal Council of Churches, along with other church groups, often has had difficulty in arranging for nondiscriminatory hotel accommodations for its meetings. But its policy is uncompromising in this matter.

The effect is illustrated in the comment of a waitress in a hotel restaurant. She asked as she served my lunch whether I had not had breakfast with a Negro. I answered in the affirmative. "I think it's wonderful," she said. "I go to Sunday school and they teach about Christian race relationships; but you people just make it seem natural to have everybody together. Some of us have been talking about whether we wouldn't feel better if we dropped discrimination in the union. After all, if we're Christians we ought to put it into practice."

It is surprising to note how little some people who think they know the churches really know about what the churches are doing. One time as I was leaving the studio after a radio broadcast of a program reporting the Church in Action, the engineer stopped me and said: "I've been handling religious programs here for five years. I've heard a lot of preaching—some of it good preaching, too. It's mostly devotional and telling people what they ought to do. But I never had any idea before what the churches are actually doing. I think maybe I ought to get into it more. Can you give me something to read that will tell me more about what's doing?"

Lest this report about the radio engineer seem to belittle the importance of preaching, let us cite another incident. A letter came from a Midwestern city addressed to Dr. Harry Emerson Fosdick, occasioned by the tenth anniversary of the conversion of the writer through a radio sermon by Dr. Fosdick. He had never written Dr. Fosdick before. He reported the work he had been doing in a Gospel Mission which he had set up and the hundreds of converts sent by the mission into the churches of the city.

Statistics of radio broadcasts, the number of stations carrying the programs, the estimated listening audiences and the mail responses are all interesting but cold. The declaration of the man converted into an evangelist, the gratitude of the hospital patient for new hope and the testimony of the prison inmate to new faith all suggest the living power of the Christian message over the radio.

If we are to understand the role of the churches in the nation today, we should take a glance at American history. In very significant respects the strength of the United States of America has been derived from its democratic faith, institutions and processes. These had their roots in the Protestant churches. In the early formative period of our national history Protestant influence was powerful. It is reflected in the records of the first settlers in Massachusetts and Virginia. It was an important factor in the impulses that led to the Revolution. In the Declaration of Independence it was the basis for grounding the rights of men in their Creator.

The essential strength of American democracy has been a citizenship deeply convinced of the ideals of liberty, disciplined in a sense of duty, and committed and habituated to voluntary service to the community. These three factors of democracy came into our national tradition primarily from the Reformation and only secondarily from the nationalism of the French Revolution.

Charles A. Beard, the noted historian, has stated somewhere that men and women brought together in the bonds of a common religious faith figured largely in the settlement of America and that by one of the strange fortunes of history their "brotherhoods" or "congregations," founded in the early days of Christianity, proved to be a potent force in the origin and growth of self-government in their new land. Beard has argued that local self-government in matters ecclesiastical helped train early Americans for local self-government in matters political.

Another distinguished historian, James Truslow Adams, similarly finds in the voluntary covenant of the "congregations" a source of our whole social organism.

So Protestantism made an indispensable contribution to democracy both in basic principles and in demonstrated forms and procedures.

Today, again, Protestantism is making a fresh contribution to democracy both by testimony and by example. Its testimony is fairly well known. But there is one notable achievement in its own life and organization which calls for analysis in terms of its relevance to the present problems of democracy—namely, the National Council of the Churches of Christ in the U.S.A.

This National Council represents nothing new in principle but rather a very important development based on long experience in co-operation among independent churches. Twenty-nine national church bodies recently decided to merge into one council eight agencies of the churches or their functional boards which had been separate. This represents a new consolidation of resources which in principle and structure point to an answer to some of the basic problems of democracy in our day.

The complexity and interdependence of modern mass society make it increasingly difficult to achieve order and freedom together and at the same time. Order is so necessary, especially in a time of crisis, that the people will even surrender their freedom to achieve it. Totalitarian systems exploit the necessity of order to gain and keep control. In time of war we Americans concentrate power in centralized authority to attain a maximum of order and efficiency.

Totalitarian systems, Nazi, Fascist and Communist, have pointed to our wartime restrictions on freedom as proof that freedom is impracticable in modern society because it leads to exploitation, injustice, waste, license and chaos.

We know from our own history as a nation how difficult it is to maintain a proper balance between order and freedom. There is a great temptation, especially in a time of confusion and fear, to increase centralized authoritarian controls.

Protestantism has been confronted with these same problems and temptations. The freedom which it has established and maintained has resulted in such a proliferation of various religious groups as to give the impression of chaos. In the face of this situation the centralized authoritarian control inherent in the Roman Catholic Church has a plausible appeal. It seems to be a system made to order for effective operation in an intricate mass society such as ours. Some Protestants envy it, and some Roman Catholics encourage the dissatisfaction among Protestants by exaggerating the alleged chaos of freedom.

It appears that there are two alternatives before modern man in politics, economics and religion: arbitrary centralized authoritarian control and voluntary co-ordination. The second is democratic. In the field of religion it is Protestant. For Protestants to try to establish centralized authoritarian control would be to deny their understanding of the will of God and to repudiate their genius and history. They could not do it if they tried. To the best of my knowledge, there is no considerable group of Protestants that wants it. Fortunately, conviction is deep and historic tradition well established.

The significance of the National Council of Churches in this respect is that it represents substantial progress in the development of the structure and procedures for the voluntary co-ordination of effort by Protestant and Eastern Orthodox churches. It is the very antithesis of centralized authoritarian control. As such, it shows the way, to the extent that it is effective, to the whole democratic system. It becomes, in this respect also, the strength of the nation.

The Council is not a body that the churches have set up to be "over" them or to direct their affairs, but, rather, an agency through which the churches themselves co-ordinate their own efforts at those points where they believe they can act more effectively together than separately. By constitutional provision, by the tradition of the council movement and by universal understanding among the constituent churches the Council has no authority over the churches that compose it. It is the churches themselves, through their own delegated representatives, acting together.

This is the democratic pattern. Freedom is guaranteed and respected. At the same time order is achieved by the voluntary decision of free people in their own groups, agreeing among themselves as to where common action is needed and where separate actions are better.

In the National Council of Churches, the churches now have an agency through which they may achieve voluntary co-ordination more effectively than before when there were eight separate agencies.

The churches which constitute the National Council have had long experience in this process of voluntary co-ordination. The National Council represents nothing really new in policy. Rather, it represents an evolution in structure which brings organization into closer conformity to policy already accepted in principle and

verified by long practice. It continues and extends the work of the
eight agencies that were merged into it: the Federal Council of
Churches, International Council of Religious Education, Home
Missions Council, Foreign Missions Conference of North America,
Missionary Education Movement, National Protestant Council on
Higher Education, United Stewardship Council and United Council of Church Women. The nature of the National Council may
be explained best by analyzing its parts, even though the whole is
something more than the sum of all its parts. Let us, therefore, review briefly the work of the parts that were previously separate.

One of the eight agencies was the instrument of co-operation of
the denominations themselves; the other seven were specialized,
representing particular functions or interests. The general agency
was the Federal Council of the Churches of Christ in America. It
furthered the co-operative work of the churches in all areas of
program except those assigned to the specialized agencies. It combined, therefore, generalized and specialized functions.

The generalized functions are now the functions of the National
Council. When the churches themselves wish to act or speak together, they do so through the National Council. In so far as any
one agency can represent "the voice of Protestantism," the National Council is that voice, always recognizing that no one agency
can ever speak for all Protestants so long as the Protestant principle of freedom of conscience prevails.

Specialized functions, previously assigned to the seven specialized agencies or to departments of the Federal Council, are now
the responsibilities of various units of the National Council, all
operating under the control of the Council's general governing
body.

The following outline description of the Council is intended to
give an impression of the scope of its work rather than of its detailed structure:

GOVERNING BODY

The governing body of the Council is the General Assembly,
composed of representatives elected to it by the 29 communions
which constitute the Council. Between the biennial or special meetings of the General Assembly, the General Board—likewise com-

posed of representatives designated by the constituent communions
—has interim authority. Representation of communions on both
the General Assembly and the General Board is proportional to
the membership of the communions.

DIVISIONS

The principal program units of the Council are the four Divisions, which operate with a substantial measure of autonomy but
under the authority of the Council. The members of the General
Assembly are assigned in approximately equal proportions to the
Division Assemblies, which are the governing bodies of the Divisions, with interim Executive Boards. In addition to the members assigned from the General Assembly, the Divisions may have
members from agencies of denominations not members of the
Council, if their denominations subscribe to the preamble of the
Constitution of the Council, which requires belief in "Jesus Christ
as Divine Lord and Saviour" as a condition of eligibility to membership.

The four Divisions and their principal subunits are as follows:

DIVISION OF CHRISTIAN EDUCATION

Commission on General Christian Education

In 1949 the total enrollment in Sunday church schools of the
co-operating religious bodies was 18,122,302.

Children's Work. Assists state and city councils, denominational departments, committees on children's work,
church-school leaders' conference and other training enterprises dealing with the religious education of children;
promotes projects to enable children to send gifts to
children overseas; provides handbooks and bibliog-
raphies of materials for children's work.

Young People's Work. Promotes regional and local conferences for adult leaders of youth; organizes United
Christian Youth Councils; provides executive leadership
to the United Christian Youth Movement with its wide
program of summer conferences, youth service projects
and education.

Adult Work. Serves as clearinghouse for pastors and denominational and interdenominational leaders responsible for development of educational programs and

production of materials for adults; assists in training leadership and promoting conferences.

Curriculum Development. Administers planning, preparation and production of the "uniform series" and the "graded series" of lesson materials for church schools, adult-curriculum and home-curriculum resources.

Leadership Education. Promotes leadership-education programs; produces the Standard Leadership Curriculum and materials, such as leaders' guides and audio-visual units.

Church-School Administration. Produces guides to help the director of religious education and the church-school superintendent to administer the total program of religious education in the local church.

Summer Camps and Conferences. Furthers the development of better standards and more adequate training for directors and leaders of summer camps and conferences for the several age groups.

Vacation Religious Education. Promotes leadership training for teachers; provides curriculum materials, film strips, handbooks, and assists in conferences. In 1949 there were 54,949 vacation church schools in the United States, with 3,705,238 pupils enrolled and 470,619 teachers and officers.

Weekday Religious Education. Assists churches to set up programs that will be legally valid and educationally sound; promotes training of teachers; produces instructional materials.

Audio-Visual and Radio Education. Supervises radio and television coverage of special events such as National Family Week, Religious Education Week and National Youth Week; sponsors workshops in audio-visual education, production conferences and leadership cultivation.

English Bible. Sponsors the understanding of, and the use of, the Revised Standard Version of the New Testament; interprets the work of the Standard Bible Committee; stimulates interest in Bible reading and study.

Religion and Public Education. Seeks to assist the churches to define policy and exert appropriate influence in the matter of religion and public education.

Commission on Christian Higher Education

This Commission, which continues and extends the work previously done by the National Protestant Council on Higher Education, represents the Protestant colleges of the

United States and the voluntary student work of boards of Christian education in public-supported and independent colleges and universities. Its purposes are:

To awaken the entire public to the conviction that religion is essential to a complete education and that education is necessary in the achievement of purpose.

To foster a vital Christian life in college and university communities of the United States of America, including those of tax-supported institutions.

To strengthen the Christian college, to promote religious instruction therein and to emphasize the permanent necessity of higher education under distinctly Christian auspices.

The Commission functions through the following departments:

Christian Institutions
Ministerial Training
Campus Christian Life
The Interseminary Committee

Joint Commission on Missionary Education

Continuing and extending the work of the former Missionary Education Movement, this unit serves as "a co-operative channel through which denominational home and foreign mission boards, departments of missionary education, boards of Christian education and other agencies responsible for missionary education in the United States and Canada can strengthen and carry forward their work."

The principal functions of the Commission are to publish missionary education materials, hold training schools and conferences and assist in the production of radio, television and other audio-visual materials for missionary education.

DIVISION OF CHRISTIAN LIFE AND WORK

This Division continues and extends much of the program work formerly carried by the Federal Council of Churches. Its function is less specialized than that of the other three Divisions. Among its purposes are these:

To enable the churches to proclaim the Gospel of Christ and to permeate the life of the community with the Gospel by means that are more effectively utilized in co-operation than in separation.

To secure a larger combined influence for the churches of Christ in all matters affecting the spiritual, moral and social conditions of the people, so as to promote the application of the law of Christ in every relation of human life.

To serve as a mediating and reconciling influence in situations of tension or conflict within the areas of concern of the Division.

To serve as an agency through which the churches may exert their influence in relation to other community agencies and enterprises.

To make more effective the witness of the churches in the struggle for world justice and peace.

The Division operates largely through the following Departments:

International Justice and Good Will. Provides study materials and messages for use by the churches; seeks to develop a concerned and enlightened opinion among church members and thus assist the churches to bring the influence of Christian principles to bear on questions of public policy; sponsors study conferences on the relation of the churches to world order.

Pastoral Services. Assists the churches to develop more effective pastoral services; publishes aids to pastors on such matters as personal counseling, the ministry to older people, dealing with grief and delinquency; through its Committee on Religion and Health brings pastors, physicians, nurses and psychologists together to share insights and counsel with regard to the relation between religion and health; through its Committee on Ministry in Institutions seeks to improve standards of chaplaincy service in prisons and hospitals.

Race Relations. Promotes the observance of Race Relations Sunday and produces materials for use on that occasion and generally in the study of race relations; co-operates with denominations in clinics and institutes on the church and race; represents the interests of the churches—when authorized by the General Board of the Council—in connection with matters of public policy involving justice for minority racial or cultural groups.

Social Welfare. Assists the churches in developing a clearer and more effective Protestant policy with regard to social work and social welfare, including child welfare; represents Protestant interests in relation to such other groups or enterprises as the National Social Welfare Assembly, the White House Conference on Child Welfare, the National Conference on Citizenship, conferences on juvenile delinquency, alcoholism, housing; assists in administration of the Church Conference of Social Work; sponsors conferences on Protestant Homes for the Aged.

The Church and Economic Life. Being composed in three fourths of its membership of laymen and lay women who are leaders in business, labor, agriculture, consumers' organizations or who are professional economists, it helps the churches to develop a policy with regard to economic life; produces study materials and messages on Christianity and economic life; sponsors national study conferences; directs long-term studies of basic ethical and moral problems in economic life; assists with local study conferences of clergy and laity on the program of the churches in relation to economic life.

Worship and Fine Arts. Conducts workshops and seminars in which ministers from the various churches, with their different traditions of worship, share their insights and special emphases for the general enrichment of worship; prepares and publishes materials for special uses, *e.g.,* hymnbooks for rural churches and for use in prisons and aids for family worship; prepares worship services for such special occasions as Reformation Sunday and ecumenical services; assists in developing an appreciation of the religious uses of music, architecture, drama and the other fine arts.

DIVISION OF FOREIGN MISSIONS

This Division continues and extends the work previously done by the Foreign Missions Conference of North America. It provides for conferences of representatives of foreign mission boards, for investigation and study of missionary problems and for the performance of specific tasks as agreed on by the boards, through their representatives. It facilitates co-operation between two or more boards in any foreign missionary endeavor in which they may desire united action.

Consultation with regard to problems in various regions and the furtherance of co-operative or united work is achieved primarily through representative area committees. Such committees serve the interests of various boards in the following areas:

Africa	Okinawa
Europe	Philippines
China	India, Pakistan and
Japan	Ceylon
Korea	Latin America
Southeast Asia	The Near East

The Division also operates through program committees that are concerned with special missionary interests that are not peculiar to any one region:

> *Associated Mission Medical Office.* Conserves the health of missionaries and staff workers of administrative boards and agencies, including immunization of travelers to foreign fields. Statistics for 1949 indicate 1,538 examinations done in the office, 2,264 health conferences, 544 treatments, and review of 1,311 examinations made by other physicians.
>
> *Christian Medical Council for Overseas Work.* Advises doctors and nurses from many countries regarding programs of postgraduate study and clinical experience; assists in securing opportunities for such study and experience; counsels furloughing missionary doctors and nurses; strengthens Christian medical colleges; advises interchurch medical committees of national Christian councils; provides courses of medical training for nonmedical missionaries.
>
> *Rural Missions Co-operating Committee.* Assists in the establishing and guidance of rural and agricultural missions, and of rural service and training centers; publishes *Rural Missions,* which is distributed to 2,500 missionaries and Christian nationals; assists in the recruiting and training of personnel for rural missions.
>
> *World Literacy and Christian Literature.* Promotes the education of missionaries in literacy and literature techniques; assists experts such as Dr. Frank Laubach in the preparation of literacy charts in 30 languages; advises regarding the production of literature for new literates; co-operates with national governments in the promotion of literacy campaigns.

DIVISION OF HOME MISSIONS

Continuing and extending the work of the Home Missions Council, this Division provides for conference, consultation and co-ordination of denominational home mission work and for co-operative action. Through consultation in the Division the several denominational boards are enabled to plan their programs in relation to the total Protestant effort, the activities of other public and private agencies and in relation to national trends. The Division administers certain projects on an interdenominational basis at the request of the boards. The scope of the Division's work is indicated by the following units of operation:

Conference and Consultation

> *Committee on Alaska.* Provides a clearinghouse for boards operating schools, hospitals, orphanages and churches in Alaska; furthers exchange of information on disease among native races, economic needs, transportation problems; arranges some interdenominational religious services.

> *Committee on City and Bilingual Work.* Brings together board executives in charge of city work; makes surveys of city areas as basis for comity agreements.

> *Committee on the West Indies.* Includes representatives of boards administering work in Cuba, Haiti, the Dominican Republic, Puerto Rico and the Virgin Islands; has a resident rural co-ordinator in Puerto Rico to correlate the various denominational projects into a comprehensive program.

> *Committee on Co-operation in the Intermountain Area.* Holds annual conference of denominational leaders of the Western mountain area with board executives.

> *Committee on the Christian Approach to the Jews.* Correlates the work of the boards interested in establishing Christian relations with Jews.

> *Committee on Missionary Personnel.* Brings into consultation board executives responsible for personnel work; develops methods of recruiting, selecting and training personnel.

> *Committee on Youth and Student Work.* Strengthens presentation of home missions to youth; co-ordinates various types of youth summer service projects.

Administration of Work Done Co-operatively

> *Co-operative Ministry to Migrants.* Provides program of religious ministry in agricultural migrant labor camps in 25 states with a staff of 20 full-time trained ministers and community workers during the crop seasons, supplemented by 200 summer workers.

> *Christian Service to Sharecroppers and Tenant Farmers.* Develops program for training local leadership among sharecroppers and tenant farmers in 13 states; co-operates with state colleges of agriculture; sponsors extension classes for rural pastors and for women; includes nine Negro staff members with graduate training.

> *Committee on Indian Work.* Employs religious work directors at ten government schools of the nonreservation

type; sponsors Cook Christian Training School at Phoenix, Arizona; sponsors the National Fellowship of Indian Workers; conducts a literary training program among the Navahos on the Reservation.

JOINT DEPARTMENTS

In addition to the Departments which operate primarily within the structure of one of the four Divisions of the Council are seven Joint Departments which are functionally related to more than one Division but which are administratively related to one Division. Of these, Benevolences, Evangelism, Religious Liberty and Stewardship are related administratively to the Division of Christian Life and Work; Christian Life Service and Family Life, to the Division of Christian Education; American Committees Overseas, to the Division of Foreign Missions.

The functions of these Joint Departments are as follows:

American Committee Overseas. Seeks to provide an appropriate Christian ministry overseas for American diplomats, businessmen, merchant-marine personnel and tourists who are going to many parts of the world in increasing numbers; advises, and provides or encourages support for existing churches or groups seeking to establish churches.

Christian Life Service. Serves the churches in presenting the appeal of Christian life service to youth; assists in recruiting for the ministry of the churches at home and for missionary service at home and abroad; produces promotional materials and conducts conferences for youth to assist them in making their choice of vocation.

Evangelism. Enables the churches to make a united evangelistic impact on a community, utilizing mass meetings, the press, radio and other means not available so readily, if at all, to the denominations separately; assists in training laymen and organizing campaigns for visitation evangelism; sponsors University Christian Missions.

Family Life. Produces special educational and other resources for use in developing a more Christian family life and maintaining the integrity of the home; sponsors training conferences for leaders; assists in promoting institutes on family life.

Religious Liberty. Studies and reports threats to religious liberty anywhere in the world; interprets problems of church-state relationships; arranges for appropriate representation of the Council to the government on matters of concern to the churches.

Stewardship. Correlates the work of the denominations in the cultivation of the habit of stewardship of all resources and in education in stewardship; produces special materials for education; provides a place of fellowship and mutual assistance for denominational secretaries of stewardship.

GENERAL DEPARTMENTS

The Divisions with their Departments, as well as the Joint Departments, have special functional responsibilities within the Council. Two General Departments have special responsibilities in connection with special constituency groups—laymen and lay women.

United Church Men. This General Department does not represent the continuation of a previous agency. It is a new unit, organized without precedent at the Constituting Convention of the Council. It is composed of the laymen who are members of the Council, together with representatives of the boards of lay activities or other laymen's organizations of the member denominations. It seeks to correlate the work of the Council and the interests and activities of laymen.

United Church Women. This unit continues and extends the work of the United Council of Church Women, one of the agencies which was merged into the Council. It works with 1,600 organized state and local councils of church women. It sponsors nation-wide events for rallying church women and has its own special projects which are supported by women, but it promotes the total interests of the Council.

CENTRAL DEPARTMENTS

Several Central Departments, related to the general administration of the Council and serving all its units, are distinguishable by their specialized services:

Architectural Services. Provides professional counseling services to local churches and to mission and church extension boards in connection with building projects; encourages structures matched with financial resources, conducive to worship and adaptable to other functional uses.

Broadcasting and Films. One of the largest units of the Council in terms of production and administration, it directs interdenominational broadcasting of many national-network radio and television programs; produces recordings; produces and distributes moving pictures and slides for educational and promotional use.

Church World Service. Assists the churches to achieve a coordinated program of relief and reconstruction, aid to churches overseas, service to refugees, resettlement of displaced persons, gathering, processing and shipping of contributed supplies; represents the interest of the Council's constituency in such co-operative programs as CROP and CARE.

Ecumenical Relations. Correlates the relations of the various units of the Council with world ecumenical organizations; supervises scholarship exchanges for theological students and others from abroad; administers the Interchange of Preachers between other countries and the United States.

Field Administration. Provides a counseling service for nearly 850 autonomous state, county and city councils of churches and religious education; helps to organize regional inter-denominational offices; correlates the field programs of the several units of the Council among themselves and with the field outreach of the denominations.

Research and Survey. Serves the Council as a whole and its units in research and special studies; provides a field survey service to the denominations to guide them in the strategic distribution of churches in relation to population and to make available data on which to base comity agreements.

Several other Central Departments which serve the Council as a whole are adequately characterized by their names: Finance, Public Relations, Publication and Distribution, and Treasury and Business Management.

Having in mind the broad base of the total resources of the churches as well as this new agency, the National Council, which they have constituted to make their influence more effective, we should analyze the challenge and opportunity with which the present world crisis confronts them. The analysis is not easy. For more than a decade we have been preoccupied as a nation with war and its attendant problems.

One of the worst things about war is that it so concentrates the attention of people on military effort that they become habituated to military patterns of analysis and strategy. More basic factors are neglected, if not forgotten. A war map of Korea, during the military campaign there, could show very graphically the changing position of opposing armies, but it could not register the attitudes of the Korean people and other Asiatics toward the powers represented by those opposing armies.

The basic issues of our world will not be settled ultimately by military means alone, as was observed early in this chapter. Military strategy is only one aspect of a total strategy in the struggle for the minds and hearts of men.

Dr. Charles Malik, the delegate from Lebanon to the United Nations, is highly esteemed in that body as one of its leaders. He is taken seriously because of his competence and character, obviously not because of the military or economic potential of the nation he represents. When he was President of the Economic and Social Council in 1948, as Chairman of the Assembly Committee, he led in the difficult task of formulating the Declaration on Human Rights. Much credit is due him for that significant achievement.

As a member of the Commission of the Churches on International Affairs (of the World Council of Churches and the International Missionary Council) Dr. Malik is making a contribution in Christian circles also.

In a speech before the important Political Committee of the United Nations on November 23, 1949, this Christian spoke on war and peace and the responsibilities of Communism and Western culture. This is not an unusual topic for a speech these days. But most of the speeches we hear are cold-war speeches—indicting or defending, defaming or extolling. Thoughtful analysis is rare. Dr. Malik pleads with both East and West—not that he is neutral, for he is not. It is his plea to the West, with his analysis, that gives us much to ponder.

Speaking "in all humility," Dr. Malik decried "a tragic dearth" of men who are "so genuinely in touch with the truth and with the hearts of their fellow men as to have only to open their minds to be loved and believed and followed. The world desperately cries for masters; for it is only the voice of conviction and truth that is going to save us. There is a corresponding bankruptcy of fundamental ideas."

As a result there is "an unequal struggle for the hearts of men between Communism and the West." There is no ideological passion in the West comparable to that of Communists for their "set of generic ideas," which are "for the most part false." In the West "the talk about democracy, freedom, representative government, is woefully inadequate; it deals for the most part with pure form, sheer external machinery. It does not satisfy man's deepest cravings for friendship and understanding and truth and love. . . .

"The only effective answer to Communism is a genuine spiritualized materialism which seeks to remove every trace of social injustice without loss of the higher values which constitute the very soul of the West. . . .

"If your only export in these realms is the silent example of flourishing political institutions and happy human relations, you cannot lead. If your only export is a distant reputation for wealth and prosperity and order, you cannot lead. . . .

"We must hope and pray that there will develop in the Western World a mighty spiritual movement which will rediscover and reaffirm its glorious hidden values, and fulfill mankind's longing for a more just order of things, a more beautiful world, a New Heaven and a New Earth. . . .

"If the Western world can show a way to eradicate the shame and scandal of poverty, of exploitation, of oppression, of greed, without resort to social revolution and class struggle and dictatorship; if it can place these material values in their proper subordinate place within the context of a mighty spiritual movement which will be revolutionary without being subversive and which will draw its substance from the infinite riches of the Western positive tradition, then the necessity for Communism will vanish, and the specter which now walks the earth will be laid forever." [1]

Probably no nation in history has had so grave a responsibility for maintaining the values of human civilization that enable man to live in dignity and develop his God-given potentialities as America has today. In material wealth and power she has unprecedented resources. In scientific knowledge and inventive genius she is unsurpassed.

But has America the moral stability, the mature insight and the spiritual dynamism to give her real power and enable her to meet the challenge Dr. Malik defines? Unless she develops these resources in greater measure, she will fail and the world may well despair.

Whether America develops these most essential resources de-

[1] New York *Herald Tribune*, November 28, 1949.

pends on the churches primarily. As America's responsibility is
crucial in the world, so the churches' responsibility is crucial in
America. History has, therefore, given to the task of our churches
an almost staggering import. We might almost say: as the American churches go, so goes the world.

The church people are awaking to the significance of their task.
The most convincing evidence of the vitality of the churches is
found in the increasing participation of the laity in leadership. This
applies to both men and women.

Women have been active traditionally in "aid societies" and missionary societies. They have studied what the churches were doing
and have raised money to support them. But they have not had
much voice in determining policy.

Today lay women are serving on the official boards of many local
churches. They are on the mission, education and general boards of
the national denominations. Both the American Baptist Convention and the Congregational-Christian churches have more than
once elected a woman to the highest office in the denomination.
Women hold full professorships in several of our leading theological seminaries.

When it was merged in the National Council of Churches, the
United Council of Church Women had 1,600 state and local affiliated councils which took an interest in questions of church policy
and public affairs as well as missions, education and social welfare.

Traditionally laymen have participated primarily as managers
of the business activities in connection with the churches' work, as
trustees of property and investments, as financial contributors and
solicitors, as Sunday-school teachers and leaders of youth and
boys' clubs.

Today, while continuing to serve in these capacities, they are
also taking more active leadership in determining policy and program not only in the local church but also in the national bodies.
The change is not in denominational structure and procedure, for
Protestant churches have generally given the laity at least as much
voice in the national legislative body of the denomination as the
clergy has had. The recent change has been in the degree of active
participation.

In determining the position of the churches on matters of pub-

lic policy, the influence of the laity has often been predominant.
Laymen were largely in control of the National Study Conference
on the Church and Economic Life at Detroit in 1950. Of the total
of 381 delegates, 248 were laymen and women. They have been
in leadership at the National Study Conferences on the Church and
World Order. The Federal Council of Churches had recently a lay
president and lay chairmen of the departments of Christian Social
Relations, International Justice and Good Will, and Race Relations.

It is no longer unusual for a denomination to have a layman as
its highest elected officer. There are many lay presidents of local
councils of churches. Some of the principal staff officers of denominational and interdenominational agencies are laymen.

Perhaps even more important than these developments is the
increasing participation of laymen in the fundamental work of
spreading the Gospel. The testimony of the average church member
among his neighbors and associates is more common than it was.
Lay visitation evangelism is one of its organized aspects.

Men are taking more and more pride in telling about their work
in the Church. The change may be illustrated by two men who left
good positions in secular work to join church organizations—one
fifteen years ago, the other recently. Both entered a church occupation out of conviction as to its strategic importance and at considerable sacrifice of income. The first found it somewhat difficult
to explain his decision to his old associates; they regarded him as
a sentimentalist or an "idealist." The second, fifteen years later,
had no difficulty in explaining to his colleagues why he was going
to a church organization; some were envious of his opportunity.

The man quoted at the beginning of this chapter is not unique.
On the contrary he is a symbol of a new understanding of the role
of the Church in American life and in the world. He is probably
a more significant index of the state of the Church than are all the
census and membership statistics.

What hope is there, then, that the churches will be adequate? We
have indicated that they are exerting a wider influence—but not
enough. Statistics indicate that they have a larger constituency
than ever before—but not enough. They have immense institutional resources—but not enough. More laymen are taking an

active part in the work of the churches—but not enough. The National Council of Churches provides an agency for effective voluntary co-ordination of strategy and influence—but it remains to be seen whether it will be adequately utilized and supported.

It requires no extraordinary insight or historical perspective to arrive at the conclusion that the most strategic and effective investment of life—time, effort, money—that a person can make in serving this day and generation is the investment made in the churches.

Most of the analysis and reasoning that have brought us to this conclusion have been rather pragmatic. The basic reason for hope that the churches may meet the crucial test is that they are more than human institutions. It is because God's power is in the churches when they are faithful and loyal that we dare hope.

To the extent that the churches have gained in real strength, the gain is attributable to God's power. Just as the layman testified to a power at the Detroit Conference that he likened to Pentecost, so we testify that any real achievement of the churches is the achievement of God.

So the summons is to men to be co-laborers with God in the churches of which Christ is the Head. If the strength of the nation is to be adequate to the needs of the world, it is required of us only that we be faithful.

Europe—Survival or Renewal?

3

By W. A. VISSER 't HOOFT

CAN Europe survive? That is the question which is asked not only by statesmen around the conference table but equally by young people who wonder whether they may not have more chance to live meaningful lives in other parts of the world. The question is not always stated explicitly, but it is always there underneath the surface.

A keen observer from India wrote recently: "Europe gives the impression of a tired old man, too tired and too old to have any hope in the future." There is truth in this statement. And it is not difficult to understand why Europe feels this way. It is such a very short time since Europe was the central creative and dynamic element in the world situation. And it is hard to get accustomed to the new position, in which Europe's destiny depends so very largely on the decisions and actions of extra-European powers. There is furthermore the deep fatigue which the second World War has left behind it—very particularly among the very best Europeans, the gallant band who fought the battle for Europe in the resistance movements against National Socialism. And there is also the paralyzing effect of the separation of Europe by the ideological frontier, which cut it as a whole into two watertight compartments, but which also divides great nations into blocs between which no true conversation is possible.

Now there is no lack of doctors who seek to cure the patient. Serious and not wholly unsuccessful attempts are being made to save Europe. The wise and generous action of the American people has already had the provisional result of staving off a total collapse. European statesmen and economists have gone far in working out possible solutions of some of the most crucial problems which the continent faces. The movement toward European federation has met with a real response and given new courage to many.

But somehow all these useful and necessary measures do not seem to go to the root of the problem. Their common aim is the *survival* of Europe. But do civilizations survive when they make mere survival their aim? Is it not a law of human life and history that survival depends ultimately on the presence and strength of the reasons for survival? Can Europe live unless it finds a purpose to live for?

To my mind the answer to these questions is clear. Europe cannot live merely for the sake of Europe. Whenever it has been truly alive, it has lived for something greater than itself. However egotistic it may often have appeared to the peoples of other continents, it has (even through its crusades and conquests) sought to give as well as take. And it suffers today from the fact that so little is expected of it. Even though, at first sight, Europe's sickness is due to such tangible causes as war, social conflict and economic disintegration, the basic trouble is in a less tangible realm. It is that Europe has lost its sense of vocation. And no plan to save Europe is therefore adequate unless it deals with this root problem. Europe can survive only if it rediscovers its calling—in other words, if it is renewed in the very core of its existence. It is not a question of survival or renewal. Europe can survive only *by* renewal. And the great question is whether in the tired old continent there are forces at work which can give it that purposeful new life without which no civilization can live.

The forces exist, and the purpose of this chapter is to describe some of them. Owing to the limitation of space and the limitation of my range of contacts the description does not pretend to be complete. I will deal especially with those new spiritual forces which have arisen within the Christian churches and, in particular, those which co-operate in the ecumenical movement. But in order to see these forces in their proper perspective, we have to look first of all at the background of the present spiritual situation in Europe.

Since the days of Constantine the Great, Europe has been the Christian continent par excellence. The story of the Church and the story of European culture had become so intermingled that no one could disentangle them. And it became difficult to decide whether in Europe Christianity had succeeded in embracing society or whether society had succeeded in embracing Christianity. The attempt of the Reformation to arrive at a clearer demarcation between the Church and the world was only partially successful. For a long time after the Reformation, in certain churches even up to our time, the fiction has been maintained that they lived (or live) in a Christian environment. They continued (or continue) to speak and act as if they were surrounded by a world which was (or is) fundamentally in agreement with the central affirmations of Christianity.

A terribly dangerous fiction! For in the meantime large areas of life and culture and great masses of men had already turned away from the churches and established new frameworks of thought and life which had only the remotest relation to Christianity. Almost overlapping with the Reformation there had been the great movement of emancipation called the Renaissance—but it had not touched the masses to any considerable extent. A second far more radical wave of secularization came in the last decades of the seventeenth and the first decades of the eighteenth centuries. From that time onward the creative intellectual forces of Europe were no longer inspired by Christian convictions. The tremendous development of the sciences in the nineteenth century succeeded in creating the impression that the Church was definitely outclassed as the leader of mankind. Science seemed to possess the key to the future.

It was of course inevitable that when the dynamic intellectual forces proved to be non-Christian, the intellectual classes found themselves in fact living outside the life of the Church. But the Church might have remained the church of the people. Its position as the spiritual home of the workers and peasants was, however, undermined when the new social movements arose, toward which the churches took a negative or at least noncommittal attitude. Moreover the type of socialism which came to dominate the working classes was the Marxist one which declared religion irrelevant or even hostile to social progress. Thus by the second half of the nineteenth century the most dynamic elements of European continental society were living outside the reach of the churches and losing increasingly their rootage in the common Christian heritage. And the churches were left with that hard-to-describe middle class which represents certainly a solid and stable element of society, but which cannot be said to shape the destiny of the nations or to be a truly creative element in society.

If it is remembered how far the "reducing process" of Christianity had advanced, it is less surprising that after the first World War there occurred the great open outbreaks of the totalitarian and fundamentally non-Christian spirit.

The first of these outbreaks occurred in Russia and since Russia had always been considered a country which followed her own specific historical laws and did not really belong to Europe, it was at first not taken too seriously. When it was found, however, that the new revolutionary society acted as a powerful center of attraction for considerable sections of the labor movement, and when it was realized how far the Communist party had gone in the liquidation of the Church, the reaction was one of deep concern. But there were not many Christians who understood the full and far-reaching significance of this first radical breaking away of a "Christian" country from its spiritual tradition. In any case the churches did not show any signs of getting ready for a total showdown with the world.

The second outbreak was that of National Socialism. Though in its earliest stages it sought to cover up its fundamentally pagan inspiration by using the misleading term "positive Christianity," it soon made it abundantly clear that it could conceive of the Church only as a servant of an absolute State which was a law unto itself and which had its real motivation in the myth of blood and soil. It was the second outbreak of unrestrained paganism which showed how much of European culture had become rootless and empty of spiritual content. It was typical that for a time there appeared in Italy a magazine with the significant name *Anti-Europa,* and that the ideological spokesman attacked every one of the great traditions of European history. It was terribly revealing that such a large number of the intellectuals in different walks of life responded like sheep to the new slogans. And during the occupation years there were enough men and women in the occupied countries who collaborated with the new masters of Europe to make it clear that no European country could dismiss this attack on all that Europe had stood for by claiming that "it can't happen here."

The Christian churches were utterly unprepared for a conflict with paganism. They had not been unaware of the increasing secularization, but they had never adjusted themselves to the new situation. They continued to live in the fictitious Christian world, the fool's paradise of that *"Corpus Christianum"* in which Church and Nation were believed to be co-extensive. Thus they sought to conserve at a time when aggressive evangelism was called for. They sought to defend their increasingly small realm of influence at a time when a concerted attack on secular culture was required. They paid their respects to the modern world at a moment when that world was on the way to spiritual bankruptcy.

Thus when the open attack upon the churches began there was at first utter confusion. It seemed unbelievable that the Christianized European world could behave as if it were the pagan world of old, the *kosmos* of the New Testament which hates the Church of Christ. The confusion led to the attempt on the part of some to adjust the Christian message even to the National Socialist ideology and so to produce an unholy amalgam of Christian and primitive racial notions. But it was precisely this manifestation of the radical danger of a complete sellout to the world which provided the necessary stimulus for a gathering together of all who knew about the true and only *raison d'être* of the Church of Christ. Thus the "confessing church" was born within the official Church. The year 1934, when the protest against the attempted violation of the Church was first clearly heard and the "Barmen Declaration" with its clear and sharp definitions of the true nature of the Church was proclaimed, deserves to be remembered as a crucial date in European history. For the new church struggle meant nothing less than after centuries of false peace the Church became again manifest as a *militant* church, as a church which accepted the challenge of the world and which set out to meet it.

The story of the church struggle in Germany and later on in Norway, Holland and other countries is by no means a story of pure Christian heroism. Yes, there have been wonderfully pure witnesses and even martyrs, for whom we must continuously be grateful. It is a great blessing for our generation to have been contemporaries of men and women who have actually preferred death to denial of their Lord and His will for them. But with regard to the Church as a whole the story of the conflict is one in which certainty and confusion, courage and compromise, are strangely mixed up. Nevertheless, the very fact that the Church was called again to fight for its existence has made a vast difference to all those who had the privilege of being involved in the spiritual battle.

There are certain discoveries which the Church cannot easily make when it is more or less at peace with the world, but which strike home with amazing force when it is up against it. The most important of these is that the Word of God is not bound— or, to put it otherwise, that the freedom which the Lord of the Church gives to His people is a freedom which no one can take away. This sounds highly paradoxical, but it is a simple fact that it takes the loss of the ordinary civil liberties to make the Church realize that there is a deeper freedom which the Lord Himself defends and uses.

Thus we see the surprising phenomenon that the same churches which in peaceful times had not spoken out clearly begin to speak courageous words for Christianity when such action implies conflict and the paying of a high price in further suffering. At the same time the discovery of this unassailable freedom brings a new joy to the churches: it is seen that the great promises of the Gospel of Christ, which had seemed to be so very remote and unreal, are literally and actually true. In the hour of need the Church and its members receive the word which must be spoken.

Thus the time of conflict brought new life to the churches. Some of the narcotic effects of their silent alliance with the world were at last shaken off. The realities of the situation became clear. The churches found out that they had to fight or die. It was no time for mere defense. And at no time during recent centuries have the churches found such an eager and grateful response to their message as in the days when they stood out as the only solid front against a total paganization of European culture.

When the second World War ended it seemed at first as if the churches would get their great opportunity to hold a thorough spring cleaning, to start afresh in their own life and to undertake their long-neglected task as pastors and prophets of the peoples. There was reason to hope that a new day had dawned and that an immense spiritual revival would take place. Would the great judgment that had come over the nations not lead them to true repentance? Could so much suffering fail to produce a new obedience? Would the churches, which had learned again to bear witness and had done so when evidence of faith was costly, not continue to speak clearly to the nations in the days of freedom?

This total renewal which was hoped for, and this widespread revival which was expected, did not come. As we will see later on, the years of war produced fruits—but the great promise which they seemed to bear was not really fulfilled. The movement of renewal met with the formidable countercurrent of the desire for restoration of the prewar conditions.

It is not difficult to find more or less plausible reasons why the visions of the war years did not materialize. There was the huge physical and spiritual waste of energy of the hard years. There was the misery of the postwar years. There was the general phenomenon which occurs after all wars—the search for the security of old established traditions. But somehow these explanations do not seem quite adequate. For the question remains: if this great judgment of God did not bring His people to a total renewal, what further judgment will be required to teach them complete obedience? And to that question there is no human answer. We can only hope that God in His infinite patience will not reject His people, in spite of their unwillingness to respond totally to His call.

The upshot of the war years was then a spiritual situation which was partly static and partly dynamic. The new and the old were strangely intermingled, and in almost every church in Europe there was the conflict between the forces of conservatism which sought to return to the ways of the good old days and the forces of renewal which realized that the churches were called to newness of life, to reformation of all that had become deformed in the course of their history and to a total mobilization for the new evangelistic task.

My purpose in this chapter is, however, to describe the new

forces in Europe and to show that, in spite of the weight of the decrepit and anachronistic elements in European life, the movement of rejuvenation continues to exert its reforming and transforming influence in many realms.

This is not the place to enter deeply into problems of theology,[1] but it is impossible to describe the contemporary Christian situation in Europe without reference to the fundamental change which has taken place in theological thought. This revolution had already begun in the twenties and thirties, but its full effect became apparent during the war years. In fact, the stand taken by the Church during those years could not possibly have been as definite and clear as it was if the new theology had not provided the necessary substance. The name which is most prominently connected with this theological renewal is, of course, that of Karl Barth. And it is indeed hard to exaggerate the influence which he has had, not only on his followers, but also on those who, while not accepting his conclusions, were forced to answer the fundamental questions which he asked. Nevertheless, the movement cannot carry the name of any single theologian, for it had many different sources. For our purpose the important point is what influence this theological revival has had on the life of the churches. I believe that this influence can be briefly described in the following three points.

First of all, it brought the churches back to the living message of the Bible. After a period in which the historical approach to the Bible had concentrated on the origins of each individual book and of its composite parts, but had obscured the cohesion of the Bible as a whole and the unity of God's plan revealed in it, the new theology opened the eyes of many once again to the total Biblical message and showed to theologians and laymen alike how indispensable and supremely relevant the study of the Bible is to the life of the Church and of each of its members.

In the second place, it gave to preaching once again its original and proper place. It dared maintain that the true sense of preaching is not the holding of lectures on religious experiences or problems, not the exposition of Christian dogma, but the proclamation of

[1] For a full report on the recent theological development in Europe see W. A. Visser 't Hooft, *The Kingship of Christ* (Harper & Brothers, 1948).

the living word which God speaks to His people today. It would be untrue to say that the full implications of this truth have been generally understood and accepted, but it has given new power and significance to the preaching of many ministers.

In the third place, it has helped powerfully in the rediscovery that the Church has its own history, which is intermingled with but ultimately not dependent on the history of the world. It thus delivers the Church from that nervousness which expresses itself in constant attempts to keep up with the world or in a fear of what the future may hold. When the Church knows that its life is not in the hands of men but in the hands of God, it can have that quiet confidence which enables it to speak to the world with true authority and conviction. This is not to say that the churches have truly reached that point, but that they have been powerfully reminded of this truth.

It is dangerous to generalize about spiritual events among great masses of men in many nations. But it would seem that almost everywhere in Europe it may be said that since the war the intellectual climate is decidedly less impenetrable for the Christian message than it was before the war. This is not surprising. The outbreak of a lawless totalitarianism had destroyed the artificial structure of humanitarian idealism and belief in progress through scientific advance which had been the "secret religion of the intellectuals." The extraordinary ease with which the various new ideologies had captured proud universities and gained control over the world of science, art and letters had made it abundantly clear how unreal, weak and incoherent had been the various philosophies and ideologies on which modern intellectual culture was based. Thus many who had discovered the lack of any foundation for their life, and who were struck by the fact that the seemingly outmoded churches had in the moment of crisis stood the test, became ready to reconsider their facile rejection of the Christian message.

This is especially notable in the university world. There was a time—not long ago—when a Christian university professor was a rare bird and considered by his colleagues a more or less eccentric phenomenon. Today this has largely changed and it has changed most clearly in a country like Germany where the spiritual conflict has been felt most deeply. Similarly there is far greater openness among the student body to a direct Christian appeal. To those who have known the small Bible-study circles among students in Germany before the war, it is a great surprise to find a regular attendance of hundreds of students at Biblical lectures in the main universities. Similarly the realm of literature is no longer exclusively dominated by the advocates of a pure vitalism to whom Christianity is abhorent because it interferes with pure and unrestrained self-expression. Their successors, the existentialists, have raised the question of the meaning of life in such an acute and desperate form that they almost force their readers to wonder whether God does not exist after all. In this situation the Christian authors, dramatists and poets meet with a new response. The present European situation leaves little room for in-between positions. And so the voices which carry weight are those announcing a definite and clear-cut conviction concerning the meaning of life. This becomes specially clear when the attempt is made to bring together the outstanding representatives of the main contemporary philosophies. Thus at the "Rencontres Internationales" held annually at Geneva the deepest impression is made by the Christians—both Protestant and Roman Catholic—and by the Communists. And Karl Barth, who took a prominent part in those discussions in 1949, could rightly speak of a new phenomenon which he had observed—a certain inferiority complex of the participants with regard to the Christian position. No one should think that this means that the intellectual life of Europe is on the verge of being converted. On the other hand it would seem that the process of increasing cultural secularization has passed its climax and that a new opportunity is given to the Church to reoccupy the intellectual areas which it had been forced to give up.

When a society has been very largely secularized the Christian layman finds himself in an almost impossible position. The convictions which he holds as a Christian seem to be completely out of place in and irrelevant to the society in which he carries on his daily task. As long as his church presents Christian faith as a purely other-worldly message which affects only the inner life, or as long as his church advocates a far-reaching adaptation of Christianity to the canons of modern culture, he may not become conscious of the duality in his life. But when the Church becomes again a militant church and proclaims the Lordship of Christ over all realms of life, he cannot fail to become aware of the tragic tension between the demands of the Christian religion and the realities of his daily environment.

It is therefore not surprising that in the years following the new mobilization of the Church, Christian laymen in many European countries simultaneously, though without any previous consultation with one another, began to struggle with the problem of fulfilling the Christian vocation in their various professions and occupations. The Christian professional associations or movements which they formed were not conceived as attempts to make laymen more active in church life (that was taken care of in many other ways) but as a training center for the leadership in the struggle against non-Christian and anti-Christian standards of secular culture. Nor was this task conceived as a merely ethical one. For it was soon discovered that the real issues between Christianity and modern civilization lie in deeper realms. It proved necessary to analyze the underlying philosophies of industry, of politics, of law, of art, of the sciences, to confront these with Christian truth and formulate a Christian strategy with regard to these fields of human endeavor.

There is probably no other field of activity in which so much new ground has been broken and which has met with such remarkable response. It was a great help that these spontaneous movements could find their natural center for co-operation and mutual enrichment in the Ecumenical Institute near Geneva which had been opened in 1946 by the World Council of Churches. For in this manner Christian men of one and the same profession could share their insights across the frontiers. It was not unusual that men who had known one another professionally suddenly discovered in this new environment that they had a deep common desire to give Christian meaning to their lifework. Members of the medical profession try to work out what it means to treat patients as total human beings whose spiritual problems are no less important than their physical symptoms. Lawyers turn from a purely technical and pragmatic conception of law to an understanding of law as the expression of the eternal order of God. Employers and workers seek for ways and means in which work in industry may be given new meaning.

The new approach to the problems of the laity is, however, not confined to the relatively small groups which are able to do the necessary pioneering work. Through the printed page and through larger meetings wider groups are reached. The most remarkable example of the attempt to mobilize the laity for its task in the world of today is the annual *Kirchentag* in Germany. Its organizers had hoped to reach large numbers. But they had never expected that in their second year they would already meet with such overwhelming response. The great closing meeting of the series of meetings of laymen at Essen in September 1950 was attended by 180,000 men and women from all walks of life. It is by no means easy to ensure that such a vast meeting does not deteriorate into a typical mass meeting with emotional appeals and popular slogans. But it proved possible to avoid such dangers. The enormous crowd, assembled in the stadium specially built (out of the rubble of the ruins) for the occasion, listened with remarkable concentration to the speakers who shared with them the conclusions of the various working groups on the specific responsibilities of Christian laymen in the life of our sick society.

Before the second World War it was the exception rather than the rule that the European churches as such expressed themselves publicly with regard to burning national or international problems. Today the churches know that it is their duty to give guidance to their members on vital political and social problems in which spiritual or moral issues are at stake. But it is one thing to realize that the Church is called to speak a liberating word; it is another to find that word and to proclaim it. During the years of conflict the front was clear and the issues were sharply defined. In the postwar era the political and social situations are full of moral ambiguity. And since the voice of non-Roman churches can never be the voice of one single church leader or of a very small group of church leaders, the churches find it often impossible to speak out definitely because of the divisions in their own midst.

In these circumstances it is all the more remarkable that in a number of cases the churches have spoken very clearly. And when they have thus spoken, their word has met with very real response. A case in point is the well-known "Stuttgart declaration" of the Council of the German Evangelical Church in 1945. This declaration has been very widely debated, but there is no doubt that it has exerted a real influence in clarifying the moral and spiritual atmosphere in Germany. Similarly the resolutions on the Jewish question and on peace adopted by the synod of the same church in Berlin in 1950 and representing the convictions of church leaders of both Eastern and Western Germany have made a deep impression, because they rendered it clear that peace need not necessarily be conceived in the terms of the political propagandists and can be built only on spiritual foundations.

In the purely social realm the voice of the Church has been less clear. Churches in Holland, France and Germany have spoken out on the subject, but their statements have not carried great weight because they lacked in concreteness and incisiveness. In this connection the question arises again and again how far the Church has a right to go in dealing with social and political issues. If it becomes very concrete it is accused of meddling in politics; if it speaks in general terms its word is felt to be irrelevant. In some countries Christian political parties—sometimes confessional, sometimes interconfessional—exist and the application of the convictions of the churches is left to them. But there is a very great danger that the more or less fixed programs of such parties with their Christian label create the impression that the Church is identified with one particular political and social viewpoint.

The direct impact of the Church through its work of reconstruction and relief has been more effective. This has been an opportunity to demonstrate in a very tangible manner that the churches do not live unto themselves but are ready to serve all who are in need. And there have been many emergency situations in which the churches rather than any official or secular organizations have helped first and most effectively. The relief action of the churches at the time of the famine in Holland, the vast network of reconstruction and rehabilitation created by the *Hilfswerk* in Germany, the work of the *Cimade* in the devastated cities of France have brought the churches right into the midst of the life of the nations and at the point of greatest need. And the churches of the "giving" countries outside and inside Europe have through their generous support of all these activities not only given relief to the needy, but also helped powerfully to enable the European churches to demonstrate their concern for the nation as a whole.

The hardest and biggest task which the European churches have had to undertake in this connection is the service to the millions of refugees. The refugee problem in Europe is by no means a mere problem of relief. It is also a crucial social and political one. But it is in the last resort a spiritual issue. For the refugee is almost bound to become an element of disintegration unless he finds a new spiritual home. Here then it is the task of the churches to provide that home and to prove to the refugee that in spite of all he has lost he is not forgotten by God and men. In this field the European churches have accepted responsibilities which far exceed their strength in man power and money. Thus it is a blessing that the American churches as well as churches in Canada, New Zealand and Australia have come to the rescue and provided remarkably generous support.

Another important approach to the problems of Europe is made by the Ecumenical Commission for European Co-operation. During the war years the Christians in the resistance movements had given a good deal of time and thought to the working out of plans for European federation. And it is remarkable that a considerable number of the pioneers for European co-operation in the governmental and nongovernmental organizations set up for this purpose are men who are rooted in the life of the Church. But the churches as such had been slow in giving their members any lead in this matter. The Ecumenical Commission for European Co-operation, which is composed of politicians and economists, now seeks to define what specific message the churches should convey. For it is very clear that there will be no progress toward greater unity in Europe unless spiritual forces are released which will overcome the psychology of fear, of self-seeking and of mere conservatism that still dominates the political negotiations.

The question remains, however, whether any of these new manifestations of Christian faith and life affect the lives of the masses and very especially of the industrial workers, who form such a vast part of modern society. Owing to the lack of imagination of the churches and to the materialistic inspiration of the continental European Socialist parties, an almost unbridgeable gulf had arisen in the second half of the nineteenth century between churches defending the ethos and morals of a preindustrial society and the workers living in the technical and impersonal world of big industry. The fellowship of the labor union and the loyalty to the Socialist—later also the Communist—cause seemed to take the place of the Church and the Christian faith. Between the two wars André Siegfried defined the situation as follows: "While the educated classes return to the Church, the masses turn away from it."

Have the experiences of the second World War made any difference in this respect? Yes—but only in a limited sense. In the first place, the churches now realize what has happened and are beginning to face the facts. The real situation is no longer covered up. Studies which have been made in different European countries have revealed that the overwhelming majority of the workers live in an environment in which almost no trace of the Christian heritage remains. And the conscience of the churches is troubled by these stubborn and inescapable facts.

There is today in the European churches a strong desire to make up for the sins of omission and commission of the past, and to bring the Christian message to the workers. But at this point it becomes clear how deeply the Church has been affected by its more or less unconscious acceptance of an alliance with specific forms of society. For it is the common experience of all who seek to reach the unchurched masses that the social, moral and spiritual structure of the Church as it is makes it practically impossible to bring it in vital contact with the men and women or young people who live in the completely different world of the industrial workers, and who do not see why in accepting Christianity they should at the same time accept a style of life which would alienate them completely from their fellow workers. In this realm nothing less is needed than a liberation from the sociological imprisonment in which the churches find themselves. In the meantime, gallant efforts are being made to reach the workers within their own framework of life. Such pioneering efforts have very great significance as reminders to the Church of its true task. But they will not have very considerable results until the churches have learned that evangelism means, not inviting outsiders to imitate the members of existing congregations, but rather going out with the one purpose of sharing the Christian truth and letting that truth create new forms of life and fellowship in the actual environment in which men spend their lives.

Another difference which the war years have made is that the gulf which separated the churches from the Socialist movement is no longer as great as it used to be. On the one hand, the Socialists have come to recognize more and more that their original brushing away of religion as a "private affair" and their dialectical materialism weaken rather than strengthen them in their struggle for social justice on a democratic foundation. On the other hand, the Churches have begun to understand that they must listen to the demand for social justice, even if that demand comes to them in unfamiliar and secular forms.

. So far I have said little of the Eastern European churches. Their situation is so completely different that it must be discussed separately. I have already underlined how deeply the whole life of a church is affected when it moves out of the situation of being accepted and respected by the world into the situation of conflict with the world. Now for the Eastern European churches that change has come in a very radical and dramatic manner. For they lived in nations which in spite of all secular tendencies had continued to give them special protection. And most of them were in one way or another linked to the State. When the change of regime came they found themselves suddenly in a completely unknown world, the official philosophy of which was openly anti-Christian. The new State declared that it stood for religious liberty; it did not mean the unhampered activity of the churches in all fields of their work, but only freedom of worship within the walls of church buildings. At the same time the churches began to meet with considerable difficulties in their religious education and youth work.

Now the first question to ask about churches in occupied areas is not the one which our generation, obsessed as it is with politics, generally asks first, namely: "What is their attitude to Communism?" The primary question is: "How does the Church accomplish its central task, and how does it live in this situation?"

And, however surprising and even shocking this may seem to many, the answer given unanimously by churchmen from these countries and confirmed by those who have had occasion to visit their churches is that they have gained greatly in vitality and meet with a deeper and wider response than they have known for many decades. In Western countries the stories about the persecution of religion in Eastern Europe have left a general impression that the churches have practically ceased to exist. As a matter of fact they not only continue to exist; they speak as with one voice of increased attendance, of a new sense of fellowship in the congregations, of greater readiness on the part of the laymen to bear responsibilities and even of new opportunities for evangelism.

This is not to say that the obstacles created by a hostile ideology do not exist, and even less that perfect religious liberty in the full sense of that term reigns. On the contrary it is easy to draw up a long list of all the restrictions placed on the churches, ranging from interference with the choice of their leaders to difficulties put in the way of religious instruction and the imprisonment of pastors and priests. And one has to add, as the most important point of all, the formidable power of a rival ideology which has the whole centralized state machinery, as well as the press and the school system, at its disposal.

What then is the explanation of the new life in these churches? It is that once again—as in other parts of Europe in the time of their conflicts—the Church is making the great discovery of its deepest freedom. It finds to its joy and surprise that it does not depend on the good will of its environment, or of the powers that be. It realizes the simple Biblical truth which Pascal expressed in the phrase: "It is a wonderful situation for the Church when it depends on God alone." Its lack of civic freedom is overshadowed and compensated by the daily experience of another freedom which no one can take away.

Karl Marx predicted that religion would automatically disappear when the new Communist society had been established. To him religion was "illusory happiness" and would have no place in a "situation where there is no need for illusions." But the fact of the matter is that by cutting the bonds by which the churches were linked to society the Marxists have unwittingly been instrumental in the renewal of the churches. This is even true in Russia itself. It was not a churchman but a leading Eastern European Communist who stated recently that somehow Marx's prophecy about the future of religion had not been fulfilled, for religion was as alive as ever in Russia and even exerted considerable attraction among young people. In a conversation which I was privileged to have with a Russian Christian living in the interior of Russia, he told me one story after another about the amazing vitality of the faith among Russian Christians of the different confessions.

I finally asked this question: "Is there according to your experience today less spiritual life or more spiritual life in Russia than before the revolution?"

His answer came without any hesitation: "There is more."

There is then little reason to fear for the future of Christianity in Eastern Europe. The Christian faith manifests its true depth and vitality when it is confronted with a definite adversary. Moreover in Eastern Europe the Church is in a very unique sense the guardian of truths about men which no one else defends. When I asked some youth leaders in one of the countries concerned to explain why in spite of all the obstacles put in their way young people were still coming to the church youth groups in such considerable numbers, their answer was simply: "They say that the chuch is the only place where they are treated as human beings." That is a wonderful situation for the Church to be in, and it is thus not so surprising that in spite of all the hardships of their daily life leaders say: "God has placed us in a glorious epoch and has shown us a glorious goal for our pilgrimage. If we work with our eyes turned backward we shall perish like Lot's wife. If we fight with the means of power we shall be crushed. But we can call on the Lord and bear witness and speak up for mercy, humanity and justice."

But there remains the question of what attitude the churches take to the dominating official ideology and to the system based on it. A full answer would require a very thorough analysis of a complex, fluid situation. But this much can be said. There is no attempt in the churches concerned to compromise with dialectical materialism or to adapt the contents of the Christian message to the Marxist ideology. The one important movement which had such a purpose—"the living church" in Russia—failed miserably. On the other hand, in the matter of the practical attitude to the new social and political regime there is considerable variety, ranging from the far-reaching collaboration of the Russian Patriarchate with the Russian government to the very fundamental and definite protest against the imposition of an anti-Christian ideology made by the Protestant churches in Eastern Germany in the spring of 1950.

On the whole the churches in Eastern Europe distinguish sharply between the ideological and the social-economic aspects of the regime. And while by their preaching they take a clear stand against the former, they feel that they must find their place in the new society. There are those who do so with the naïve expectation that the new regime will create a more just social order; there are those who do so in the sober conviction that it is sociologically impossible to return to the prerevolutionary order and that a purely negative attitude condemns Christians to utter sterility.

The churches have little opportunity to make public protests against the harsh and inhuman sides of the system, but that does not mean they do not seek in many other ways to exert that Christian influence which makes for "mercy, humanity and justice." We can perhaps best characterize the attitude of Eastern European leaders by reporting this reflection of one of them, made publicly before an audience which included Communists: "You Communists seek to create a new and better society. But you try to do so on a materialistic basis, and that is impossible. Someday you will find out that you need the spiritual forces and you will come to us for help."

Most of the Eastern Orthodox churches are in the countries under Communist regimes and share in the suffering and also in the joy. But special reference must be made to the role of Eastern Orthodoxy in Greece and in Western Europe. For here also very real forces of renewal are at work. In Greece the various movements for evangelism and religious education reach a very considerable part of the population. And there is a remarkably lively movement of Christian laymen, "Aktinis," which seeks to bridge the gulf between the Church and modern culture and which is in close touch with the Christian lay movements in other parts of Europe. I was told in Athens that the proportion of readers of religious periodicals is higher in that city than in London or New

York. And this is not surprising, for the Church in Greece has a strong influence on the whole nation. When the Archbishop of Athens recently made an appeal for help to the refugees from Northern Greece, he received within one day 266,000 parcels of clothing.

The role of the Orthodox emigration to Western Europe has been quite out of proportion to its size. This has been due not only to the high quality of the emigrants but also to the fact that they brought to Europe the insights gained in the great spiritual battle through which they and their churches had gone. They became interpreters of the signs of the times and helped European Christians to understand that the "Constantinian era" of relatively peaceful coexistence of church and society was drawing to a close, and that the Church should prepare itself for a period in which it would have to fight for its life. Nicholas Berdyaev's prophetic warnings concerning the revolutionary character of our time, and his call to the churches to shake themselves free from all entangling alliances and to stand in the full freedom with which Christ has set them free, have opened the eyes of many in Europe to the realities.

It is obviously not possible to give in this chapter an adequate description of Roman Catholicism as a spiritual force in the life of Europe. On the other hand the above picture would be quite out of perspective if it is not seen in relation to the Roman Catholic situation. For Roman Catholicism is an extraordinarily powerful element. It is true that some great strongholds of Catholic life and culture such as Austria, Poland and Spain have been reduced to a minor role, and that the process of secularization has gone even further in a largely Roman Catholic country like France than in Protestant countries. But all this is compensated for by the great outburst of religious, cultural and political activities, all of them co-ordinated from one center, which has taken place in recent years. The main question is, however, how far Roman Catholicism is a force of renewal in European life.

There can be no doubt that within the Roman Catholic Church forces of rejuvenation are at work. The turning to the Bible and the thorough work on theology, the growing concern with the "sources" and particularly the study of the early fathers, the crusading spirit of the associations of young Roman Catholic

workers, the spiritual courage with which priests identify themselves with the workers, the renascence of Roman Catholic art
and literature and the keen new interest in the ecumenical problem
—these are some of the most tangible signs that a new spirit is at
work in important sectors. And if this spirit were allowed to permeate the Church as a whole there would be no doubt that Roman
Catholicism would make a great contribution to the renewal of
Europe. For these manifestations of Catholicism are based on the
assumption that the real battle to be fought is not a battle for
external power but a spiritual battle.

But there is another side to the picture. There is the ecclesiastical
machine which has by no means given up its dream of a return to
a church-dominated society. There is the involvement in politics,
and often in politics with a reactionary bias. There is the timorous
attitude of the Vatican toward all fundamental renewal, as expressed in that depressing recent encyclical "Humani Generis."
There is the tendency to follow the line of least resistance with
regard to the cruder forms of popular devotion. And there is the
ambiguous attitude toward such basic human rights as the right included in the "Universal Declaration" of freedom to manifest one's
religion or belief.

Thus the Roman Catholic Church is today a body in which there
exist great potential and actual forces of renewal, but in which these
forces are very often arrested or even crushed by countercurrents
of a reactionary character. Some of the finest aspects of cultural
and social activity in Europe are due to Roman Catholic inspiration, but there is also the sad story of the violation of religious
freedom in Spain and of the pure power politics carried on by several Roman Catholic political parties. Thus the answer to the
question whether Roman Catholicism will ultimately prove a force
of renewal in Europe will depend on the outcome of the inner conflict within that church between those who think primarily in
terms of laying new spiritual foundations and those who think
primarily in terms of the survival of an ecclesiastical system.

It remains to say a word about interchurch relations. Here
again the experience of the war years made a considerable difference. Before the war there had been little true fellowship between
the European churches, and the political tensions exerted a strong

influence on their relationships. But the common need and the common resistance created a deeper desire for communion. After the first World War it had taken ten years before the issues of war guilt could be removed from the agenda, but after the second World War that issue was definitely disposed of in the discussion in 1945 at Stuttgart and subsequent meetings. Thus the postwar years have seen an unprecedented development of interchurch contacts. Leaders and members now have a considerable number of opportunities to know each other and to learn to work together —the courses of the Ecumenical Institute, the health center at Locarno, the meetings of the Interchurch Aid Department and of the Youth Department of the World Council, the Franco-German conferences, the Scandinavian-German convention, the German-Dutch meetings, the meetings of the Lutheran World Federation, the Presbyterian World Alliance and other confessional bodies and a host of *ad hoc* conferences on specific subjects. Thus a process of sharing has begun which will have a deep influence on the participating churches. The narrow space in which they had lived is widened and new horizons are opened up.

In this process interchurch aid plays a very considerable part. It has not merely practical significance. A lonely and needy congregation in Germany, or Italy, or Poland, which receives help from the churches of Switzerland, Sweden or Great Britain, gets a new conception of the meaning of common membership in the Church of Christ. And now that the churches of Norway, Denmark and Holland have also begun to help more needy churches, the network of mutual service has become very widespread. By far the most substantial help comes, however, from the American churches, and this, together with the many personal contacts which have been established between European and American Christians, has created a far better appreciation of Christianity in America. There remain considerable differences between the American and European churches, but they no longer look on each other as strangers and are far more ready to learn from each other.

This outburst of ecumenical activities is the manifestation of a new understanding of the Church as the one and united people transcending national differences. But what of the relations with Roman Catholicism? The Roman Catholic Church does not participate in the ecumenical movement, and the official collaboration between Roman Catholic and Protestant church leaders which existed in several countries during the war years has not been maintained since. Nevertheless, unofficial relationships through informal discussions on questions of common interest exist in many places, and on both sides serious attempts are made to know each other. It should not be thought that this means a softening of attitudes in the profound differences. The same Protestant leaders who take part in such meetings have, for instance, expressed themselves in no uncertain terms about the promulgation of the dogma of the Assumption of the Virgin. But it is believed by ecumenical-minded men on both sides that, without minimizing the question of truth, Protestants and Catholics must overcome their age-old habit of abusing each other at a distance and enter into a serious and searching conversation with each other, even though no one expects that within the foreseeable future it will bring tangible results.

In concluding my discussion of the survival or renewal of Europe, I ask the searching question—will the forces of renewal which I have described succeed in reversing the process of disintegration and produce a new and stable foundation for European civilization before it is too late? The answer depends on the definition given to "too late." If we take it to mean "before some further political catastrophe happens," then we must say that it is by no means certain that the creative elements are strong enough to cope with the equally strong destructive forces of reaction and of anarchy. This is not a reason for defeatism or passivity and cannot be used as an excuse for writing off Europe. On the contrary. This is a reason for giving more imaginative and energetic support to the truly forward-looking and constructive builders of a new Europe.

But if we take the words "too late" in another sense—as referring to the disappearance of the fundamental values of European life—then our answer can be much more positive. In that case we dare to say, on the basis of all that has happened and is happening spiritually in Europe—and especially in the part of Europe under totalitarian regime—that there is a living church within the churches of Europe which believes and knows by experience that no force in the world can prevail against the Church which is founded on the rock of faith in Jesus Christ as the Son of the Living God. Already the Church is in some parts of Europe the one remaining guardian of the greatest spiritual gifts which humanity has ever received. We may hope that it will fulfill that role for Europe as a whole.

Faith and Fear in the Near East

4

By GLORA M. WYSNER

WE ARE afraid! We are afraid of the kind of world that man's intelligence has made. The more we know about the atomic bomb and its power to destroy, the more we fear this work of man's mind. We sit in fear and shudder at the danger that stalks the world. This danger confronts us because man's spiritual and moral character is as nothing compared with his intellectual capacity. If we are not to fear, we must have a new kind of men.

We are afraid! How often these words are heard in the Near East. Even more frequently are they unuttered, yet they are real to the people. Is it not significant that in this part of the world where fear is so prevalent, where many kinds of fear haunt the minds and chill the hearts, the angels announced to the shepherds on the Judean hills the birth of Jesus with the words, "Fear not, for behold I bring you good tidings of great joy which shall be to all the people"? The Founder of our faith, born in this very area of the world, came where people were afraid—came to expel fear and establish faith.

In the ancient "Near East" people feared hunger and illness; they feared their rulers; they feared evil spirits. These same things Near East people fear today. Thousands fear hunger. They go to bed every night without having had sufficient food for the day. The fear that their children will be hungry haunts most parents day and night. Hungry people are learning that there is enough food in the world to feed all. They know that there are those in their own countries who "live off the fat of the land." They are growing more restless. They will listen to those who promise them sufficient food, and yet in the end they may find themselves victims of an enslavement far more bitter than their hunger.

There is fear on the part of the rich in the Near East. They sense the restlessness of the poor. They realize that men cannot be kept always in abject poverty. But there is little concern on their part to do much to alleviate the condition of the masses. Considering the fatalistic theology of Islam, how can one expect a motivation that will spur those who have a large share of material things to use them unselfishly for those who are poor?

There is the fear, also, of political leaders who have become enmeshed in intrigues and jealousies which are keeping them in conflict with opposing leaders. As we were riding through an area of conflict in the Near East not long ago and were rounding a curve on a beautiful mountain road, the driver pointed out a place where only a few weeks before a high-ranking government official had narrowly escaped death. Plans had been carefully made and a time bomb had been set, but changes in schedule sent another car over the road first and an innocent man was killed. This story could be repeated many times.

There is fear of aggression in many countries of the Near East. Arab leaders realize that armistice agreements do not furnish the stability which is needed between the Arab States and Israel. They are fearful lest the great influx of refugees into Israel may eventually lead to the expansion of the State of Israel beyond its present borders. Israel, on the other hand, trying to establish a stable government, struggling with the overwhelming problems of resettling thousands of refugees, fears that if the Arab States become strong enough in military might they may move over the border into Israel again. These fears are fanning the flames of continued bitterness and are delaying indefinitely the constructive co-operation which is needed for stability.

Thousands live in the fear of evil spirits, often called "jinn." In the time of Jesus, people feared evil spirits and believed that certain men were possessed of demons. This is still true, especially among non-Christians. It is the custom of many Moslems to say "In the name of God, the Compassionate, the Merciful" on locking the door, or when going to bed. They believe the reciting of these words is a talisman against the jinn. Charms are often employed as a protection against evil spirits. Verses from the Koran are believed to be the most efficacious way of warding off jinn. They are often placed in little leather sacks and tied to the belt, to the baby's cap or hung around the neck. When a child is born in Algeria, a plant is placed over the cradle to keep away evil spirits. A knife, a piece of salt and a pail of water are put at the cradle head for the same purpose. Water is considered a good protector. The fear of spirits is very real. Merely the conflicting ideas of those who do not believe in the jinn will never banish the fears of those who do. It will take patience, kindness, understanding and sympathy to lead such people to freedom from fear.

Another fear that hangs over the heads of most Moslem women is that of divorce. How frequently they hear, "I divorce you." And if it is repeated three times, they are divorced. Feminist movements in some countries of the Near East are giving primary attention to legislation which will make divorce more difficult. If it comes, one tension in the lives of Moslem women will be lessened.

There are conflicts and fears peculiar to Christian groups. One of the great fears of many a Christian concerns his employment. Even though he is well-trained and efficient, if there is one position and two applicants—a Christian and a Moslem—the Moslem gets the job. A Christian is often replaced by a Moslem less capable, since the latter belongs to the official religion of the country. This keeps good wage earners in constant fear of finding themselves among the unemployed. It develops a "minority-group complex." Under the sense that discrimination is being practiced, feelings flare all too frequently into conflict. Thus bitter misunderstandings rise between religious groups.

Peoples in the Near East have the same fear that is haunting other parts of the world—the fear of Communism. Turkey and Iran are next-door neighbors to Russia, and Communistic propaganda is flooding all Near East countries. A well-known journalist picked up from his desk a new book printed in Arabic. It had come to him from Russia. "Why," he asked, "don't the democratic countries translate more of their best books into Arabic and send them to us? There's a battle for men's minds going on in this country." The battle isn't being fought only on the level of the intelligentsia. It is being fought among the poverty-stricken peasants in the rural areas. It is being waged in the refugee camps. It is gripping the imagination of labor in the industrial centers. People are restless, disillusioned, frustrated.

To understand the peoples, we dare not pass over their fears. Fear itself is frequently the key to why men act and react as they do.

Moslems are finding themselves faced with conflicting loyalties. Shall they give their support, their first loyalty, to those promising them economic security but who belittle religion, or to their faith, whose leaders have scarcely lifted a finger to better their economic condition? Shall youth give their first loyalty to the family they have been taught to reverence and respect, or to new social mores of which their parents heartily disapprove? Is the conservative mother, still loyal to tradition, willing to agree to a career for her daughter, instead of insisting on her taking a husband chosen for her?

Conflicting loyalties, conflicting ideas, conflicting ambitions among political leaders, conflicting beliefs, internal conflicts and conflicts with neighboring countries—all these are a part of the Near East today. True, these problems are not peculiar to that section. Basically, they are found wherever people must learn anew how to live together in a world that has grown suddenly small.

The history of the Near East has been woven in the warp and woof of religious and racial tensions. This does not mean that the conflict has always been destructive. Often it has been constructive, for progress has been made at times through the help of conflict.

It is a sad paradox that the area of the world which has had the greatest influence on the history of mankind is less known and understood in America than almost any other. Most fairly well-informed Christian groups in America know some facts about China, Japan, Africa, the Philippines or Latin America. But real knowledge regarding the Near East is all too meager.

The peoples of the Near East are as a rule religious. The name of God is frequently on their lips. A simple greeting is always given in His name. A friendly farewell sends one away with the peace of God invoked on a departing friend. The beggar asks for help—a crust of bread or a coin—"in the name of God," and most Near Easterners will toss him a coin and call down the blessing of

God on him, feeling comfortable in the thought that they are building up for themselves merit in heaven.

To understand most of the problems in the Near East, we need
to understand its religions. Out of this area came the story of creation. Here the Jews developed the ethical code and moral law which
have been the basis of monotheism. Here it developed, struggled
and established itself, first in the religion of the Jews, later in
Christianity and finally in Islam.

Some of the stories so familiar in Bible times have their counter-
part today. From Ur of the Chaldees Abraham went forth, "not
knowing whither he went." Was he a refugee, a displaced person
or only a pilgrim? Like Abraham, Fahlim and his family went
forth not long ago, not knowing whither they went. These Palestinian Christians—and there are many of them—suddenly found
their home surrounded, and they too had to leave quickly, forsaking
all their possessions. They tramped for days and finally joined
friends in a refugee camp. Still, after three years, they do not know
whither they can go. Their home has been a tent where they have
lived through the rigors of the Palestinian winter and the heat of
the summer. They have been clothed only in garments that have
been given them. They have been fed by United Nations rations.
Their children are unable to continue education. The father has lost
all his tools and he has had no work. Fahlim and his family often
ask, "Do our fellow Christians care?" How proud we are of the
faith of Abraham that led him forth and made him the father of the
Jewish faith and of the Christian faith! Dare we forget there is a
Christian faith in Palestine that has kept this refugee, and his an-
cestors, faithful to God and to Christ down through the years?

Refugees are not uncommon in these lands. The Israelites fled to
Egypt. Joseph took Mary and the young child Jesus to Egypt, and
thus they too became displaced persons. Armenians, refugees by
the thousand after the first World War, have settled in nearly
every country here. Numbered among the refugees also are large
numbers of Assyrians. Today the State of Israel is trying to care
for thousands of Jewish refugees from Europe and in addition is
lifting people out of Yemen and North Africa and other parts of
the Near East to place them in the narrow land of promise. In the

Old City of Jerusalem, in Lebanon, Syria, in Palestine and in Jordania are some 800,000 Arabs. "When do we go home?" is the tragic question on the lips of thousands.

Anyone who has worked with refugees will see the great difference between those in the Near East and those in Europe. In the D.P. camps in Europe they cluster around the leader of their religious faith. They find strength and courage to keep on in almost impossible circumstances, often sustained by their faith and the ministry. The Arab refugees consist of Moslems and Christians. The scattered Christians in Palestine establish themselves near their leaders when they can. But for vast thousands of Moslems there has been no steadying religious influence. Bitterness and disillusion eat at their hearts, making them more adverse than ever to any co-operative work that might help them. A tremendous opportunity belongs to the Christian Church today to minister to these people.

It was in an ancient land of the Near East that Cain killed Abel, and Cain's question falls all too frequently on unheeding ears: "Am I my brother's keeper?" Does the landowner have any responsibility to the poor farmer eking out a bare existence on his land? Does the student with a rare chance in life bear a responsibility toward the thousands of illiterates found in all these countries? Is the Jew, in his creation of the State of Israel, responsible for the Arabs now without home and work and sustenance? Does the Orthodox Church, which has lived for centuries on the defensive, surrounded by Islam, feel responsible for carrying the Christian message to its Moslem neighbors? How much obligation do the people of the world who are benefiting most from the discovery of oil acknowledge by concerning themselves about those from whose land the oil is taken?

How right those Christians in the Near East were when they recently issued a call to prayer and stressed the need for better men—men whose moral and spiritual character will use their material and political achievements for a blessing and not as a curse! Such thoughts are frequently expressed these days. And in this there is hope.

A Christian in the Sudan put it this way: "What we need in the Sudan is new brains, new and progressive ideas, new standards of living. If people are interested primarily in making money instead of working for God, then we'll not do our best work."

An Arab leader expressed it thus: "Our countries today need leaders, leaders who do not consider first and only their own comfort and gain. We need men who will seek the good of other people, especially the poor, who will serve their country without hope of reward, who will do all this for the good of all men because in it all they magnify God."

Many recognize that for peace here and throughout the world a stable Near East is needed—a Near East where governments are strong, where the leaders command respect, where co-operation through honest endeavor is possible. For this we need better men!

Many students, having studied abroad, come home resolved to bring to fruition some of the things they have learned that will improve health, better economic conditions, raise educational standards. But all too soon they become frustrated and discouraged. They cannot find kindred spirits who care to help them make their dreams come true. The students are becoming aware of the need for better men.

But the picture is not all black. Some students have caught a new vision of service as they have participated in social-welfare activities in Christian institutions. Many parents are seeking out Christian schools for the education of their children. Not that they are eager to have their children educated in the Christian faith, but they see in the young people of these schools a strength of character which they covet for their own. It is far more to the credit of a Christian institution to be known as a place where character is built than to give a statistical report that looks good.

The Near East has many leaders whose lives have been molded more than they appreciate by Christian environment and teaching. Perhaps there has been no world organization in which the Arab nations are so proud to be members as the United Nations. Of the 35 Near East representatives attending the organizational meeting at San Francisco, 29 had been educated in Christian schools. Their ideas and ideals had in many ways been shaped by the impact of Christian teaching. An outstanding record of Christian statesmanship and wise leadership is being given at the United Nations by one of the outstanding Christians of the Near East—

Dr. Charles Malik. As has been mentioned in an earlier chapter, he worked tirelessly to shape the impressive and inspiring Covenant on Human Rights.

Many non-Christians in the Near East are motivated by Christian ideals, and their thinking and actions are colored by the unconscious impact Christianity has made upon them. Of course they do not think of themselves as in any degree Christian, nor would they dream of becoming identified with the Christian Church. But the leaven is at work, slowly changing attitudes, ameliorating motives, molding characters.

In most of these countries one is registered at birth according to the religious faith of one's parents. This is regarded a much more important classification than whether or not one is Arab, Armenian, Kurd, Kabyle, Sudanese or Samaritan. As you travel you frequently hear someone ask, "What is your nationality?" If you reply that you are an American, they are almost sure to say, "I don't mean your country; I mean your nationality." It may take several questions for the stranger to realize that what they really want to know is your religion. They want to identify you with the religious community to which you belong. They cannot understand why this information is not found on your passport as it is on theirs.

This association of religion with community is the ground for much of the conflict in the Near East. Furthermore, it gives to most of the people an attitude toward conversion hard for Westerners to understand. To change your religious community is looked on with severe disfavor. Those who do so are almost always accused of having economic or social motives. Hence, to change one's religious faith is not a matter of conversion; it is a matter of convenience. This strong attitude toward conversion has even resulted in some Eastern churches not favoring the conversion of a Moslem to Christianity. In fact some of them believe that a sincere conversion is impossible. Hence, and tragically enough, the declared convert to Christianity is regarded with suspicion.

Loyalty is always to the particular religious group to which one belongs. Adherence to it has often been more important than loyalty to the person and teachings of Christ. Frankly, Christianity has made little appeal to non-Christians.

What is more, economic fears and social pressures lead some Christians to embrace Islam. There is little doubt that many of them do this with little or no real religious conviction for Islam. One may wonder how much Christian conviction they had. But before one criticizes too quickly, it may be well to examine one's own faith and ask if one's Christianity is so deep that one would not succumb, too, if the economic security of the family was at stake. Are we certain that social pressures are not sometimes stronger than our faith?

For some twelve centuries the churches of the East were cut off from fellowship with those of the West. The Eastern churches, consequently, were practically untouched by the revolutionary movements which brought new vigor and vitality to the Western. The Eastern churches concentrated all their efforts on survival, and they succeeded—with the exception of the church in North Africa. But they developed a rigid conformity to the past—in their traditions, manner of worship and doctrine.

To understand the Christian Church in the Levant, we need to go back to the beginning of church history.

Who of us has not been thrilled by the stories of Saint Paul as he established Christian churches in many parts of the Near East— on the Island of Cyprus, in Pamphylia, Cilicia, Cappadocia, at Antioch, Lystra and Derbe. Conflicts arose in the earlier centuries and divisions came. A schism which ended in a definite break established the Nestorian or East Syrian Church. This was a great enterprise whose vigor was due, for the most part, to its missionary zeal. Christian teachings were first carried to many places by ardent Nestorians.

In fact, it was in the Near East that the pattern for Christian missions was first laid. It began in Palestine in the days of our Lord. Today His ministry under the aegis of the Cross has spread throughout the world. The sick are healed in Africa, the eyes of the blind are opened in China, the refugees are cared for in Korea, new hope is brought to bomb-blasted Nagasaki—all in the Name of Him who began a like ministry in Palestine.

We must not leave the early church without a look at North Africa. Its rise and fall there is a fascinating story, and at the same time a very sad one.

When the Roman Empire was still intact and the Mediterranean still a Roman lake, Christian congregations sprang up all along the coast of North Africa. They were not counted by the score or by the hundreds, but by the thousands. This was largely a Roman, not an indigenous, church; but many of its members and some of its most famous leaders were North Africans. It was proud of its great figures. Their writings have wielded an influence down to our own day. Who has not heard of Augustine and Tertullian? They kept the faith in all sincerity and helped to spread it all along the shore.

There is a tradition out of North Africa which is significant. When the Church was seemingly strong and flourishing, a certain leader was meditating in quiet and calm on his faith as a Christian. Suddenly he said aloud: "How happy I am here under my olive tree enjoying my religion! Let the rest of the world go by!" Had he opened his eyes and looked up and beyond he would have seen, not far away, the curling smoke rise from huts in the tiny villages which dotted the mountains. Most of the people there were pagans. They were of no concern to the Christian under the olive tree. He was enjoying his religion, undisturbed for his neighbors who needed him, whose hearts and souls were restless because they had not found his God.

It wasn't long after this that the Arabs swept across the continent. They came in the name of a new faith, a faith that had already conquered thousands, the Moslem faith. The Church, torn by dissension, enjoying its faith and having no concern to make Christ known to its next-door neighbors, fell before the onslaught of Islam. North Africa became known as the "Land of the Vanished Church." Christianity today needs to remember the tragic end of the once glorious Church of North Africa. When it loses its missionary vision, its spiritual power is gone.

When the American churches began to send missionaries abroad early in the nineteenth century, they included the Near East in their plans along with China and India, and the first American Board (Congregational) missionaries landed in Beirut, Syria, in 1820. Later a foothold was gained in Turkey and in Persia, and gradually Christian missionaries entered Palestine, Egypt, North Africa, Mesopotamia and Arabia. In several of these countries, notably in Egypt and Persia, British societies also opened work and a few small missions were established from the continent of Europe. Except for Palestine, however, which until recently had proportionately more missionary groups than any country in the world, it cannot be said that any of these fields has been adequately occupied. Today only six of the larger American denominations maintain work in the Near East and one or two of these have little more than token representation.

Because of Moslem opposition it was at first possible for missionaries to work only among the minority Christians of the Eastern churches. In Turkey, for example, Congregationalists served the Armenians. In Persia, Presbyterians opened the "Mission to the Nestorians." (The Nestorians themselves had carried the Christian faith from Syria into Persia and on east as far as China.) In Egypt, United Presbyterians began work among the Copts. Schools were opened in these and other countries for boys and girls, and hospitals were established. Arabic, Persian and Turkish translations of the Bible were soon available for distribution. The American Press, a Christian missionary agency which was established in Malta in 1822 and moved to Beirut in 1833, has had an extraordinary record in the variety and quantity of its publications and in their circulation throughout much of the Moslem world.

Undoubtedly the aim of these pioneer missionaries was twofold: to bring enlightenment and spiritual deepening to their fellow Christians of the Eastern confessions and, particularly, to win Moslems to the Christian faith. In both purposes, however, they met with frustration. While the Eastern churches have, by and large, been greatly influenced by the presence of Evangelical missionaries, no great reforms in them have occurred, and most individuals who accepted the Evangelical teaching no longer felt at home in the older churches. The inevitable result was the formation of separate Evangelical bodies. Today we have a strong Evangelical church in Egypt, Syria and Lebanon. In Turkey a movement for reform had begun in the Gregorian Armenian Church before the missionaries arrived. A thriving church of Armenian Evangelicals was the result. But before and during the first World War it went through the fire of massacre and exile. Today its members are scattered all over the world, though many of them are found in the Union of the Armenian Evangelical churches in the Near East. Both Nestorians and Armenians share in the Evangelical Church of Iran. These and a number of other churches are members of the Near East Christian Council and have a part in the ecumenical movement through the International Missionary Council and the World Council of Churches, to which latter several of the Eastern Orthodox churches also belong, including the Patriarchates of Alexandria, Jerusalem, Antioch and Constantinople.

Missionaries have needed unwavering faith to hold firm to their purpose of reaching Moslems with Christianity. First one by one and then in increasing numbers, Moslems in the early years came to the missionary dispensaries and hospitals which offered medical service far superior to anything else available. As Western education in the Christian schools proved its worth, Moslem parents braved criticism by enrolling their sons and later even their daughters, until today in many of these schools Moslems outnumber Christians and those of other faiths. The very presence of missionaries over several generations, establishing Christian homes and teaching and exemplifying Christian truth, has done much to soften traditional Moslem opposition and, as has been said, the ideals of thousands in the Near East have been molded closer to the Christian pattern.

Conversions are still relatively few. Missionaries in Persia worked for 50 years before the first Christian convert was won. He proved a giant in intellect and faith. In the years since, hundreds have followed his lead and form a strong element in the Evangelical church. In other Near East countries the enormous family and social solidarity in Islam usually compels anyone who is baptized to seek refuge in some other land. Yet there are exceptions, as a missionary makes clear in writing from a large city in one of the strongest Moslem countries: "The new Christians have been very faithful. We feel humble before these men who are braving persecution, boycott and even personal injury. One has been distributing Scripture portions and tracts on his own time. This year he distributed more than 6,000 pieces. During these trips he has been brought into the police station many times, has been stabbed, and has been stoned. Once he was knocked completely unconscious by a blow on the head." The courageous faith of such men as these, along with the leavening influence of Christianity throughout the Near East, is the hope of the faith. Persistently it touches all of life.

In some countries not only conversion but other forms of missionary effort have been severely restricted. But, as in Turkey, for instance, there have been thriving Christian educational work and considerable distribution of literature, including very popular modern translations of the Bible into Turkish and into Latin script. Moreover, the personal influence of missionaries continues. In Arabia education and medical service have won their way, and recently medical visits to the very center of Arabia have been possible with a Christian evangelist in the party. In other fields Christian schools and colleges turn pupils away for lack of room, hospitals are filled, and the circulation of Christian literature increases rapidly. One series of 30 pamphlets, presenting the Christian answer to basic questions regarding God, man and society, written for the Moslem with a modern education, has had total printings of hundreds of thousands of copies in Turkish, English, Arabic and Persian. The author, Lufti Levonian, is one of the best-known writers in the Near East.

Christian student hostels and centers have been opened recently in Iran. There is a Christian experimental farm in Syria, a rural rehabilitation project in Lebanon and adult literacy programs in several fields. As women become more emancipated, they respond more readily to child clinics and to projects for the improvement of their homes and family health. Everywhere the missionary is laying those moral and spiritual foundations which are the basic need of the Near East.

That the Christian missionary is usually welcomed when understood was made dramatically evident during the recent period of hostilities between Israel and the Arab states. Though in the latter there was intense feeling against Britain and the United States because of their alleged pro-Zionist bias, and in some cases violent demonstrations took place, not one missionary or Christian institution was threatened. The long years of devoted missionary service and the exemplary life of most Christians in the Near East have made generally clear the distinction between Christian faith and political influence.

Let us take a look at a few intimate stories of Christian faith at work, conquering fear.

In a certain Christian school in North Africa there was one Jewish girl, one Christian and some 30 Moslem girls. The teacher wanted to show them something of the true meaning of Christmas.

"What do you do in your village when a baby is born?" she asked.

"If it is a boy, we fire guns," the children replied.

"Yes? What else?"

"The women clap their hands and give the yu-yu calls."

"Yes? What else do you do?"

"We take gifts to the new baby and its mother."

"What gifts?"

"Coffee, sugar, figs, oil, eggs."

With this background it was not difficult for the children to understand the story when the teacher told of the visit of the wise men to Jesus and their gifts. Then she spoke of how they might celebrate Christmas in their own village, how they might bring gifts for others on the birthday of Jesus. The children were eager to have a part.

Christmas Day came and the little girls, excited by their new adventure, sat cross-legged on the grass mats in the classroom. In story and song the Christmas message, old but ever new, was told, this time by the children themselves. Then two baskets were placed on the mats, for the children came from two villages and each wanted to do something for someone in her own village. Joyously they sang as they placed in the baskets the gifts they had brought.

To appreciate the sacrifice in their giving, one needs to remember that most of these girls were always hungry. One little tot reached her hand down inside her dress and pulled out three figs which she placed in the basket. Another pulled out a piece of barley bread. It was bread she would have loved to eat herself. One who was a little better off than the others contributed an egg. Each out of her poverty gave what she could. They enjoyed it, and the most fun came when they started for the two villages, proud of their baskets with the humble gifts. One basket was given to a blind orphan boy, who lived by begging from door to door. In the other village the children chose a very old and exceedingly poor woman to be the recipient. For weeks after Christmas the girls talked of this experience. Many times they were asked by the villagers why they had taken gifts to the blind boy and the poor woman. They answered by telling the story of Christmas.

The next Christmas the children were ready to go one step farther. Instead of giving their gifts in their own villages, they decided to go to a neighboring community. Their figs, eggs and bread were sold to the missionaries. The money received was sent to one of the Christian dispensaries ministering to needy people.

By the following year the children's horizons had been stretched even farther, for they had been studying about other parts of the world. They had heard stories of children in India, China and America. They had built in their sand table an Indian village and then a Chinese one. They had been especially touched by the stories of war orphans in China. So now they asked if they could send their figs and bread to China. It was explained to them that it was impossible to send their food such a long distance. They kept asking if some way might not be found. Then they began earning a little money by gathering olives. It is the season of the year when all of them are expected to earn something. The money must be used for many necessities, to buy clothes for the year and meal for their bread. They planned to put aside a few of the pennies they earned and bring them to the Christmas service. They made little baskets in which to put their offerings. A worship service was prepared which the children presented. They told the Christmas story in Scripture and song. And then these Moslem children brought their gifts, from their poverty-stricken village. Every child brought a few pennies, adding up to $5.00 to go to China for relief! They had found something of the meaning of Christmas.

Living in a country like America or Great Britain where one has freedom of choice in so many walks of life, one finds it difficult to realize what putting faith into action means in a land where a Christian is so often in conflict with non-Christian relatives and neighbors.

Akli grew up in a Moslem village. As a very young man he went to a Christian student hostel to board while attending a government school. There was no school in his own village. His mother was a widow. She was proud of her son, who, being the eldest, had the family reins in his hands. When he announced that he was going to a near-by town to study in the government school his mother knew it was no use to protest. This made her even prouder of him.

He was such a likable boy that he soon had many friends both at the school and at the hostel. His curiosity often led him to read books on subjects of which he had heard and he was eager to know more. Among them was a copy of the New Testament. He had long discussions with some of the Christian leaders. He argued fervently with fellow Moslems who would have nothing to do with the books he was reading and who warned him that he'd soon be in difficulty if he kept on. Finally it happened as they feared it might. Akli became a follower of Jesus Christ. Not long after he asked for baptism. Then came the time of testing.

The observance of Ramadan, fast month for the Moslems, soon began. Akli refused to keep the fast. His school colleagues tried to prevail on him, but in vain. Relatives tried to persuade him, but he remained adamant. He held firmly to his convictions throughout the 30 days of Ramadan. Not long after, Akli returned to his village for a visit. His mother had heard of her son's behavior and had laid her plans. A dead Moslem son would be far better than a live Christian one. She prepared a meal for him which looked tempting and tasted good, and Akli ate heartily. But it was poisoned and he became desperately ill. Fortunately his mother had miscalculated and the poison was not enough to kill him. Akli lived but suffered for years.

He grew in stature as a Christian. From among the girls at a near-by hostel he chose a wife, one of the very first women in that country to be educated. She was a Christian girl, trained in homemaking. Akli and Semina established a Christian home of their own. The first time they went to visit Moslem relatives soon after their marriage, in order to avoid a quarrel they succumbed to demands that Semina be veiled. A few hours later, however, they thought better of their decision. The young husband took the veil from his wife's face, declaring that never again should she wear it. They must be true to their faith. This meant more than any

Westerner can appreciate. It went hard with Semina and Akli, but they held firm and their relatives had to respect them.

Akli qualified for a government post where he won the respect and the love of all his colleagues. They knew he could not be bought off by any group and that in all business transactions he was thoroughly reliable. They knew their own positions were never in jeopardy through any influence of Akli, for he was jealous of none of them. They soon learned it was of no use to invite him for a drink on the way home, unless it was a drink of coffee. They found he had no time for vile stories. They came to respect him, love him, counsel with him. Akli was never ashamed of his Christian faith. He frequently talked with his Moslem colleagues of what Christ would do for them. He had the supreme joy of bringing some of them into the fellowship.

Probably one of the happiest days of his life was when his son was baptized. Present at that ceremony and rejoicing in it was his old mother who years before had tried to kill him rather than see him a Christian. All through the years she had found him so much more thoughtful for a mother's welfare than the sons of her relatives and neighbors that she knew his religion was not a curse but a blessing.

Not long ago Akli died. His Christian funeral was a testimony to the esteem in which he was held in the town where he had lived and worked for many years. The church would not hold the hundreds who came to pay their last respect to an honest, upright, humble man. Hundreds of Moslems thronged about the church. On the lips of all were expressions of sorrow for his death and words of gratitude for his good life.

Many a Moslem, when he has been persuaded to study the life of Jesus for himself or to join a discussion group based on the Gospel, has found Jesus so appealing that he has become a Christian. But you will probably not often find their names written on church registers like Akli's and Semina's. Their identification cards still label them Moslems. But they are a definite part of the leaven of Christian faith at work in the Near East. They really do not think of themselves as Moslems. In their hearts they consider themselves followers of Christ.

"We need new men" is the deep concern of leaders in every department of Near East life. Better men are not made overnight. But lives are being gradually molded to finer issues by Christianity in varied action.

We may not think of games as a very telling way of helping young people understand the Christian life. They have their place, however. Croquet was introduced to a group of shepherd boys, the first organized game they had ever played. At first they would wrap their bare feet around the ball and push it in front of the wicket. Each time the director detected the sly move he asked the boy to return his ball to its right place. This went on for quite a while. During class periods the boys were learning lessons in honesty and discussing ways to practice it in everyday life. But they did not seem to realize that these lessons should be applied on the playground.

Finally the teacher announced that he had brought back the balls long enough; from then on any boy who used his foot to push his ball into a better position would be out of the game for that day. He must go home. The boys had learned to love the game. After getting up at daybreak to take their sheep out onto the hillsides and coming back when the sun grew too hot, they looked forward to the fun of play. But habit was stronger than a new lesson. They had been brought up in homes where dishonest practices had gone on for generations. They tried hard, but——

One of the boys, Ariziki, suddenly saw an excellent chance to get ahead. Supposing himself unobserved, he slyly put his foot on his ball and pushed it into easy position for his next shot. "Sorry, Ariziki, home you go!" his astonished ears heard. Surely friend Tom must have "jinn"—with eyes that see every move. Ariziki asked to sit on the side lines, but Director Tom was adamant. Home he must go. This was truly a risk on Tom's part. Did he have the boys' interest and respect so that the others would stay, or would they follow Ariziki? Tribal loyalty conflicted with love of the game. The game won.

Tom wanted Ariziki to have another try. He promised him a place on the team the next day. Anxious to make good, Ariziki sent his sheep out with a friend and was on the playground hours before game time waiting patiently.

Later on, the boys who had been playing all summer were explaining the game to some newcomers. They were heard to say, "You know, we've learned not to cheat here. This is a Christian playground. Christians don't cheat." Had they become Christians? Not in name, not by label, but they had caught an idea of the quality of Christian living.

The Christian Church is active in the midst of conflict in the Near East and its Christian work is more vital and more real than the world in general realizes. The measure of the Church and of the Christian impact is by no means revealed in a tabulation. Results are found in new attitudes—young people planning to spend their summer assisting in some project of village improvement; teaching the farmer how to improve his crops, introducing better breeds of chickens, conducting literacy campaigns, forgetting self in the joy of service, having no ulterior motives. Plans are made for many such programs in Christian schools and they are carried through. Co-operating in them have been a great variety of races— Arabs, Armenians, Kurds, Americans, Afghans, Iranians—and many faiths—Jews, Christians, Moslems and others—united in a common task, learning, consciously or unconsciously, of the spirit of our Master.

Christian women in the Near East have pioneered in the work of prison reform. Beginning when conditions were unspeakable, they met obstacle after obstacle. Sometimes it was unco-operative officials, sometimes corruption, sometimes lack of social understanding in the prison workers. Discouraged, yes. Defeated, never. Changes have come all too slowly, but the Christians kept on, hearing ever and again the words: "I was in prison and ye came unto me."

In lands where marriage has been looked on as the sole vocation for a girl, the Christian Church has taught the dignity of work. Christians have pioneered in the training of nurses—encouraging a few brave Christian parents to allow their girls to enter the vocation. In some areas the first teachers were trained in Christian schools. Christians opened the way in places where the government has now taken over, and, prejudices overcome, is educating an increasing number of nurses, teachers, social workers—in fact, young women for all walks of life.

Graduates of Christian schools and colleges, fired with idealism, go out to open clinics for the sick, to organize day nurseries, to plan and encourage village improvement. Sometimes their enthusiasm wanes. At other times they become disheartened by the obstacles they encounter—unsympathetic family and officials, unscrupulous village leaders. But a growing number bring the tasks to fruition. Their country is better for their labors of love.

Not Christian? Perhaps not by label. But surely their motives are Christian, their lives have been influenced by Christian ideals, their vision stretched by an awakening to the needs of their fellow men. Their social sensitivity has been prodded into responsibility and action. Someday they or their children or their children's children will come to know fully that Jesus Christ is Lord.

Many are afraid—afraid of the uncertainties and insecurities of life, afraid that aggressors may invade their land, afraid of the unknown, afraid of political upheavals, afraid of poverty and hunger, afraid of modern trends, afraid of emotional tensions, of divorce, of conflicting loyalties, of social and religious pressures. The peoples of the Near East live with fear. They need emotional stability, confidence in themselves and others, courage to live out their ideals, strength to follow higher moral precepts, and loyalty to a cause that will challenge the best that is in them. They need to be understood and loved. Most of all, they need to know Jesus Christ. He is saying: "It is I; be not afraid."

William Norris Wysham, chairman of the Near East Committee of the Division of Foreign Missions of the National Council of Churches, collaborated in the writing of this chapter.

Africa in Revolution

By Emory Ross

IF AFRICA is in revolution—and that is to be looked into—responsibility appears to lie heavily on the Christian Church. For Christianity has been of such prime influence in relation to Africa that it cannot off-load now its share of responsibility for whatever happens in and to Africa.

That plenty is happening seems at least vaguely felt by not a few Americans. But is it revolution? In a world of cold war, of Korean war and Indo-China war and East Indies war, of China revolution, of German and Austrian and Near East disturbance, of the total Communist struggle, can Africa be said to be in revolution?

The answer is no, if by *Africa* is meant all parts of, and only, the continent so called.

The answer must also be no, if by *revolution* is meant an organized, armed, violent revolt by the governed against the governing Powers.

But the answer is yes, quite clearly it seems to me, if what is meant by "Africa in revolution" is this:

That hundreds of thousands of Africans, out of perhaps 150,-000,000 total, and a large number of foreign friends, in groups of greatly varying proportions in the major areas of Africa, are undergoing and pressing for further radical changes in Africa's thought, religion, society, economics, political organization and world relations; and

That impressive numbers of people in nearly all other parts of the world are, in one way or another, in speeded-up movement and change in their attitudes and actions concerning Africa and Africans.

These two conditions do exist. Both inside and outside of Africa there is resistless change, amounting in degree and pace to revolution, and there is growing pressure in the thought and action of Africans, and of others regarding Africans.

In Africa's case this second factor involving people of other countries, this "external" revolution in the mood and deed of others about Africans, is of special importance. For Africans, almost all of them, are still under colonial rule. They are unorganized; are—masses of them—quite illiterate; are not in charge of their own economy; have in wide areas little effective participation, and no control, of their own governing; are of course unarmed; and are unable, except locally and sporadically, to apply or even threaten the use of organized physical force.

Thoughts, ideas, ideals, spiritual convictions, moral force, public opinion inside and outside of Africa are therefore of critical importance in Africa's revolution.

These things, as we look back, have always been basic in revolution. But only infrequently in history have they alone sufficed, has revolution come without the blast of bombs, the bath of blood and the heritage for a generation or more of fear and hate, impeding and sometimes preventing the growth and full use of the new gains. To have this armed battle, this implacable fear and hate come to Africa, and into today's world, would be a major defeat in the current, unceasing struggle in which we are joined for justice, freedom and advancement of all the peoples of the earth, for the loyalties of men's minds and the commitments of men's souls.

Hence the critical African question now is : Can Africa's revolution be accomplished without war?

A firm yes or no cannot be given. But consider here a basic proposition inherent within the theme and purpose of this book: the Christian mission is power. Let us see what such power has already done—and failed to do—in and about Africa, and what further it can and should do.

This chapter's reasoning is framed by three statements :

First. The Christian Gospel in 2,000 years, and particularly for Africa in the past 200 years, has opened the eyes, widened the vision, kindled the hopes, lifted the aspirations and directly aided the greatest fulfillment of the highest potentials in more men of more races than any other power in human history.

Second. But enough Christians of every generation and in every land, as individuals and as a church, have so far failed to carry through the daily and inclusive *practice* of Christianity in millions of individual contacts, and in our socio-politico-economic fabric, as to help bring crises, disillusionment, frustration and despair to whole nations, conditioning them to become deluded victims of Godless "isms" which promised them many of the very things Christianity had first shown them but had failed fully to give.

Third. Therefore: the terrible and unprecedented disequilibrium of Africa and the world today, the revolution which is upon Africa, is a direct and special challenge to Christians, whose failures through the generations have tragically contributed to its cause and whose God-given and world-embracing Gospel supplies its only cure.

A person probing into the first of these three statements in relation to Africa will, I believe, find almost 100 per cent agreement among Africans and foreigners who know Africa—including those of both groups who do not like much of what has happened there —that the Christian mission has been, in the broadest field of education, the greatest force in the past century. And by education is meant the whole realm of spiritual, intellectual, professional, technical, social and cultural teaching, experiment and practice which forms the base for practically everything today.

In no other great area of the world or among so many people has this in our day appeared so clearly and indisputably true. Why?

There are five major and visible elements making for this greater clarity and wider acceptance of the basic and pervasive power of Christianity in contemporary African life than in any other continent.

First. Africa, south of the Sahara, at the very beginning of its contact with Christianity, was more in arrear socially, culturally, politically and spiritually than any other large mass.

Second. Only one or two of the more than 800 languages had been reduced to writing, and illiteracy was almost total.

Third. Education in either Eastern or Western forms was unknown among the African animists. The missionaries have put more than 400 languages into writing and almost everywhere have been pioneers in education of nearly all types. They continue to carry perhaps 85 per cent of the total educational load, sometimes with and sometimes without government aid.

Fourth. In the modern world Christianity has made its most massive gains in Africa. There are now 20,000,000 in the African Christian community out of a population of about 150,000,000, as compared to about 19,000,000 out of a total of some 1,170,000,000 in all the "non-Christian" countries of the Near, Middle and Far East combined.

Fifth. This unprecedented quantitative change is thrown into clearer relief by two timing factors: (a) it has been accomplished in a shorter time than Christianity has had in most of its other modern missionary areas; and (b) it has been accompanied by faster and greater social, cultural and economic changes than any people of comparable mass has ever undergone.

The situation in Africa was a most primitive one (in a sense a more "simple" one, though primitive and simple are often far from being synonymous); the change was more profound, more rapid, more visibly measurable within a given generation or so; and Christianity was more distinguishable and more influential in Africa than the few other forces which entered from outside in the first six or eight decades of the past century.

This is the combination of circumstances which has perhaps enabled more neutrals and skeptics to distinguish, identify and agree on Christianity as a realistic and actually basic and pervasive force for change there than in much of the mass social advance elsewhere.

Africa therefore appears to furnish pretty clear evidence to support the rather sweeping terms of the first of the three statements which frame this chapter. It may be that some Christians in these circumstances find it pleasant and soothing to feel that Christianity is recognized by so many as the great constructive power in this century's changing life in Africa.

But complacency should be totally routed when we see the truth of the second of those three statements: that there have been so many personal and collective failures of Christians, in and out of Africa, as to bring disillusionment, frustration, bitterness and despair; and of the third statement, that the Christian Church, because of its demonstrated power in African hearts and actions and its likewise proved shortcomings—shortcomings due so largely to human pride, selfishness and sin—has still a huge job of inner change and outer action of the very highest importance to Africa and to the world in its relationships and service with millions of African Christians and non-Christians.

The late Dwight W. Morrow said a very homely thing one day: "Any party which takes credit for the rain must not be surprised if its opponents blame it for the drought." There are many Christians, and many opponents of Christianity, who see in Christians' failures the greatest dangers Africa faces in these days of revolution. Let us look at certain of these major and critical problems.

There is the breakup of communal society. Almost the whole of African animistic society has been communally organized. The individual, with few exceptions, has been subordinated to what traditionally had come to be regarded as the will and the good of the group—usually of the family, clan or tribe.

Within this communal society, religion—the primitive religion of animism—was the chief, the intimate and principal control. Generally speaking there was nothing in African life too small or too great, too private or too public, too weak or too powerful to escape animism's control. It was the communal whole which prevailed, and the religion—animism—was the most pervasive and powerful ingredient in it.

The fact is that all aspects of African communal life are so tightly and completely integrated and meshed that it often seems rather hard for the nonspecialized Western mind to understand it at all. I myself am a nonscientific layman speaking with laymen about it. I do not pretend to be an expert in comparative religions or theology or anthropology or sociology. Experts may dissect and analyze communal society in the general pattern of the laboratory, though not at all with the same scientific accuracy possible in physics and chemistry. I am not competent and do not attempt to do that here. What is attempted is to suggest something of the African's traditional and complete acceptance of the fused whole which is his communal society, and of the splitting impact Western Christianity, and other Western forces largely molded by Western Christianity, have had on it.

For Western Christianity led the initial and basically the most penetrating and disruptive assault upon the communal-animistic structure of African society. Christianity's emphasis on the individual, on human personality, on individual freedom of choice, and indeed not only on mere freedom of choice but on the individual's *responsibility* for continuously exercising it—this whole range of accent on the individual was a powerful and disruptive frontal attack on communal society.

It was true that Christianity coupled with its emphasis on the individual its emphasis also on the individual's responsibility for others, on the individual's role and responsibility in building Christian community. But that factor was not so new to the African; communal society also imposed responsibility for others, even though the individual's own volition didn't have much call to operate. To the African the really new and striking thing which Christianity brought in to start with was the emphasis on the individual, on individual choice and decision, on the power of individually choosing a new way of life. This was heady and daring stuff—releasing, exciting, challenging, untried. It was not unnatural in view of this that Christianity's emphasis on responsibility for others was sometimes rather overshadowed in the Africans' conception of this strange new Gospel by its heady emphasis on the individual.

Missionaries, in their understandable commitment to win men to Christ, perhaps stressed the doctrine of freedom of choice, freedom of abandoning animism and of choosing Christ, rather more than the doctrine of accountability for others. In any case the initial individual act of choosing Christ was a definite, single act. The doctrine of responsibility for others is a resulting lifelong continuum of great variety and complexity. It has been quite possible for others besides African animists to adopt the Christian practice of freedom of choice without practicing too consistently responsibility for others, the responsibility of the Christian community.

To be remembered also is the fact that Christianity entered Africa just when stress on the individual, on the God-given freedom of individual choice was mounting to hitherto undreamed of heights in many of the Western countries which invaded Africa. That stress had been in considerable measure an outgrowth of Protestant Christianity. It was already beginning to result, among

other things, in what came to be called a system of *laissez faire*
that produced a human mixture of good and bad in Western
society. Those Western countries were themselves in many respects
failing to stress responsibility for others. The "community" of the
Christian Gospel was often pitifully weak. In retrospect one should
not be too surprised that Western Christianity in those early days
of battle with animistic communalism in Africa succeeded better
in one part of the job—a degree of emancipation of the individual
—than it did in another part—the working out of a new pattern of
responsibility for others, the building with maximum skill and
strength of *Christian community*.

It by no means entirely failed in building Christian community.
The mere act of sincerely accepting Jesus Christ can bring one a
certain sense of community, even though one does little about it.
As a matter of fact Christianity appears to me to have become the
greatest force in Africa south of the Sahara in drawing Africans
together across language, tribal, geographical and political lines,
and I shall later try to give reasons for that belief.

This does not, however, negate the statement I have made that
Christianity's chief manifestation in its early decades in Africa was
to call people to the freedom of individual choice. For many hundreds of thousands of Africans the decision to choose the way of
Jesus Christ may have been, indeed must have been, the first
major, individual, noncommunal or anticommunal decision ever
made by them. No matter how mixed the motives or imperfect
the understanding, the choice of Christ was an individual act of
colossal importance in this solid communal society. In quality and
in quantity it can, I believe, be said to be the first major break in
the communal structure of African society.

It was violently opposed in many places, this daring flouting of
communal controls. Ostracisms, persecutions, perhaps at times
even death resulted. But the breach grew, and the outward flow
increased of individuals freed at least to the extent of making a
basic personal decision.

The making of this breach was aided by several other forces
from outside which also were entering Africa.

"Book" was one—the whole unimaginable process of reading,

writing, communicating by hand and eye. It was pure magic. And yet ordinary individuals, daring to take the required individual decisions and actions, could master it. Thousands did.

Western medicine was another. African medicine was powerful, but Western medicine and surgery were in important respects of another order entirely. Yet African individuals, even those not in the hereditary line of witch doctors and medicine men, could acquire some skills in it as orderlies, nurses, dispensers—provided they took the necessary individual decisions and actions. And as knowledge of and confidence in Western medicine grew, with its reliance on microscopic examinations, laboratory tests, individual diagnoses, individual medication, successful surgery, the fear and thralldom of the evil spirits believed by animists to cause all disease were lessened, some of the most powerful sanctions of an animistic communal society were weakened, and the individual took another step on the way to greater freedom of body, mind and heart.

Western education was another powerful breachmaker in animistic communalism. Its primary human unit was the individual, *always* an individual who had had to make a prior individual decision for Western schooling, sometimes to the curtailment or omission of traditional African schooling. In all of this and in subsequent steps in Western schooling there was great emphasis on individualism, though community was by no means ignored. But even this community concept, Western-style, was new in that in principle it required the free assent and choice of individuals; and in practice, if it was to be built, it required the best thinking, planning and voluntary co-operation of scores or hundreds of newly free individuals. So even community in its new style emphasized individualism, as compared with animistic communalism.

Western education sharply accentuated individualism in another fashion. African traditional education, usually of the group type, had often developed special skills in individuals—fishing, hunting, weaving, smithing, carving, dancing, divining, pleading, withing, governing and other lines. But all of those lines were traditional lines. They were all solidly laid in the communal fabric. They were all firmly controlled by the communal sanctions. No matter how proficient an individual became in any skill, he did not escape the communal control. It and he were controlled. His initiative was curbed. His self-expression was limited. His self-advancement in his special skill was bounded—by traditional communalism which appropriated his skill and prescribed its use.

In Western education he likewise acquired special skills, certain of them quite new: teaching (Western-style), preaching, clerking, printing, nursing, carpentry, masonry, machining, engineering, accounting, translating. Many became very skilled indeed in these new things. And their individualism was strengthened, their self-expression and initiative grew, for this reason: that *these new skills very largely escaped communal controls.* They were not traditional skills. They were not solidly laid in the communal fabric. They were new, and foreign. There had never been any clerking in the modern pattern, or teaching, or nursing, or machining, or printing. The implements and techniques, and even some of the materials, in Western carpentry and masonry and engineering were new and so traditionally uncontrolled. Thus both these new skills and the "new" individuals were more and more escaping the communal animist pattern and controls.

It is perhaps instructive here, and it certainly is very important, to note that of all the new skills acquired in these decades of revolutionary Western contacts, new agricultural skill has perhaps shown the least degree of freedom to dare and to expand, to breach the communal wall. Agriculture is not exceeded in importance by any material skill. It is of the most fundamental importance to the whole future well-being of Africa, spiritually and physically. It is a skill on which life itself depends.

Yet it has progressed so little in this new Africa that recently a world-renowned Western agriculturist said of southern Africa that he saw little hope of sound agriculture there unless a great influx of Europeans took place and Europeans practically took over the agricultural management of the subcontinent.

This appears to deny, or to despair of, the power of Jesus Christ to enable man—African man—to master his earth and his environment. It certainly clashes head on with British colonial policy which, obviously if but indirectly, is derived from the principle that man, African naturally included, *can* master his earth and his environment.

The agriculturist who made this judgment is a committed Christian. He has seen man in unfavorable positions elsewhere in the world make effective strides in improved agriculture. Why did he pronounce as he did about southern Africa? The answer might go a long way in revealing some of those weaknesses and failures of Christians that have contributed to disillusion, frustration and despair in Africa, and which if not overcome may lead to armed and bloody battle.

I suggest two special elements of Christianity's relation to land and Africans that require deeply understanding and co-operative action.

The first is that Christianity must really deal with the earth. Up to now it has scarcely come to grips at all with that problem except maybe in a half-dozen widely separated spots. It has taught gardening and agriculture, of course; and contouring and rotation, and diversification and seed selection. But that is not the problem of the earth in Africa. The problem of the earth in Africa is spirit. The earth is at the very heart of animism. To the African animist, earth is the great mother of all. Mother Earth produces all life, sustains all life, receives all life. The earth is absolutely indispensable to every individual and to the whole tribe. Therefore, the earth simply must be, and consequently is, *spiritually and physically,* the property of the whole tribe. There are certain qualifications to be introduced here, African conquest and migration being among them, but by and large the above statements seem to me true.

In the face of such a spiritual and communal concept of the earth, Western man moves in, and this core relation of millions of Africans to Mother Earth is blown to bits by the theory and practice of the private ownership of land and of much that has grown out of it. Even the "public" ownership of vast tracts is no spiritual or practical parallel to communal ownership, since by "public" is meant a government of aliens and not of the people, and since "public" ownership is often but a way station on the road to private ownership in the Western style, or to "native reserves" or "locations" which are too often inferior in quality, inadequate in extent and increasingly unacceptable ideologically.

Christianity is seen by Africans too often as irrevocably connected with this kind of spiritual rape of Mother Earth, since it has helped establish and sanction it in its own countries and has helped introduce it into Africa. It has obtained private ownership in Africa of communal land for its own Christian uses (the Catholic Church in particular having acquired vast reaches of land in some parts of Africa far beyond its direct spiritual and social-service potentials for its African followers). It has too generally failed to assist Africans in effective resistance to land exploitations and deprivations of many sorts. This whole matter of "earth" has special and dangerous potency in the revolution in thought and action now under way in and concerning Africa.

The second element in this deeply understanding and co-operative action relating to Mother Earth involves Christian community and the lack of progress made in creating it. In very few places in Africa has the Christian Church achieved accepted success in creating a new-pattern rural community possessing both Christian cohesion and Christian dynamic. Ninety-five per cent of the people are rural people. Throughout much of this huge population the communal pattern with animist core appears on its way out. And the community pattern with Christian core seems scarcely yet in sight. Do we wonder why insecurity, suspicion, tension, fear and often hatred develop in the face of this apparent delay and failure of Christianity?

Africans have responded to the Christian emphasis on the worth, place and power of the individual. They like it, as do many other people. But, like other people too, they want community. Their communal society for many generations provided a certain amount of security. It at least permitted survival, even if at the expense of individual flowering.

Christianity has made a wonderful promise: of individual fulfillment *and* of community solidarity. It has proved its high potential in individual fulfillment. It has till now not convincingly demonstrated to millions of its followers and to non-Christians its power in developing a solidarity of community. Its failure to do so is perhaps most clearly seen and keenly felt in this matter of a needed new relationship to the earth. A right relationship here is absolutely essential to that newly glimpsed Christian community for which consciously and perhaps unconsciously millions of Africans, Christians and animists, long and search. If Christianity fails much longer in aiding the African in his agonized search for the new community, the promissory program of Communism stands prepared and beckoning. And revolution in blood can come.

This Christian-community relationship to the earth is basically not at all a question of plowing or irrigation, of manuring or seed selection, of contouring or diversification, of wise animal husbandry and sensible soil conservation—things which rural mass inertia and animist fear resistance in Africa make difficult and often unobtainable in today's atmosphere. What is primarily and fundamentally involved is the *soul* of the community and the *soul* of Mother Earth, and the satisfying spiritual union of the two.

Now above all we are not, here in the West, to shrug this off. We are not to say, Oh, this is just dreamy vaporings of backward and superstitious and impractical Africans; all that's required agriculturally is scientific farming and mass education and some additional good land laws and perhaps increasing mechanization—or a flood of Europeans who will take over the land, put the natives to work and produce bumper crops.

In considerable areas today a European take-over effort of that sort would probably be one of the surest ways yet devised to drive unarmed Africans eventually toward self-annihilation by violent rebellion and revolution. And in the world scene such results could tip the scales for defeat of a Christian way of life in this generation.

No, we must first of all understand as well as we can the African mind, soul and aspiration. We must remember and be penitent that with all Christianity's quantitative successes in Africa, with all its demonstrated power of individual emancipation and individual fulfillment, with whatever success it has had in building a church in many parts of the land, it has largely failed as yet to create *Christian community*. What is required must be at once strongly cohesive and powerfully dynamic; must replace and immeasurably surpass the animist communalism of such strength throughout all remembered African life; and, among other indispensable services, must create a sense of deep union between the soul of the community and the soul of the great supplier of all life, the good earth. Is it too much—and too late—to ask Christianity still to try to render this service to millions of its new disciples who deeply feel its need as they strive for individual fulfillment *and* community solidarity in the world opening before them?

Intimately related to the concept and use of Mother Earth are other aspects of the economic-spiritual developments which have occurred and are occurring in Africa, and especially those which lie just ahead. They constitute a very large factor in the revolution in and concerning Africa.

I say "economic-spiritual" developments despite the fact that for many of us in the West the idea may be hard to define or perhaps even to entertain. In many ways Western civilization has gone very far in trying to separate the purely material from the spiritual. If in the enormity of our suffering in this generation— two World Wars, deep economic catastrophe between, the terrible ideological struggle following—we in the West begin to see that there is little "purely material" in this life, and that all materials are impermanent and of small worth unless right spiritual controls are accepted, then we may, in our travail, come closer than ever before to the African in his.

In broad lines the African's struggle and ours are but one struggle for one objective. We seek to regain the spiritual bases we too largely forsook while making our great material strides. The African, on today's threshold and seeing us, hopes and tries to get and retain sound spiritual values while striving for the material advancement which he glimpses and wants.

The common objective is a *wholeness* of matter and the spirit. It is, if it can be had in any degree in modern society, that intimate fusion of spirit and matter which is the communal heritage of most of the African people.

Westerners find it easy to see that Africans have much to learn from them. It is not so easy to see, and to assent, that from the African spirit the West may have something to learn and to adapt. I believe this to be true. And I believe the Christian, African and Westerner, the committed Christian individually and collectively, is best sensitized, oriented and empowered to pioneer further in this delicate but promising interpenetration in aid of warless revolution.

There are many others who share this belief. Let me quote three sentences, received the very day I write these lines, in a letter from a senior official of 24 years' experience. Mr. Kenneth Bradley, C.M.G., has been colonial secretary of the Northern Rhodesian and Gold Coast governments and is now editor of *Corona*, the journal of His Majesty's Colonial Service. He writes:

We have indeed reached a turning point in the history of African development. In its early stages Africa needed pioneers in practical endeavor and later it needed pioneers in science, but now it needs pioneers of the spirit who are equipped and ready to devote their lives to opening up the swift-growing and entangled jungle of human passions and ideas. Into this jungle there is only one road, the heart, and the only weapon which can clear that road is faith.

In this swift-growing and entangled jungle of human passions and ideas of which Mr. Bradley writes—a jungle that stretches far beyond Africa, of course—there is a factor of fatal power if it is not downed. Race and color.

In colonial Africa nearly all the governed peoples are colored and nearly all the governing peoples are white. The Portuguese began this relationship about five centuries ago. After 500 years of white governors and black subjects in some parts of Africa and the gradual spread of that colonial color pattern to all parts in the past few generations, it ought not to surprise us if many Africans come to view the whole colonial system pretty much as a white-black struggle.

It can be—and has been—argued that this is not true, that color is merely incidental. Such argument doesn't make headway with many sensitive Africans today, or with other peoples of color. They see whites ruling and blacks ruled; social and residential color segregation in many places; what looks to them like black labor discrimination in wages, housing, conditions of work; very few Africans indeed getting equal pay and perquisites for comparable training and work.

They see the inequities in land and the whole frightening insecurity regarding Mother Earth very largely as part of this black-white struggle. "When the whites came," they say, "we had the land and they had the Bible. Now we have the Bible and they have the land." The statement has inferences which cannot be rationally supported. But that makes little difference. This whole color business isn't rational at all on either side. It belongs to the entangled jungle of human passions and ideas.

Even on mission stations and in the church, color barriers are too often felt by the Africans. Color can divide even Christians. Witness the United States where the Church, in its *practice,* is one of the severest segregators. Witness the Union of South Africa where the largest church of all is perhaps the most militant proponent of apartheid (complete segregation), and has given one of its clergymen as the nation's present head and high leader for white racial domination in nearly every human relation.

One of the grave results of irrational color prejudice is that where tensions exist every difference of opinion, every clash of ideas, every incompatibility of persons, every real or fancied slight and ill can be attributed automatically and irrevocably to color. The entangled jungle of human passions thickens.

Thus it is that in the Church when devolution of responsibility from missionaries to Africans is judged by Africans to be slow, or any other differences arise, the emotionally easy act is to charge it to color prejudice, or to white paternalism born of color bias. The color factor thus grows by feeding on itself, the emotional surcharge increases, and every problem becomes harder than the last to solve.

Christians *must* come to grips with this matter of color if Christianity is to make its victory contribution to the world—to the whole world. And the first place for American Christians to take fresh hold is at home.

The other day a brilliant African scientist came to see me. He had been in this country perhaps ten weeks, doing special work at one of our leading schools. He had been invited to our nation's capital. Four days before his visit to my office he had tested and been seared by the color barrier in Washington. He had immediately left for New York and his government had, at his pressing demand, secured emergency place for him on an Atlantic ship. He was leaving.

With tense voice and burning eyes he said he would never be back. "I shall not again see America. I wish never to hear of America in future. The whites who can do this, the blacks here who can take it—they have nothing for Africa, none of them. When we are free we shall sever all relations, bar none, with this country. We can have no faith here."

Emotional? Irrational? Suppose that be granted—then what? The fact can still be that his heart will remain like forged steel; white-heated, pounded, chilled—a barrier, a weapon against anything America may do. And the case is not unique.

It may well be that over these years when tens of thousands of foreign peoples of color are visiting our land and our capital, many of them with high hopes and yearning hearts, the color discrimination of private citizens—sometimes a single case—may register more than a dozen acts of Congress for foreign grants in aid. Human hunger for appreciation and love is of a different order, but it is not less strong than hunger for bread and wealth.

Africans want bread, of course. But I should judge they want community as much or more. Bread in Africa they *can* get for themselves. Community depends partly on others. If bloody revolution ever comes in Africa it will be, in my judgment, because others have failed Africans.

Americans have a special obligation not to fail Africans. No other land has put more treasure and life into education and the Christian evangel in Africa. No other land has 10 per cent of its people from Africa. No other land has been so enriched by its citizens out of African heritage. No other land has taken stronger pledges for human freedom. No other land has experienced more melting-pot action. None is now able to do more in world councils for and about Africa.

Goethe pointedly remarked that "it is easier to perceive error than to find truth, for the former lies on the surface and is easily seen, while the latter lies in the depth where few are willing to search for it."

That observation is widely applicable in human affairs. But it has perhaps some special applicability to Americans in relation to

Africa. It is easy for Americans, this one included, to perceive error in many past and present policies and practices in Africa—errors of governments, of industry, of missions (ours and others), of Africans; of commission and omission; of ignorance and design. If one doesn't perceive the errors readily enough there are a dozen, a dozen dozen, books that set them out clearly. I find it fairly easy, after 38 years in and with Africa, to catalogue errors. *Vide ut supra.* And don't think that is all.

The conclusion of the syllogism earlier in this chapter is that, despite the errors, Christians through the God-given and world-embracing Gospel have what is needed to retrieve many of the errors, to overcome the results of others, and to press forward to success in Africa. And by "Christians" I mean Africans fully as much as Westerners.

How now do we find the truth lying in that depth where few are willing to search for it?

The first remark must be that no individual or short group search will reveal the whole truth about Africa. Would it about North America, or France, or Russia? Africa is vast, diverse, inchoate, at myriad stages. The whole truth is perhaps even unobtainable. But the presentation of a few truths may be attempted in hope of leading to bettered action for continued nonviolent "revolution."

One. There is hope and progress in some of the government policies and programs. In Liberia the administration and certain economic and educational factors are more hopeful than they have ever been in the 38 years I have known that republic. In Nigeria and the Gold Coast, in the midst of great tension, self-government by Africans, with only a few powers reserved to the British Crown, is coming steadily nearer. Favorable signs may be seen in other parts of Africa, but not so clearly.

Two. The principle of responsible international concern for all colonial peoples is making progress. For "trust" territories (formerly "mandates") the principle of international accountability is now established. The sole resister is the Union of South Africa, which defied world opinion and the Hague Court in joining South West Africa to the Union.

Three. Education in a number of areas is making gradual progress. Not so in others. The British are leading, with three university colleges (last stage before becoming a full-fledged member of the British and Commonwealth university system) already open (Gold Coast, Nigeria, Uganda) and a fourth about ready (Sierra Leone). The French have higher schools at Dakar and Brazzaville. The Union has appreciably increased its grants for non-European education, but there are about 9,000,000 to serve and there are still great strides to be made, not least in mutual confidence and faith. At present these qualities seem almost nonexistent. Liberia College (government), Cuttington College (Episcopal), Booker Washington Agricultural and Industrial Institute (union) and the College of West Africa (Methodist), all are expanding in the Republic of Liberia. The first three have American Negroes at their heads. Elementary education is still the order in Congo Belge, with some promise of more higher-school work. Except for Protestant missions there is little education in Portuguese areas, and practically none in Spanish. Ethiopia is putting serious effort into its schools.

Four. There are about 600 African students in America, the majority from British West Africa. This is in addition to 2,155 in Britain, and perhaps about the same number in France (including those of non-Negro stock from French North Africa). There are practically no Africans studying in Belgium, Portugal or Spain, except a handful preparing for the priesthood and two Protestant graduate men in Portugal, one in sociology, the other in medicine. The graduate study abroad of persons from areas having no facilities for higher education is a matter of the highest importance.

Five. Christian consultation, functional co-operation and spiritual solidarity are all growing within the Protestant Church. Four Christian Councils (Congo Belge, Union of South Africa, Portuguese Angola and Nigeria) have full-time officers serving all participating missions and churches. The Congo Protestant Council (formed as the Congo Continuation Committee in 1911) is the oldest field organism in existence in the pattern of the 1910 Edinburgh Conference, and it is now one of the most inclusive. In all there are 15 Christian Councils in Africa south of the Sahara, 11 of them with only part-time and honorary secretaries. It is regrettable that in the oldest field of all, Liberia, where American responsibility is proportionately larger than in any other field, there should be later and scantier co-operation, with the exception of literacy work, than in any other African field.

Six. Specialist training courses for all foreign Protestant missionaries are organized in Brussels, Paris and Lisbon to orient and better equip missionaries going to overseas territories. During the three years 1947, 1948 and 1949, 608 missionaries of eight non-Belgian nationalities spent a total of 90,961 days of study in Belgium. In 1950 there were more than 200 missionaries studying there. In France there are some 105, and in Portugal 35. This is wholly on the initiative and at the expense of the various sending boards, except that in Belgium a government per-diem grant is given missionary doctors and nurses as they study.

Seven. The African ministry and teaching personnel is increasing generally throughout Africa. These men and women face ideological, educational, spiritual and economic problems of great range and difficulty. Their training opportunities are for the most part deficient. Their duties are large and must become larger. And their support is often distressingly meager. A careful study of the training of the ministry in Africa is being made. But the whole social, economic and even political life in each area is involved, as well as their training. The churches abroad will need to find more adequate and effective means of co-operation with the African Christian community in solving these problems of supply, training, operation and support of the preaching, teaching and other African staff personnel.

Eight. Let me close this incomplete search for truth about current African life with a word further on the subject of Christian community. As I have mentioned, we have thus far failed in large measure in the relationship of Christian community to land and rural life.

But Christianity nevertheless appears to me to have become the greatest, as well as the earliest, force in Africa south of the Sahara in drawing Africans together across language, tribal, geographical and political lines. Within an area there were from early days more and more meetings and friendships of African strangers in the tempering atmosphere of common Christian commitment. The first Africans to go overseas from a given area were often Christians, who experienced abroad and brought back home spiritual assurances of solidarity with other Christians. Then interterritorial conferences began, exchanges of more or less regular correspondence followed, a few interdenominational and intradenominational periodicals were circulated. Christian students were given study scholarships abroad. Attendance of a few at international Christian meetings outside of Africa was arranged. And through nearly all of this the pervading, binding love of Christ operated. It seems to me clear that no other force has done so much as the power of Christ to bring the feel of this kind of common community and mutual commitment to so many Africans. The days ahead should be used to their full to expand this sense of Christian community.

The chapter must close on what has come to be called since January 20, 1949, Point IV, or "technical assistance to underdeveloped areas." The world press in the days immediately following President Truman's unprecedented proposal for "a bold new program" gave evidence of its nearly universal acceptance with a speed and eagerness perhaps never before matched in history. This came despite the fact that Point IV might be turned into a huge and inequitable exploitation of the resources and people of underdeveloped areas, as Soviet spokesmen promptly announced it would be. Why was it so quickly and widely accepted in principle?

For one thing there was the critical and even desperate economic need of nearly every country in the world.

A second feature was the known power, the "know how," of the United States to produce greater quantities of more things out of its resources than any nation in history, a knowledge greatly spread by the world's visual experience of seeing millions of those things scattered prodigally in nearly every quarter of the globe in the World War II years.

But there was a third matter. The first two had little in them to down the fear of raw exploitation. The third consideration was of a different order.

It was four generations of unself-seeking international services to some fourscore countries of the world. The United States and Canada had joined Britain, Western Europe and Scandinavia in these services, which have combined to create an acceptance attitude of great import for Point IV aid. While the fears of imperialism and exploitation are by no means wholly downed, and Soviet and other forces are trying to increase them, this essentially Christian-motivated, unself-seeking international aid, in which America has been the largest single contributor of personnel and funds, has not only performed its own direct services, nearly all of them of sound Point IV type, but it has in addition helped lay foundations for the broadest and at the same time most intimate peacetime co-operation ever officially proposed by a powerful nation.

What has been the nature of that Christian-motivated aid?

First. The oldest, most widespread and most consistently maintained assistance has been the Christian missionary enterprise. There are at work overseas some 15,000 North American Protestant missionaries alone. With their European colleagues and the growing national churches of the other countries, they have nearly everywhere been the pioneers in technical help, as well as in those cultural, social and spiritual endeavors without which technical help is of little avail.

Second. There have been the great philanthropic foundations, undertaking many aid projects in underdeveloped areas, almost always with that unselfish attitude which tends to dispel suspicion, win confidence and bring pay dirt to the surface everywhere.

Third. The many universities and colleges and service programs which have been set up abroad either by direct Christian initiative (as the Christian colleges in China, certain of the Near East colleges, the Service Committees of the Friends, the Brethren, the Unitarians and others) or under the dynamic of Christian commitment (as Yale-in-China, Pekin Union Medical College, Oberlin-in-China).

Fourth. Even services of certain United States government departments and agencies (as the Department of Agriculture and the United States Public Health Service) have been rendered overseas under much the same impulsion as the others above mentioned, and have tended to build confidence and co-operation.

One effect of all this truly generous, Christian-motivated aid may be seen now in new perspective: it has helped psychologically, morally and spiritually to lay, both in America and overseas, the broad foundation without which there would likely have been no spontaneous and predominantly favorable world reception of "a bold new program" of enormous import.

Acceptance, however, is but one of the first steps. Between acceptance and accomplishment there is a long road. Solid experience in constructing the first sections of that road is already acquired by Christian-motivated service groups of the past century. Four things stand out clear in that experience:

First. Christian principles are those on which sound development and accomplishment can be achieved. No other principles are so practical, proved, nearly universally acceptable and enduring.

Second. Private commitment and initiative are indispensable both in the aiding countries and in the aided. Governments may facilitate, but they can by no means do all or even most of what must be done. They should be encouraged and guided by democratically minded peoples to do their necessary part. But it would be tragic and, I believe, fatal to the highest success of this bold new program if the Christian-motivated, sacrificial private initiative and energy which have achieved the greatest successes should, through confused counsels, spiritual poverty, low faith or damning human inertia, yield to a predominantly materialistic and political handling.

The greatest dangers to the program at this moment are greed in many American and foreign hearts, and the unconcern and inaction thus far of the great American religious community, Protestant, Roman Catholic, Jewish. Resolutions have been passed and forwarded. Relatively little else has been even attempted.

Third. Up the long road from acceptance to accomplishment the bulk of a nation's people must pass. The engineers cannot go alone, or the politicians, or the scientists, or the children, or the men, or the farmers, or the lawyers, or labor, or the scholars. The Hindus cannot go alone, or the Protestants or the Moslems, or the clergy, or the laity, or the yellows or the whites or blacks. That long road is the road of *human* rise.

Fourth. A Point IV program, therefore, cannot possibly deal in underdeveloped countries with a narrowly defined "technical assistance" program alone, or with "materials" alone, or with "production" alone. Man is a whole, society is a whole, the world is a whole. We see that now as we never have seen it before. And there is global proof that Jesus Christ is the greatest "holist" the world has known.

A bold new program can have no sufficient boldness unless it is basically Christian-motivated. It can have no convincing newness to millions unless it is essentially unself-seeking. It can be no program of high promise unless it includes the whole of man.

Experience of the past century and of the past three years shows that no major success can come in dependent, underdeveloped areas either from a specialized-agency approach through unrelated or unco-ordinated projects covering a considerable range of needs, or from an approach through the single channel of economics.

The British groundnut scheme in East Africa gives vivid proof of the impracticability of a concentrated, speedy, solely economic approach. It was conceived, mapped out, proposed on March 28, 1946, and managed for the first two years by Lever Brothers, perhaps the world's most widely experienced private producing agency in tropical countries. It was the largest agricultural scheme ever undertaken. It had practicality and ideals well mixed. There was, to begin with, an unprecedented and promising welding of socialist government and capitalist management. But the first annual report issued on November 1, 1949, shows that to accomplish up to March 31, 1949, 1.5 per cent of their five-year objective in acreage, or .08 per cent of that objective in production, they used 30 per cent of their time, and expended 85 per cent of their appropriation of £25,000,000. They were not able even to keep their financial accounts—not even, apparently, when Lever was in charge.

Why? Very largely because everything had to be imported from outside and maintained at the end of an 8,500-mile line; because almost the only things available on the spot were unprepared land and unprepared people; because there were no carpenters, no bricklayers, no cabinetmakers, no contractors, no truckers, no water system, no sewers, no houses, no shops, no shoemakers, no clerks, no stenographers, no nurses, no doctors, no electricians, no mechanics, no garages, no spare parts, no chemist shops, no recreation, no ironmongers, no schoolteachers, no foremen, no skilled laborers, no sawmills, no woodworking shops, no foundries, no blacksmiths, no community, no group spirit, no spiritual cohesion—no one of these things and no one of anything in sufficient quantity to provide a matrix, to provide a *whole* in which such a groundnut scheme would have comprehension, support, nourishment and aid, sufficient for its successful progress.

North America and Europe are too prone to assume that the techniques and processes of their economic production can be transplanted wholesale to other societies. That is false. Techniques and processes of economic production depend on the minds and hearts of the people of a nation; on the kind of freedom and self-discipline which they have; on their vision, daring, health, education, recreation; on the complex social and spiritual stimuli which are theirs; on the resultant willing co-operation and confidence to take and share the vast stock which God has put into this world, and co-operatively strive to do what, but yesterday, seemed impossible.

Yesterday, as a matter of fact, this bold new program would itself have been impossible. Think of the scorn poured, a half-dozen years ago, on Henry Wallace over the much less pretentious "pint of milk a day for every Hottentot" idea!

But today is a new day. It is a day of acknowledged need such as man has not known. It is a day of spurring fear which drives us to new daring. It is a world split two ways that hungers for a oneness agonizingly glimpsed.

The bold new program seems to promise a oneness of striving, of common labor, of mutual sharing, of united achievement, the richer aiding the poorer to lift, the stronger helping the weaker to climb. To millions it seems a new door to a new earth. If really we open our souls to God and our persons in service to our fellow men, it can be, for them and us, a new heaven *and* a new earth.

But never, never can even the approximation of a new heaven and a new earth come through "technical assistance" or "economic development" alone.

It is a *wholeness* which is desperately needed in this earth. It is to help meet this need for wholeness that world organization, as I understand it, has come to be recognized as a matter of grave concern. It is the fundamental human need for wholeness which keeps tired and sometimes bitter people together, hour after hour and month after month, in the slowly shaping framework of the United Nations.

It is wholeness which the people of Africa also want. They have had it in large degree in the traditional society of their tribe, but even that is seriously threatened from outside. They have rarely had it in intertribal relations. They have never had it in international relations.

If Africa is to be assuredly spared violent revolution the Christian commitments outlined in this chapter and a wisely sponsored Point IV and technical-assistance program should be evaluated most seriously and in suitable form combined with sound government actions everywhere in Africa. A high degree of international action is necessary. This is all exceedingly massive and complex and beset with pitfalls.

But there is a very simple thing to remember about it all: straight through this thorny problem there is only one road, the heart; and the only implement which can clear that road is Christian faith.

There Are Many Christians in Asia

6

By CHARLES W. RANSON

CHRISTIANS have been in Asia for a very long time. An Alexandrian businessman, traveling in the sixth century A.D., found Christians in Ceylon and in India, with bishops and clergy from Persia who ministered to them. In "the land called Male, where the pepper grows," he found an organized church, which remains to this day. This is the ancient Syrian church of Malabar, which cherishes the tradition that it was founded by the Apostle Thomas. In the year 635, when Christianity was first beginning to take root in England, a Persian bishop crossed the mountains and deserts of Asia to carry the Gospel to China. For Chinese and for Anglo-Saxons church history begins at the same time, though its subsequent course has been very different in widely diverse cultures.

The vast majority of the Christians in Asia accepted the Christian faith in comparatively recent times. The greatest period of missionary expansion since the Apostolic age has been the last 150 years.

"When Waterloo brought the Napoleonic Wars to their close," writes Professor Latourette of Yale, "the new tides of life swelled to a flood. Protestant Christianity became more vigorous than ever before. The Roman Catholic Church experienced an unprecedented revival. The expansion of Europe continued at a quickened pace, and paralleling it . . . Christianity spread more rapidly and over a wider area than ever before. Upon the culture of occidental people, Christianity continued to have a profound effect, in some places more pronounced than at any previous time. Among non-occidental peoples, Christianity became more potent as a transformer and moulder of individuals, of groups, and of cultures, than at any time in its history. Christianity entered upon the century of its greatest influence." [1]

One result of this phenomenal expansion of missionary effort is that the Christian Church has taken root in almost every part of the Asiatic Continent. There are countries where, though there may be Christians, there are no organized churches. Afghanistan and the Asiatic region of the U.S.S.R. are closed to Christian missionary work. So are Tibet (to which Sadhu Sundar Singh, the Indian mystic and evangelist, set out on a missionary journey from which he never returned) and Nepal (cut off by mountain fastnesses from the outside world and traditionally hostile to its influences). There are a few islands and countries in which the Gospel of Christ has not yet been preached. But with these exceptions there are Christian churches in all the countries of Asia. Many of them have in recent years been tested by almost incredible difficulties. They have stood the test. Isolated by war and revolution from their fellow Christians in other parts of the world and thus deprived of missionary aid, they have proved their power to survive and to grow under the most adverse conditions. Through all the years of trial they have kept alive their faith and have cherished their place in the fellowship of the universal Church.

Immediately the war was over, the old fellowships began to reassert themselves. The International Missionary Council convened a world meeting at Whitby, Ontario, in the summer of 1947. Those who shared in that gathering will never forget its profoundly moving quality. Here were men and women drawn, in many instances, from countries which were still technically at war with one another, rediscovering the reality of a community that transcends nationality and which had proved indestructible through six years of bitter, total war. This experience is best described in their own words:

Though separated from one another through six years of war, Christians have known by faith and in experience the reality of the universal Church. Now fuller expression is being given to this reality as Christians are again able to meet one another and to learn how each has fared in the days of storm and whirlwind. The

[1] Kenneth Scott Latourette, *Three Centuries of Advance*, Vol. III of *A History of the Expansion of Christianity* (Harper & Brothers, 1937-1945), p. 457.

first joyful realization is that in no country or wide region of the world has the Church been obliterated by the war. . . . In some ways the strain of war has been of service to the spiritual life of the churches. When earthly helps are taken away, men are compelled to rest on God alone. . . .

Some churches under the pressure of tyranny have suffered and resisted in the unshaken knowledge that Christ is the Lord of history. Amid imminent peril and uncertainty they have remained steadfast in the certain hope of His final appearing as Lord of Lords and King of Kings. The Bible has proved itself in new ways to be the Word of God, not only as the historical record of revelation but as a living contemporary word spoken sometimes with almost painful actuality into the situations of today. Throughout the war, the spiritual unity which binds in one the Body of Christ has never been broken. In country after country, those whom man's laws had made enemies found that it was beyond the power even of the desperate crises of war to make anything but brethren in Christ.[2] . . . Under the stress of trial, Christians have been driven to realize as never before the oneness that underlies their divisions. Harsh reality tends to reduce to triviality many of the things that once seemed important; all have been forced to test again the essential and the accidental in their creeds; many have found that without disloyalty to conscience and without placing expediency before principle, they have been able to work alongside other Christians in a fellowship that in other days would have been regarded as impossible.[3]

Of no churches in the world are these words more true than of the churches in Asia. Yet they do not tell the whole story; and it would be a gross distortion of the picture to suggest that the years of war and revolution have brought nothing but gain. There have been grievous losses in many Asiatic lands. The ministry of some churches has been depleted by death. Training has suffered by disorganization or total suspension. Institutions were frequently scattered or destroyed. The weariness of prolonged strain left its mark upon the immediate postwar leadership of the Church.

[2] For detailed illustration see Kenneth Scott Latourette and W. R. Hogg, *World Christian Community in Action* (International Missionary Council). An account of the world of the Orphaned Missions Fund of the International Missionary Council.

[3] Charles W. Ranson, ed., *Renewal and Advance* (Edinburgh House Press, 1948), pp. 206-7.

The last few years have seen a remarkable recovery. Amid far-reaching political changes and continuous revolution, enlivened in many countries by sporadic disorders and in a few by actual civil conflict, the churches of Asia have sought to repair the ravages of war. Organized church life has, in most areas, been fully restored; institutions which had been interrupted have been renewed, and the influence of the Church has been widely extended.

Yet the Church in Asia fulfills its task in conditions which differ greatly from those which prevailed during the century and a half preceding the second World War—the period in which, as we have seen, the Christian Church witnessed its most dramatic geographical extension. It is a fallacy to suppose that the Church depends for its survival and expansion on conditions of external tranquillity. The most creative periods in history have often been marked by political and social upheaval, and the long story of Christian expansion has shown, again and again, that the Church has been at its best in periods of storm and has been most effective when conditions appeared most adverse. There is plenty of evidence in the modern history of the Church both in Europe and in Asia to support this view.

The changes which have taken place in Asia during the past few years are so profound and sweeping that they have already affected in a variety of important ways the life and activities of the Christian Church. These changes are still in process and their ultimate results no one can at present foresee. Any estimate of the position and prospect of the Christian churches must take full and realistic account of the contemporary Asiatic revolution. The ingredients of this revolution are not easy to describe in a few brief paragraphs. There is a danger of misinterpreting an extremely complex picture by compact generalization. The elements in the picture include the background of ancient tradition, the legacy of Western empire, the aftermath of war, the new heritage of political freedom, the sweeping social changes, the rising tide of Communism and the clash of divergent ideologies.

It is impossible to understand what is going on in modern Asia without some sense of the long sweep of Oriental history. Western commentators tend continually to project their own conceptions of society and of political and social change into the Eastern scene, at once oversimplifying and distorting the contemporary Asiatic picture.

Modern Asia is like a palimpsest—an ancient vellum manuscript from which the original writing has been partially erased to make room for successive inscriptions. The Asiatic palimpsest has not been wiped blank by the events of the last ten years. The writing of earlier periods is clearly visible. But successive layers of cultural influence have been superimposed on one another so that the total result is variegated and frequently contradictory. We do not need to be skilled paleographers to read this Oriental palimpsest with reasonable intelligence. But if we wish to avoid superficial judgments we shall do well to remember the continuing influence of ancient tradition on the life of contemporary Asia.

In the shaping of that tradition the great religions which have their home in Asia have played a dominant part. Buddhism, Hinduism and Islam have, in their different ways, exerted a profound influence on the culture of the Orient. They have been modified in a multitude of ways by modern forces, but have proved astonishingly resilient and are still powerful forces in the life of the new nations of Asia. They are deeply embedded in the texture of Asiatic thought and form the tegument of the social structure of great areas of Asiatic life.

That social structure—rooted in religious tradition—has a common pattern throughout Asia. The vast bulk of the population is rural and agricultural. These masses are largely illiterate and desperately poor. A small, and often wealthy, ruling class is found at the top. There is no powerful "middle class" such as we know in the society of the West. This simple structure, subject to certain modifications which will be noted later, remains the governing social pattern of Asia today. It has the enduring toughness of any social system that is rooted in the land and reinforced by religious sanctions.

On this ancient heritage has been superimposed the legacy of Western dominion in Asia. During the last 400 years Asia has been exposed to the impact of Western culture. The Spanish, the Portuguese, the Dutch, the French, the British and the Americans have in varying degrees and in different ways left their imprint on the life of the Orient. They have left their mark on culture, political life and economic development. Perhaps the most pervasive and potent influence of the West on Asia has been in the sphere of economics. The introduction of Western commerce and industry has brought Asia effectively into the orbit of a world economy.

It began as a process by which the West exchanged its manufactured goods for the great wealth and variety of raw materials produced in the Orient. Even this elementary process tended to suck Asia into the coils of world commerce—a process wittily satirized by G. K. Chesterton:

> Our principal exports all labelled and packed,
> At the ends of the earth are delivered intact;
> Our soap and our salmon can travel in tins,
> Between the two poles and as like as two pins.
> So that Lancashire merchants whenever they like
> Can water the beer of a man in Klondike,
> Or poison the meat of a man in Bombay,
> And that is the meaning of Empire Day.[4]

The process of exchanging raw materials for manufactured goods continues on a tremendous scale. In a recent visit to the Philippines I was struck by the fact that in a remote village bazaar one could buy a range of canned goods, similar to that found in the average village store in the United States.

But there is a growing revolt against this simple exchange economy. The last 30 years have seen a great development in manufacturing industry in most countries of Asia. In this Japan led the way, but other Asiatic countries such as India[5] have followed hard in her train. This important development has brought about a modification of the Asiatic social structure in ways that have great significance for the future. It has created in many Asiatic countries an industrial (as distinct from an agrarian) proletariat; and it has thrown up, for the first time in Asiatic society, a *bourgeoisie* or middle class, which is still small but increasingly powerful. In the growth of an Asiatic middle class, Western education, political

[4] G. K. Chesterton, *Collected Poems* (Dodd, Mead & Company, Inc., 1933). Reprinted by permission of the publishers.
[5] India is one of the eight great industrial nations of the world.

ideals and forms of government also have been powerful influences.

The end of the second World War left many areas of Asia stricken and chaotic. Those countries which had been occupied by Japanese forces were left by the collapse of Japan with a grim heritage of political and economic disorder. In every part of Asia the events of the war had given a powerful impetus to the movement for political freedom. The five years since the war have witnessed the virtual end of the Western dominion in the continent. The United States honored its promise to the Philippines in the granting of full sovereignty to a newly formed republic. Great Britain similarly negotiated a series of settlements which have resulted in the creation of free self-governing dominions in Pakistan and Ceylon, of independent republics in Burma and India. While Singapore island was retained as a crown colony and strategic naval base, a large measure of self-government was negotiated with the states of Malaya. The Dutch withdrawal from Indonesia has been accompanied by the transfer of sovereignty over that vast island empire (save for Western New Guinea) to the new United States of Indonesia. The French in Indo-China have retained a precarious foothold. The situation there is complicated by civil war and the threat of Communist dominion. But it is clear that whatever the future may hold for Indo-China, it will not include the perpetuation of the old colonial status. Korea was released by the defeat of Japan from a long period of domination by an Asiatic empire. Here also the achievement of full sovereignty has been delayed by a conflict of the great Powers over which Korea herself had no control. It is to be hoped that out of the present bitter tragedy of war there may ultimately emerge a new prospect for a united and self-governing Korea.

In the brief space of five years, 500,000,000 or 600,000,000 people in Asia have achieved political freedom. At least seven new nations have been born.

Their birth, which has not taken place in the most stable and auspicious conditions, has released into the life of the most populous continent in the world new and powerful forces, has fanned the fires of many a smoldering social revolt and stimulated vigorous ideological conflicts.

The tremendous political revolution has accelerated the social ferment. In most countries of Asia there are all the ingredients of social revolution. The age-long tyranny of the few over the many, the economic servitude, the appalling poverty of the masses of the people are no longer allowed to pass unchallenged. Political freedom is accompanied by social revolution—varying from country to country in its manner and method, but everywhere powerful and potent. This revolution is not primarily the result of Communist propaganda or organized agitation. It grows out of conditions which have long been endemic in every country in Asia. It is true, however, that these conditions provide fertile soil for the Communist gospel, and organized Communism is exploiting them to the full in a powerful bid for the conquest of Asia. Behind all these tumultuous influences, often obscured by the dramatic march of surface events, lies the real heart of the matter. The Asiatic crisis—like the contemporary Western crisis—is essentially a crisis of faith. Asia seeks hungrily for a faith by which to live in the new, revolutionary era on which she has entered. Herein lies the relevance of the Church's mission.

In seeking to assess the Christian prospect and interpret the Christian mission in Asia it is important to bear certain figures in mind. These help not only to place the picture in perspective but to give some impression of the magnitude of the Christian task.

The population of East Asia (from Pakistan in the West to Japan in the East) is approximately 1,100,000,000. The Christian population of the area, according to the best available estimates, is something like 33,000,000. This means that roughly one in every 33 in Eastern Asia has a connection with one or another of the Christian communions. Of the 33,000,000 Christians, roughly 22,000,000 are Roman Catholic and between 11,000,000 and 12,000,000 non-Roman Catholic. The Roman Catholic figures[6] include an estimated Roman Catholic community in the Philippines of nearly 13,000,000,[7] and a 1,500,000 in French Indo-China. The largest non-Roman Catholic Christian communities are found in India and Pakistan (nearly 5,000,000), China and Manchuria (1,500,000) and Indonesia (1,750,000). Impressive as these fig-

[6] Taken from the Catholic Directory 1948 and Le Missioni Cattoliche, Rome, 1946, quoted in World Christian Handbook.
[7] The total population of the Philippines according to the census of 1948 was approximately 19,300,000.

ures are—and they evidence a very remarkable development— we need constantly to remind ourselves that the Protestant community represents only one person in 100 in the total Asiatic population.

Thomas Carlyle warned us long ago that you can prove anything by figures. It is also possible that you may prove nothing. While this brief statistical excursion has had its value in helping us to preserve a sense of proportion, it has not done much else. We need to put flesh and blood on these bare statistical bones. I have had recent opportunity for travel in most of the countries with which this essay is concerned. I returned from four months' intensive study and wide contact with representative Christian leaders in East Asia more impressed than ever before by the sheer miracle of the world-wide Christian Church, obsessed with a desire to make known what I have seen, and burdened with a sense of incapacity to do so adequately.

There is no other expression of the ecumenical idea which is comparable to the missionary enterprise of the Church. Take, for example, the astonishingly complex international character of this world-wide movement. In November 1949 Dr. W. A. Visser 't Hooft, the General Secretary of the World Council of Churches, and I, as General Secretary of the International Missionary Council, were in the hills of northern Sumatra. We were taken one day to visit a school for the blind, which is an institution of the Batak Church. The man who brought us to the school was an Indian Christian doctor who left his home in South India two years ago to serve as a medical missionary in Batakland. The blind school had been founded originally by German missionaries of the Rhenish Mission. Support from Germany was cut off by the war, but the school has continued to meet an urgent need with such financial support as the Batak Christians themselves have been able to give it. The limited nature of this support was evident in the state of the building and the meager furnishings with which it was provided. We were shown a workroom where the blind pupils—most of them adults—were weaving baskets with swift and skillful fingers. Then we were ushered into a small room with wooden benches facing a small table and a row of chairs. On the table there was a large volume. I glanced at it and discovered that it was a copy of the Gospel according to St. Luke in Braille. Underneath the title was the inscription, "Presented by the British and Foreign Bible Society."

The blind pupils then filed into the room. There were about 30 of them—men, women and children. As I watched them feeling their way to their seats on the benches, I wondered what word I could speak that might bring some renewed hope and courage to that sad-looking little company. I did not get very far with these thoughts, for no sooner were the blind scholars in their seats than they rose. A woman tapped sharply on the end of a wooden bench and the whole group burst into singing. The Bataks are specially gifted in choral singing and, under the guidance of the German missionaries, this gift has been fostered and developed in a remarkable way. They sang a lovely German chorale with a precision of timing and a richness of tone that would have done credit to the choir of a great cathedral. The words were in the Batak language. But an interpreter whispered that they were singing about their blindness and their longing for release into a world where there shall be no more night. It was inexpressibly moving.

I glanced across the table at Visser 't Hooft and could see that he was no less moved than I. He caught my eye, leaned over and whispered: "We must sing for them. Let us try 'The Church's One Foundation.'" So when the Bataks' singing ended, we stood up and sang in English. It was not very good singing. Nature has not endowed either of us with suitable equipment for the concert platform. But we sang "The Church's One Foundation." And somehow we felt that in that ill-matched response to their magnificent effort, and although they could not understand our words any more than we had understood theirs, we had a bond with those sightless Batak people that was deeper than words:

> Elect from every nation,
>   Yet one o'er all the earth,
> Her charter of salvation
>   One Lord, one faith, one birth

There in vivid epitome—in that dingy little schoolhouse among the Sumatra hills—was the Church Universal in being and in action. A Dutchman and an Irishman are taken by an Indian to visit a school founded by Germans for the service of the blind in Batak-land. They find there a copy of a Braille Gospel given by a British society and hear a blind choir sing a German chorale to Batak words. They respond by singing, in English, the words of a great ecumenical hymn. And that is not the end of the story. A brief report about this visit was sent by air mail to a secretary of the International Missionary Council in New York. He enlisted the interest of an American society for the blind, which sent a grant to assist the school, thus giving Christians in the United States a share in this ecumenical affair.

A British poet has written:

> China and Ind, Hellas and France,
> Each hath its own inheritance,
> And each to Truth's rich market brings
> Its bright divine imaginings,
> In rival tribute, to surprise
> The world with native merchandise.

What he wrote of "Truth's rich market" is true, in a deeper and wider sense than he ever dreamed, of the world-wide movement of the Christian Church. The main stream of its life in East Asia carries the "native merchandise" of the young and virile indigenous churches, which have their roots in the life and the culture of their own lands. But they are also conscious of their place in the fellowship of a church which is universal. The thing which gives visible and continuous reality to that universal fellowship is the presence and partnership of the missionary and the sustained support of the organized missionary enterprise. The spearhead of the Christian mission in East Asia is the indigenous church, and its strategy is firmly centered in the initiative and leadership of the national churches. But the Christian mission remains, in a very real sense, a partnership in which the older Christendom continues to have a share. It is in fact an immensely varied and complex international enterprise in which the "older churches" of the West (and increasingly the "younger churches" of the East) through their organized missionary boards and societies seek to "bear one another's burdens and so fulfill the law of Christ." By this means the churches of East Asia have links which bind them in living fellowship with the churches of the United States, of Great Britain, of Continental Europe and of Australia and New Zealand, as well as a growing series of links with one another within Asia. A clear apprehension of its international and ecumenical character is essential to an intelligent understanding of the Church's mission in Asia. A detailed and comprehensive survey is beyond the range of this essay. But a few thumbnail sketches, based partly on recent experience, may offer a useful means of illustrating the tasks and opportunities of the Church in East Asia. These will exclude any treatment of India and Pakistan, which are dealt with elsewhere in the volume.

Korea: Look first at Korea, a country now the arena of war. There are about 900,000 Christians in Korea; 150,000 of them are Roman Catholics. North American, Australian and British missionary societies have shared in the task of bringing the Gospel to Korea, but North American boards (Presbyterian and Methodist) predominate. At the time of the invasion from the north, there were in South Korea strong independent Korean churches, pietist in outlook, vigorously Christian and growing rapidly in numbers. They were supported by a network of Christian institutions, including colleges, schools, a medical training school, hospitals, theological seminaries, rural training centers and a variety of other Christian enterprises which served to build up and enlarge the Church and extend its influence. The National Christian Council of Korea bound together in united planning and common action the various Christian interests in the country. United planning in Christian literature and Christian education, in adult literacy and rural reconstruction, in student evangelism and in the organization of a Christian broadcasting station, was an established feature of South Korean church life.

The war in Korea has grievously disrupted the life and work of the Church. Congregations were scattered, institutions dispersed and corporate activities suspended.

One of the most tragic elements in the Korean picture is the ceaseless movement of the refugees. As the tide of battle has swept back and forth across the country it has carried before it hordes of homeless and frightened people—fleeing now in one direction, then in another. Here is a vivid description of what this means, written by Edward Adams, a missionary on the spot:

The Communist Army made a break-through east of Taegu about 25 miles, cutting the best of the two remaining highways of retreat to Pusan at a point not very far from the remaining highway. It was a very dangerous situation, but fortunately the northern forces were not strong enough or ready to capitalize on it. An order was issued to clear a strip in the refugee camp for a barbwire barricade, which was interpreted as a general order to evacuate. *Three hundred thousand refugees took to the road!* We heard about it early. The road was about ten feet wide. For the first four days the road south for ten miles was a solid block of humanity, struggling, crying, groaning humanity. The second day it started raining and rained off and on for several days. These were busy days, we did the best we could, but what a drop in the bucket was our help. I hope never again to see such concentrated and mass suffering.

We have organized with a nucleus of four pastors, the Christian Church Service Group. More will be joining. They are working without salary. They are pledged to use no relief supplies personally that are not specifically designated for them. We have already taken our hospital doctor down twice. He treats about 300 patients each trip. We have had to limit treatments to babies, because of numbers. Lately the Red Cross has sent doctors down, who settle in one location. They do not begin to cover the field, though. These 300,000 plus refugees are settled according to the geographical location from which they come. This is to prevent Communistic infiltration. They are scattered for four miles along a stream. There are many other small groups of refugees that are harder to locate.

An immense task of relief and reconstruction confronts the Christians in Korea and calls for the generous support and assistance of the whole ecumenical fellowship.

This is not the first time that the Church in Korea has been tried as by fire. During the long period of the Japanese dominion Christians had known more sharply than most other Koreans the hostile pressure of their rulers. They had had to face the challenge of compulsory attendance at Shinto shrines, the demand for the observance of loyalty ceremonies in church services, the constant shadow of police surveillance and all the odium which attached to those whose loyalty was in doubt. When World War II ended, their liberation from Japanese rule followed. But the word "liberation" soon began to have a hollow sound in Korea, for it became clear that its price included the division of the country and the unpleasant role of being a pawn in the game of power politics as played by the great Powers. Nevertheless there was a very real sense in which, for the Christians of South Korea at least, the end of World War II brought real liberation. They were freed from complete isolation from their fellow Christians in other parts of the world. They were delivered from the intolerable demands of State Shinto and the many restraints which had been laid on their practice of their faith. They were free to worship and to witness, to rebuild the institutions which had been closed or gravely hampered during the war, and to welcome back the foreign missionaries who since the early 1940's had been excluded from the country. The Church bore the scars of its long trial, and the years immediately following the war were marked by a certain amount of faction and controversy.

In the north, however, there was a different story. Above the Thirty-eighth Parallel, the writ of Soviet Russia ran and the Korean Church remained under suspicion and unrelenting pressure. Missionaries were excluded and, while many Christians stayed on —under conditions about which we have little information—large numbers trekked as refugees across the Thirty-eighth Parallel into South Korea. There they set about rebuilding their corporate Christian life with a vigor and independence of spirit which are beyond praise.

In the city of Seoul I went one Sunday morning to a Christian service. The congregation consisted almost exclusively of North Korean refugees. They were worshiping in an old Shinto temple, which had been abandoned in 1945, and the congregation overflowed through the door into the street outside. Beside the temple a new granite-fronted church capable of seating 2,000 people was half finished. Much of the labor on the building was being done by the refugee congregation. The next day I was taken by the pastor to see some of the homes of the congregation. Many of them were living in improvised huts and canvas tents—in the bitter Korean winter climate. I was shown a Japanese war factory which had been taken over by these North Korean Christians and was humming with activity, making shoes of rubber and canvas. It not only gave employment to some hundreds of men and women in dire need, but from the profits of that factory two institutions were being supported. One was an orphanage for refugee children whose parents had died or disappeared on the southern trek. The other was a Christian high school.

We do not know what will happen to these institutions and to the resourceful men and women who established and maintained them. But one thing is certain—such faith as theirs, rooted in unswerving loyalty to Jesus Christ, is invincible. Whatever the future may hold for Korea, the Christian Church is certain to play a role in it. It may well be a decisive role, for, despite the seductive appeal of Communist propaganda, the heart of Korea is open to Christian faith.

On a hill which dominates the city of Seoul, the Japanese erected a great Shinto shrine which became the most prominent center of State Shinto in Korea. I climbed to the top of that hill in December 1949 and found, on the spot formerly dedicated to the pagan rites of Emperor Worship, a museum of Christian history. I came away from that dominating hilltop reflecting on this dramatic change, and feeling, in the light of all I had seen and heard in Korea, that it represented a forecast of Korea's future.

Japan: The position of Japan is unique in Asia. A few years ago she was a formidable naval, military and industrial nation. The dramatic speed with which her armies, supported by a powerful navy, overran half of Asia and the greater part of the South Pacific astonished the world. Behind this military achievement lay a highly developed industrial system and the most literate, energetic and technically efficient people in Asia. But these remarkable achievements were not matched by political maturity. Japan's expansionist ambitions brought untold suffering to Asia and total ruin on herself.

Under a benevolent military occupation she is today trying to rebuild a shattered national life. Her people are bewildered. They have lost in defeat the faith which sustained them during the years of war. They live in a moral and spiritual vacuum. They are seeking with pathetic eagerness for the things that belong to their peace.

It is not easy to estimate with any accuracy the present influence of the traditional faiths of Japan. Buddhism is still a live force; and its characteristic other-worldly and "life-denying" philosophy may have a strong appeal to a people disenchanted by the events of recent history and the glories of building an Asiatic empire. Shinto, the primitive faith of the common people, has not disappeared. Reports suggest that in rural areas it is still an active influence in the life of the community. In more sophisticated circles, however, the traditional faith has suffered a grievous blow as a result of its employment as an instrument of national unification and of state policy. Large sections of the Japanese people are spiritually distressed and scattered and as sheep without a shepherd. This fact confronts the Christian Church with an unprecedented challenge to which it has not yet responded with sufficient vision and enterprise.

The Christian forces in Japan are relatively weak, numerically. In a population of nearly 80,000,000, there is a non-Roman Catholic Christian community of less than 200,000. The Roman Catholic Church is estimated at about 100,000.

Christian leaders shared the shock and suffering which fell on the whole country in the final period of the war. In addition they had passed through a prolonged period of domestic tension. As early as June 1941 the Protestant churches had, under government pressure, united to form the Church of Christ in Japan. There was a small, nonconforming minority; but the bulk of the Protestant churches accepted the union. For some years before the war began the presence of missionaries in Japan had become embarrassing to the indigenous church, and their numbers were steadily reduced. The Church in Japan was thus moving into a position of increasing isolation before "Pearl Harbor" abruptly severed the remaining visible links with churches in other lands.

Since 1945 these links have been re-established. Missionaries have been welcomed and Japanese Christians are eager to share in the ecumenical fellowship of the Church. As they face the unprecedented opportunity which confronts them they need and desire the active partnership of the churches of other lands.

The Church in Japan, though numerically weak, is not without assets as it faces its task. It has a proportionately larger ministry than any church in Asia. The ministry is the product of a well-established system of theological education. There are a large number of Christian colleges and schools which offer wide contact with the non-Christian community and an opportunity for Christian influence.

On the other hand the Church in Japan is inhibited by certain serious weaknesses which derive both from past history and present internal tensions. It is largely confined to the cities and towns. It is not only urban in its distribution, it is predominantly bourgeois in outlook; and it has little influence either with the urban proletariat or the agrarian population. The Christian schools and colleges are not meeting their opportunity, partly because they are content with less than the best in academic quality (they are for the most part grossly overcrowded), but also because they are not clearly and positively *Christian*. The plans now being made for a new International Christian University give promise of a new pattern for Christian education in Japan. But a drastic overhaul of the traditional educational structure is sorely needed.

Preoccupation with its internal problems has marked the life of the Church and has hindered a vigorous evangelistic outreach to meet contemporary needs and opportunities. On the cessation of the war several denominational groups detached themselves from the United Church of Christ and re-established their separate ecclesiastical organizations. This created an atmosphere of uneasiness and tension which has made co-operation difficult. The United Church remains in being and is by far the largest ecclesiastical unit in Japanese Protestantism. But the problems of readjustment to postwar conditions have been difficult and have absorbed much of the energy and time of the ablest leaders.

The most crucial problem in the Church in Japan today is the discovery of a living Christian unity. The secret of such unity does not lie in the efficient manipulation of ecclesiastical machinery, but in the rebirth of evangelistic concern. There has been a notable advance in the re-establishment of co-operative enterprises—in relief and reconstruction, in the printing and distribution of the Scriptures, in the field of Christian literature generally and of religious education, in women's work, health services and so on. The National Christian Council has been reorganized and has renewed its constituent membership in the International Missionary Council. The most urgent task before the N.C.C. is a resurvey of the entire Christian enterprise with a view to the more effective use of all available resources in a united effort to meet the spiritual hunger of contemporary Japan. It is in such an effort—in which all the churches and Christian agencies combine in concerted action —that the Church in Japan will discover a living unity and, under God, a new sense of power and purpose.

China: Although the Protestant Church in China is comparatively young and the 1,500,000 Protestants form a very small minority of China's total population of 475,000,000, the Church's strength and influence are strong factors that are recognized by all groups. The Communist government even acknowledged this strength in the selection of religious representatives to the People's Consultative Congress in Peking in the fall of 1949. From this ancient Confucianist-Buddhist-Taoist country five of the delegates selected were Protestants; the other two, Buddhists. We are not concerned here with the strategy of the Communists in seeking representatives of the Church for this congress, nor are we able to determine the good and bad effects which may result from the participation of these religious leaders. The fact remains, however, that in the choosing of religious delegates the Communists revealed their estimation of Protestantism as compared with the other religions of China.

This estimation of strength is based on the fact that more than 10,000 churches and chapels continue to carry on their religious activities. Moreover, Christian institutions in China include 13 colleges and universities, approximately 200 middle schools and more than 300 hospitals. To this list may be added seminaries, Bible schools, literature societies, schools for the blind, Bible societies, leprosariums, rural-service centers, clinics, kindergartens, orphanages, child-welfare centers and a host of primary schools.

The growth and the development of the Chinese church is the result of the work of more than a hundred Western missionary societies from the British Isles, North America, Europe, Australia and New Zealand. Indeed, China may be termed the melting pot of the missionary societies, for here is a church which reveals a fascinating pattern of church life, one that reflects all the colors and shades of Western Christianity; a panorama which includes various contrasting groups—Norwegian Lutherans and Free Methodists, Anglicans and Quakers, Irish Presbyterians and Assemblies of God, the Yale-in-China Mission and the Salvation Army.

Against the background of Chinese society this panorama is taking on a new appearance and the churches are being merged into a unity which may bring a gem of rare beauty into the Ecumenical Church. Already 17 mission societies have united to form the Church of Christ in China, a body whose communicant membership of approximately 200,000 worships in a network of churches that extends from northern Manchuria to southern Hong Kong, from the teeming millions of Shanghai to the isolated mountain fortresses of Sikang province in West China. Under Chinese initiative and leadership this church has established missionary work among the border tribes of the far west, the land of the Miaos and the Lolos.

The largest co-operating Christian agency in China is the National Christian Council with headquarters in Shanghai. It seeks to co-ordinate the work of more than 40 societies in a great variety of projects. It promotes joint programs of evangelism, supplies Christian literature for churches, encourages Christian work among industrial workers, produces visual-aid materials, promotes Christian education among government and mission schools, and keeps the churches in contact with other areas of the Universal Church.

To state that this forward-moving and forward-looking church is without perils and temptations of great magnitude is to overlook one of the major crises in the World Church of our day. The existence of a totalitarian state that zealously advocates another "religion" places Christians in a precarious position. Individual cases of apostasy and some compromising with Marxian ideology may exist. On the other hand, the presence of a great evangelical church challenges Christians throughout the world to live in a spirit of Christian expectancy, in the certain hope that God will use this day of trial not only for the purification of His church but for the actual conversion of Communists to the Christian faith.

The Philippine Islands: There is an almost startlingly exotic quality in the Philippines which marks them off from the rest of

Asia, without obliterating entirely their Asiatic flavor. Centuries of Spanish culture combined with the dominant influence of the Roman Catholic Church have left an indelible imprint on the life of the islands. Fifty years of intimate contact with the United States have overlaid the Latin tradition with a culture which has left its own distinctive marks. English is spoken universally by the educated and is the official language. Spanish is widely known and the indigenous vernaculars are used mainly in the rural areas —though even there English is understood and sometimes used. A Manila barrister was quoted to me as saying: "I speak the vernacular at home, I speak English in the courts and I speak Spanish when I make love."

The evangelical churches in the Philippines date from the beginning of the American connection, and have thus recently celebrated the Golden Jubilee of evangelical Christianity. They owe their origin almost exclusively to American missions. Today they have a constituency of approximately 730,000 among the 7,083 islands, totaling 19,500,000 in population.

Like every other Asiatic country which suffered under enemy occupation during the war, the life of the young Philippine republic has been beset by many internal difficulties—economic and political. Some of the bitter controversy that marked the tensions of the occupation has carried over into the life of the new republic and has shown itself both in political unrest in the life of the State and in surviving suspicions in certain areas of church life.

There are many unsolved economic questions, both external and internal, and these have offered a ready target for the agitator and a fertile source of revolt. The Philippines are very conscious of the Communist threat, both externally because of their geographical position and internally because of the persistent activities of rebellious elements within the country. Remarkable progress has been made in rehabilitation, and Christian institutions in particular have shown a striking recovery and a marked expansion since the war.

This is specially true in the case of Christian schools and colleges. The Philippine Federation of Christian Churches, reorganized after the disruption of the war, is one of the most effective instruments of Christian co-operation in Asia. It links the evangelical churches in active united endeavor as well as in common planning. Closely allied to it is a vigorous Association of Christian Schools and Colleges. The Federation, in addition to its central task of providing a forum for Christian consultation among the member churches, engages in a number of important joint activities. These include a department of Christian rural service, under a full-time secretary. The importance of rural training centers, of land-settlement schemes and of credit unions under Christian leadership can hardly be exaggerated in a situation where land problems are acute, poverty endemic and agrarian unrest widespread. They represent a significant contribution to rural well-being and not infrequently a means of demonstrating the nature of social justice. The Federation has also a lively youth department, well-laid plans for the united production and distribution of Christian literature, and for the development of modern means of communicating the Christian message by radio and other auditory and visual devices.

There is serious concern in the evangelical churches regarding the training of an adequate Christian leadership—lay and ordained —for the service of the Church. The losses and setbacks of the war have told heavily and have not yet been restored. Discussions have been going on for some time, and are still in progress, regarding a wider extension of united Christian training.

These activities do not, by any means, exhaust the Federation's interests, but serve to give some impression of their breadth and significance. Two of the most important tasks which devolve on this united body are the negotiation with member churches regarding comity and the geographical distribution of their work, and the vigilant guardianship of civil and religious liberties. The purpose of comity negotiations is to eliminate unnecessary overlapping and ensure the most effective distribution of limited resources in the immense task of evangelism. The necessity for the Federation's vigilance in matters of religious liberty is accentuated by a stiffening opposition to evangelical expansion.

It must be said, in this connection, that a visitor receives the impression that the present government holds in high regard the work and witness of the evangelical churches. The laity of these churches make a contribution to public life out of all proportion to the strength of the churches which they represent.

Religious liberty is an issue of crucial importance everywhere in Asia. It is threatened by Communist aggression, by the alliance of the ancient faiths of Asia with political nationalism and, alas, in the Philippines by the intolerance of the large Roman Catholic Church. There is no stronger bulwark against the threat to human rights and to religious liberty (in whatever form that threat presents itself) than the spread of a vigorous Christianity which is at once evangelical and catholic—drawing strength from the classical traditions of reformed theology and expressing a true catholicity in its living sense of continuity with the Apostolic Church and of essential oneness with the Church Universal.

The vigor and continued growth of the evangelical Church in the Philippines is thus a ground for thanksgiving and for hope. Despite its weaknesses and unsolved problems it is a stabilizing and a constructive factor of real significance in the life of the republic.

Indonesia: Let us now move south to glance briefly at the Church in the vast 2,000-mile archipelago which is Indonesia, containing a population of 55,710,000. Here we find the largest group of non-Roman Catholic Christians in Asia, outside India. There are approximately 1,750,000 Protestant Christians in these islands,[8] grouped in a series of churches which for the most part owe their origin, under God, to the work of the Netherlands Missionary Societies. The one notable exception to this is the Batak Church in Sumatra, which grew out of the work of the Rhenish Mission.

The Christians of Indonesia shared with their non-Christian fellows the rigors of the Japanese invasion and the subsequent occupation, the long strain of the postwar struggle for independence with its intermittent warfare and accompanying disorders, and the final achievement of national sovereignty. Through all these vicissitudes the Church has both suffered and grown. During the occupation it suffered isolation, the sudden cessation of all contact with the mother churches in Europe, the removal of missionaries and of financial assistance, the closing of vital institutions, the reduction by death of many ministers and Christian workers and the steady pressure of the occupying power. It suffered in the

[8] There are 560,000 Roman Catholics.

period of the revolution from the effects of the prevailing disorder and consequent demoralization, but most of all perhaps from the painful tensions which, almost inevitably, arose in relations with the Dutch missionaries to whom they owed so much. These tensions have been greatly eased, if not wholly resolved. The Indonesian churches have not yet made up their minds as to the position which they desire the missionary and the missionary-supported institution to take in the life of the indigenous Christian Church. There is, however, sufficient good will and Christian understanding on both sides to give promise of a wise solution.

But the Church has grown through all these years of stress. The latest figures available suggest a remarkable increase in the Christian community during the troubled decade, 1938-1948. Since the war there has been a continuous attempt—gravely hampered in many places by the continued internal strife—to restore the work of the Church to full effectiveness. The Advanced Theological School in Djakarta—a united institution which serves the whole of Indonesia—has been reopened. It is quite outstanding in Asia and the curriculum would intimidate the majority of theological students in the West. It produces results. The young men trained in this rigorous discipline are proving themselves outstanding leaders in the Indonesian church. One of the most urgent needs of this church, however, is for greater facilities for theological training on a regional basis and of a less advanced type.

The largest growth of the Church in Indonesia has been in the outlying islands. Metropolitan Java has vigorous churches, but they are numerically small by comparison with the great churches in Ambon, the Celebes and in Batakland. Indonesia is a predominantly Moslem country and, while Moslem influence is in evidence everywhere, it is most powerful in Java. There is also a racial difference between the Javanese proper and the inhabitants of the outlying islands, who are largely of aboriginal origin. It is a notable fact that Indonesia is the only Moslem country in the world in which Christianity has made any substantial progress.

The new government of Indonesia has adopted an enlightened attitude on religious freedom. But the provision of safeguards in a constitution is not in itself a guarantee of liberty in matters of religion. There is among Indonesian Christians a widespread feeling that, under the new political conditions, they may be called to face increasing cultural and religious pressure by the Moslem majority. They are probably right. There is also to be found among Christians an increasing recognition that nationalism is not enough, that "freedom" will not bring the millennium, but may well lay burdens on the newly freed society which it is unready to bear. The churches in Indonesia—as elsewhere in Asia—have before them a tremendous challenge and a formidable task in giving a Christian content to words which are on everyone's lips but are little more than empty shells, now that the goal of "freedom" has been achieved.

In order that they may face their arduous task with greater cohesion and unity, the churches of Indonesia have, within the past few months, formed themselves into a National Council of Churches. An interesting feature of the constitution of this council is that it states, as its first aim, the formation of a united church in Indonesia. In this they reflect a sentiment that is virtually universal in the churches of Asia—an impatience of the denominational division inherited from the West, a conviction that in face of their gigantic task in a non-Christian world the traditional divisions of Christendom are trivial, and a determination to achieve the visible unity of the Body of Christ. In this area, at least, Asia is leading the older Christendom, and challenging sharply "our unhappy divisions," which, despite their alleged unhappiness, we appear to endure with astonishing complacency.

Malaya: Malaya has a mixed population totaling between 5,000,000 and 6,000,000. Of these approximately 2,000,000 are Malays. There is a Chinese population of 1,800,000 and an Indian community of 500,000 or so.

The Christian message was first brought to the country by St. Francis Xavier, and there is a Roman Catholic community of 86,-000. Non-Roman missionaries began work in the early part of the nineteenth century and the churches which they founded represent a constituency of 47,000. One of the features of the Christian situation in Malaya is that the spread of Christianity has taken place almost exclusively among the non-Malay peoples. The Chinese predominate in the Church, with Indians forming the next largest element. There is a considerable body of Eurasians and

Europeans but almost no Malays in the membership. This is accounted for partly by the fact that the Malays are traditionally Moslem in faith, and Islam is notably unresponsive to the Christian appeal. But there have been other factors at work. The colonial government, in the period of missionary expansion, was reluctant to offend the susceptibilities of the Moslem population and, while welcoming the growth of Christian educational and other activities among non-Malay communities, did not offer similar encouragement to a Christian approach to the Malays. This fact, combined with the relative responsiveness of the Chinese and Indian peoples, contributed to the curious situation which now exists.

The church in Malaya has historical and active associations with the Anglican and Presbyterian churches of England, the Methodist Church in the U.S.A., and the Mar Thoma Syrian Church and the Tamil Evangelical Lutheran Church in India. These links were largely severed during the Japanese occupation by the internment of British and American missionaries and the severing of communication with the outside world. The Anglican Bishop of Singapore succeeded in persuading the Japanese authorities to grant him a parole, which lasted for about a year. In this period he gave himself without stint to the service of the churches and not only won the confidence and affection of the whole Christian community but laid the spiritual foundation of a deeper Christian unity. It found expression immediately after the war in the organization of the Malayan Christian Council and in the establishment of union theological training in an institution in which Anglicans, Methodists and Presbyterians combine.

There has been no sensational growth of the Christian community in recent years, though, despite the war, there has been a steady and appreciable increase in church membership. The system of Christian schools in Malaya is particularly strong and in this field there has been a general expansion since the war.

With the increasing pressure which the new regime is exerting upon the foreign missionary in China, the large Chinese population of Malaya, with its traditional responsiveness to Christianity, may well become a factor of strategic importance in the future evangelization of China. The use of Asiatic missionaries in Asia has already begun elsewhere. There may soon be situations in which this will be the only means of Christian access, and we must be ready to meet them.

Burma: "Anybody . . . when asked about the political situation in our country will answer that it is in an awful mess." These were not, as one might expect, the words of a bitter opponent of the Burma government, but of the Prime Minister of Burma. They were spoken in the middle of June 1949 and were the climax of long years of almost incredible chaos. To tell that tortuous and involved tale would require more space than is here available. But a recognition of the disorder which has marked the postwar era of Burma's history is essential to any understanding of the problems of the Church in the unhappy land. It should, in fairness, be said that since the Prime Minister's candid facing of facts (perhaps partly because of it) there have been a gradual improvement in the internal situation and a greater prospect of stability than for many years.

There is some reason to suppose that Burma has become nervous about her position in the strategy of Asia in the light of recent developments in China and Korea. This has apparently had a sobering effect. The government's support of the United Nations Security Council's resolution on Korea was, in the light of recent history and known tendencies both within and without the government, a surprising development. Burma has little desire to be "myeza grass between two fighting buffaloes." She seems to have begun to realize that her chances of avoiding this unhappy fate may be enhanced if she sets her own house in order and throws her weight against Communist aggression elsewhere in Asia.

In a total population of 16,000,000, mainly Buddhist, there is a Christian community of over 550,000, of whom about 125,000 are Roman Catholic. The churches in Burma have for the most part grown from the pioneer missionary work of the American Baptists, the missionary societies of the Church of England, the American and British Methodist missions, the Lakker Pioneer mission and some smaller organizations (including one which bears the impressive title: "New Jerusalem in the U.S.A.," which in 1938 had 200 adherents). The largest single Protestant church is that which resulted from the American Baptist work. With a constituency of about 400,000, this church, drawn mainly from the

Karens and other tribal peoples, is a force to reckon with in Burma. Strong, self-reliant and vigorously evangelistic, it has provided some of the finest Christian leadership there.

Burma suffered heavy damage during the war. It was exposed to more bitter and continuous fighting than most countries engaged. The destruction was correspondingly great and the demoralization widespread. A somber record of civil strife and continuing disorder has marked the postwar years and has retarded or rendered impossible the tasks of reconstruction and recovery. The well-known Judson College in Rangoon has not been permitted to reopen and other Christian institutions have suffered sadly in these chaotic years.

The vast majority of Burma's 17,000,000 people are Buddhist by religious tradition. The impact of the Church upon this dominant community has, hitherto, been slight. The bulk of the Christian Church has been drawn from the tribal peoples. The recent conflict between them—particularly the Karens—and the government of Burma—predominantly Buddhist—has had its repercussions on the life of the Church. Many of the ablest Karen leaders are Christians. The deep distrust which existed between the Karens generally and the Burmese had led to frequent sporadic conflicts. These culminated in an attack on Karen Christians in church on Christmas Day, 1948. It precipitated a Karen rebellion which at one time assumed very serious proportions.

As already suggested, the internal situation has improved, but the position of the Christian Church in the foreseeable future is not likely to be easy.

It is both interesting and important to record, however, that during the years of continuous turmoil and suffering since 1941, the Church in Burma has increased notably in numerical strength.

Before the war the Burma Christian Council was part of the National Christian Council of India, Burma and Ceylon. It has been reorganized since the war and has recently become a member council of the International Missionary Council, being thus recognized as a *national* council in its own right. This revived and reconstituted organ of Christian co-operation has, through the trying years, been a focus of combined Christian action. But its operations have inevitably been limited by the dislocation of communications within the country. With the restoration of travel and the possibility of renewed fellowship and consultation, the National Christian Council will be able to enlarge its effectiveness as an expression of Christian solidarity and an instrument of united Christian service.

Ceylon: Ceylon is an illustration of the curious fact that a country, like a family, which is well-behaved and capable of managing its affairs competently and in orderly fashion is not regarded by the contemporary journalist as of any interest to the newspaper-reading public. Such is the perverted sense of what makes "news" that only violent revolution and bloodshed attract attention. This is the only reasonable explanation of the fact that in all the reams that the popular press has printed in recent years about Asia, Ceylon has hardly ever been mentioned. Yet Ceylon might well be taken as a model for a lesson on how to achieve self-government painlessly!

Within a few short years the island has passed from the status of a crown colony to that of a self-governing dominion with exemplary efficiency and a complete absence of excitement or disorder. It has revealed political maturity of a refreshing rarity.

Ceylon has an exceptionally good educational system. It has achieved a higher level of literacy than any Asiatic country except Japan. Its population of 6,500,000 is predominantly Buddhist and the island has been the home of a vigorous neo-Buddhist revival.

There is a total Christian community of about 600,000, of whom 500,000 are Roman Catholics. The non-Roman churches, though numerically small, have, through their well-organized system of schools, exerted an influence on the life and thought of the country out of all proportion to their numbers.

Though not unscathed by the war, Ceylon escaped the trials of occupation which were the lot of so many Asiatic countries. The work of the Church continued with little dislocation. The training of the ministry was not suspended and the church in Ceylon is fortunate in the possession of a strong and well-educated pastorate. The growth of the church has been slow, but Christian nurture has in general been thorough and there is a more mature and instructed Christian community than in most other countries of Asia.

The non-Roman churches are mainly of British origin—Anglican, Baptist and Methodist. There are also churches of the Presbyterian order which date their origin to the period of the Dutch dominion in Ceylon; and there is an American Congregational mission in the north, and a church related to it, which now forms the Jaffna Diocese of the Church of South India.

Ceylon has its own plans for church union in an extremely well-devised scheme, inclusive of Anglicans, Baptists, Methodists and Presbyterians. If these plans are fulfilled, they will result in a Church of Lanka (the ancient name of Ceylon) which will combine the main streams of non-Roman Christian tradition in the island in one comprehensive church. Such a development will, as is the case in South India, have very far-reaching effects upon the Church in other parts of the world.

In another direction the church in Ceylon is in a position to make a contribution that may be of service to many of its sister churches in Asia. Christianity in Ceylon cannot but be conscious of the power of the Buddhist tradition and of its massive resistance to Christian penetration. The pressure of events in less favored parts of Asia, the disorganization of the Church's life, has too frequently meant that the vital task of theological reflection has been impossible. There is an urgent need for a penetrating interpretation of the relevance of Christian faith to its Asiatic environment—whether that environment be dominated by one of the classical non-Christian religious traditions, by aggressive Communism or by modern scientific humanism. There are Christian minds in Ceylon capable of making such a contribution to Christian thought. This may well be a part of Ceylon's contribution to Christian advance in Asia.

Thailand and "Bangkok 1949": The church in Thailand—a predominantly Buddhist country—is not large. In a total population of about 15,000,000 there are approximately 58,000 Christians. Of these only 15,000 are members of churches which derive from the work of Protestant missions. The largest and most influential of these missions is the Presbyterian of the U.S.A.

The government and people of Thailand have had traditionally friendly relations with foreign missionaries and have maintained an attitude of tolerance toward the Christian Church. Despite this, the Church has expanded slowly. Christian influence has been widespread and, in certain directions, powerful; the numbers who have been led to serve Christ in the fellowship of His Church are relatively small. In 1934 the greater part of the Protestant churches united to form the Church of Christ in Thailand. There is also a National Christian Council, which serves to link the indigenous churches and the foreign missions in common consultation and the planning of their total task. The magnitude of that unfinished task, as the few statistics quoted have served to show, is considerable; and its importance is enhanced by the growing significance of Thailand in the economic life of Asia and its strategic geographical location.

In recent years Bangkok has been the center of many important conferences and consultations. Most of these have met to discuss political, economic and cultural questions. None of them is so significant for the whole future of Asia as a small conference of Christians which convened at the beginning of December 1949. This was the first occasion on which representatives of the Christian churches of East Asia have met to express a common solidarity in the faith and to consider their own Asiatic problems on a continental scale. Asiatic Christians have taken a distinguished place in *world* conferences during the past 25 years. Never before had they met for a strictly Asiatic conference.

Forty-five delegates from 13 countries of Eastern Asia met in Bangkok. They were joined by representatives from Australia and New Zealand and by observers from several Western countries. Though the conference was held under the auspices of the International Missionary Council and the World Council of Churches, its planning and leadership were in Asiatic hands.

It would be difficult to overstate the symbolic and strategic significance of this meeting. It symbolized, in an Asia divided by language, race, culture and political allegiance, a unity which transcends all difference because it is born of a transcendent allegiance to Jesus Christ.

In a period of sweeping change and revolutionary upheaval, new and powerful forces are bidding for the soul of Asia. At such a time as this, it is not an insignificant fact that the Christians of Asia should meet to consider a common strategy and to proclaim with new vigor the kingship of Christ. "Amid all the turmoil of time, we bear witness afresh to the eternal truth of the Gospel, the truth that the world has a Lord, a Judge and a Saviour—Jesus Christ. Constrained by His love and directed by His plain command, we declare again that the Gospel is the saving truth for this and every generation, and we urge upon the churches of Eastern Asia the duty of making the Gospel known to every creature."

The conference was vividly aware of the threat to Christian freedom which confronts the Church in many parts of Asia. It was conscious of the challenge of Communism and of the Christian responsibility in the enveloping social revolution. It faced these issues with realism and prophetic conviction.

In relation to Communism these Asian leaders urged that:

The Christian must distinguish between the social revolution which seeks justice and the totalitarian ideology which interprets and perverts it. The Christian Church must welcome the demand of the peoples for a fuller participation in the life of society at the level where power is exercised, since this is an expression of human dignity; and the rise of Communism is a judgment on the churches for their failure to do so. Nevertheless the struggle for justice frustrates itself if the evil forces inherent in any human situation are not held in check. Because Communism lacks a conception of the independence of moral reality over against power, it denies the supremacy of the moral law over power politics and hence in the long run defeats the very purpose of the social revolution. This ideological error in Communism, which turns a social revolution for justice into a new oppression, arises out of the self-righteousness of its militant atheism; and at this point the conflict between Christianity and Communism is fundamental.[9]

This fundamental conflict will not be resolved in Christian victory merely by the offering of moral advice or the introduction of social reforms.

Moral advice and the proclamation of moral ideas are insufficient. Only that which transcends morals, namely, the knowledge of the ultimate accountability of man and society to God and of the grace of God by which men, being forgiven, forgive one another, can be the foundation of personal responsibility and respon-

[9] *The Christian Prospect in Eastern Asia.* Papers and Minutes of the Eastern Asia Christian Conference, Dec. 3-11, 1949. (New York: Friendship Press, 1950), p. 115.

sible society. The lack of the knowledge of God as the Judge of history is at the root of all tendencies towards nihilism and totalitarianism, in Asia and elsewhere. The proclamation of the Word of God, with a profound sense of its relevance to the ideological and political conflicts of the Orient, is therefore the central task of the Church in Asia.

In the final analysis, the prophetic ministry of the Church in the social and political order depends on the Church being truly a community of persons rooted in the Word of God, that is, worshiping congregations in which human worth and mutual responsibility are acknowledged and realized, and from which love goes out in work of service to the neighborhood. A true Christian congregation is the most effective prophetic witness to the divine righteousness in society, and the only answer to the challenge of political ideologies that view man solely in terms of his social and political functions. The Christian congregation has revolutionary significance in the East Asia political situation.[10]

The revolutionary significance of the Christian congregation! That in the final analysis is the heart of the matter and the only firm basis for a Christian strategy of expansion. The freedom of the local congregation to worship and to bear witness is, therefore, crucial.

The Christian Church cannot accept anything less than the freedom which allows it to be what it is, namely, the body through which the Lord Jesus Christ continually calls men and women from all nations, races and religions into communion with Himself. The Church dare not become a static minority; it must ever remain an ever-expanding, dynamic, free and open society.[11]

The Christian hope for Asia rests not on the historical situation in which the Christians in Asia find themselves today. It rests, in Asia as elsewhere, on something that transcends history—God's revelation in Christ of the destiny of man and the hope of a kingdom which cannot be shaken.

A soldier of the Red Army in Europe said to a correspondent of the London *Times* in 1946: "We are happy, not because we are rich, but because we know where we are going."

In the Bangkok Conference the Christian leaders of Asia said:

[10] *Ibid*, pp. 115-117.
[11] *Ibid*, p. 117.

We know where we are going; not to the kingdom of man, the illusion of a secular hope. We seek a city which hath foundations, whose builder and maker is God.

It is the Christian responsibility to work for or defend a political and social order, informed by the Christian understanding of man and his destiny, as a sign and witness to the Christian hope; nevertheless the breakdown of political hopes does not destroy the freedom of the Christian man and the Christian Church.[12]

Among the many Christians of Asia there are few who sit in the seats of the mighty—"not many wise men after the flesh, not many mighty, not many noble, are called."

Yet the real hope of Asia rests with these Christian communities, not because of what they are in themselves, but because they are the bearers of the everlasting Gospel. In the tremendous task to which they are called they look to the Universal Church for partnership with them in a missionary task which is both theirs and ours.

On the road that winds down from the mountains of Northern Sumatra to the coastal plain and the city of Medan there is a little village named Parapat. Normally it is a quiet spot, nestling drowsily by the lakeside in a fold of the hills. But when we entered it on a morning of late November 1949, Parapat appeared to have lost its customary tranquillity. The village street was lined with vehicles. Military trucks and civilian busses, compact jeeps, American sedans and solo motorcycles seemed to fill every available space, while a fairly steady stream of traffic flowed past them, filling the air with noise and petroleum fumes.

The primary cause of all this commotion was the fact that the Dutch army had begun to withdraw to Eastern Sumatra, in preparation for the final transfer of sovereignty from the Netherlands to Indonesia, which was to take place on January 1, 1950. The withdrawal of the foreign troops had started a minor movement of civilians and generated an atmosphere of crisis. There was a sense of excitement in the air—an odd mixture of expectancy and apprehension.

[12] *Ibid.*

Though governments change, men must eat; the main focus
of interest in Parapat was a Chinese restaurant. Its proprietor was
no partisan. He had painted across the front of his establishment
the word "Neuteral" and was busy catering for all comers. Business was booming; a motley crowd of customers was pitching
into the pilau and the omelets, the curried chicken and the mutton
chops which a smiling Chinese youth was bringing from the
kitchen in large quantities. The walls of the restaurant were adorned,
with a fine impartiality, by posters of the various Indonesian political parties and portraits of the Netherlands royal family. The
active patrons included soldiers of the Indonesian Republican
Army, a miscellaneous group of civilians and a considerable company of Dutch troops. Despite a superficial appearance of good-
natured bonhomie, one was aware of a vaguely uncomfortable
constraint in the atmosphere. The various groups, though occupying the same room, were strictly segregated. The Republican officers ate their meal with polite aloofness, while Dutch troops
gathered round a tinny piano in the corner to sing lilting army
songs. The hubbub and the heartiness could not disguise the dis-
comforts of close association or disperse the sense of its brittle
artificiality.

When our little party entered the restaurant, we were eyed with
undisguised curiosity from all sides. For we were a mixed company. A Dutchman, an Indian, an Irishman and several Indonesian Bataks eating together at a table created a mild sensation
in that cosmopolitan but deeply divided company. We were brought
together by one thing only : *we were Christians.* That bond of common faith and allegiance transcended all the differences of race and
culture, of political outlook and personal prejudice which—in an atmosphere charged with unresolved tensions—would otherwise have
tended to keep us apart. When we finished our meal we went up a
shaky wooden staircase which led onto a gloomy landing and there,
while the dishes clattered and the piano continued its staccato
rhythm, we bowed our heads and commended one another to the
God and Father of our Lord Jesus Christ. We said our farewells,
and the Indian missionary and the Batak Christians set off once
more up the mountain road, while the Dutchman and the Irishman
went in the opposite direction on the long journey which would

bring them respectively to Geneva and New York. But they went conscious that the bond of unity in a common faith transcends distance no less than difference, and deeply convinced that those who are held by that faith in the unity of the Spirit and the bond of peace are cells of hope in a divided and fearful world.

Some of these cells in Asia we have sought to describe. The description has been far too prosaic for the tremendous reality which they represent and the potential hope which they hold for Asia—and for the world.

The words of President Henry Van Dusen in *World Christianity* are a more lyrical and therefore more adequate statement of the case:

The world-wide movement of the Christian Church! There is nothing else like it in all the world. There has been nothing like it in the whole of human history. The truth is there is nothing that can so much as be compared with it. With all its divisions, its inadequacies, its apostasies, it is today the greatest power for the uplifting of the life of humanity in its every aspect and for the building of a fairer world which this planet has ever seen. Its powerful advance, with incalculable benefit to mankind, waits upon our realization of that *fact*—for it is a fact. And then upon our appropriate response to that fact.[14]

[14] Henry P. Van Dusen, *World Christianity* (Abingdon-Cokesbury Press, 1947), p. 134.

Theodore F. Romig contributed the section on China in this chapter.

The Agony of China

By THEODORE F. ROMIG

"THERE are things that could never be imagined, but there is nothing which may not happen." So runs an old Chinese proverb. The Communist triumph over the reputedly strong Nationalist government led by Chiang Kai-shek was something which could hardly be imagined, but it happened. With the appearance of such a phenomenon it is well to ask the question, "What does it mean?" An event of such magnitude must be deeply significant.

The triumph of the Communists cannot be ignored as a mere ripple on the surface of the long historical life of China nor as merely the appearance of another Chinese "dynasty" come to hold its sway for a hundred years or so. Nor should it be attacked as a dreadfully evil aberration which has suddenly appeared and must be extracted from the world much as one would pull out a decayed tooth that is giving pain to the whole body. The Communist conquest of China is no sudden unrelated and meaningless phenomenon. It is a loud voice shouting a warning to all people; it is a cry that demands our attention, a wail which speaks of the agonies and frustrated hopes of the human soul. He who cannot sense in this upheaval of an ancient society the struggle of the human spirit for a fuller life is, indeed, insensitive to the voices of the soul. The nation which fails to heed the warning of this significant revolution will itself meet a similar fate in time. For Christians to ignore the revolution as merely the work of evil men will indicate that the Church is static, complacent and devoid of prophetic insight. Let us seriously ask the question, "What does this mean?"

The events of the past four years did not suddenly come on the horizon like morning mist appearing in the skies. The Communists did not sweep over the mainland of China like a tidal wave labeled "Made in Russia." The final success of the revolution, it is true, was motivated by a systematic chain of ideas worked out by Karl Marx, for many of China's Red leaders were educated in Russia. They are undoubtedly Marxists in their thinking, Leninists in their political planning, and perhaps Stalinists in their nationalist and expansionist ambitions. Yet the revolutionary embryo has been in China for more than a hundred years. Periodically it has tried to break the shell and mature into a full-grown revolution.

To change the figure, the revolutionary spirit has been like a team of horses harnessed to a bogged-down and ditched chariot which has been shattered by the stamping and kicking steeds wildly seeking to free the chariot from the binding mud and the treacherous ditch. The chariot gradually emerges from the ditch, but into the driver's seat jumps Karl Marx, who directs the horses down the one-way highroad which he has discovered. Eager to be guided to freedom and triumph, the horses respond to the touch of their master. But make no mistake about it: this one thing is certain, namely, the horses are pure-bred Chinese steeds, determined, powerful, and hungrily racing for a place in the world's great arena. The durable chariot was made by Chinese hands from the wealth of China's good earth. More than once in the past hundred years the horses have emerged from the mud and raced violently to be free, ending only in meeting an unseen trap and slipping back into the mire.

A series of convulsions and sporadic revolutions, frustrated attempts to free the chariot, have swept over China. The most important of these is the almost forgotten T'ai P'ing Rebellion spreading over the years from 1850 to 1864. A contemporary writer speaks of it as the largest and most significant war in the history of the world prior to World War I. Yet this uprising which probably cost the lives of at least 20,000,000 Chinese is ignored and almost forgotten by the West. It is like the tremendous earthquake which recently shook the foundations of Tibet and swallowed entire villages, failing to impress us because the place seemed so remote.

Nevertheless, the Communists themselves claim the T'ai P'ing Rebellion as the beginning of the people's liberation. No longer in China dares one speak of it as a "rebellion," for it has been given dignity by being termed a "revolution."

The man who jumped into the chariot seat of this race was Hung Hsiu Ch'uen, a religious fanatic whose religion consisted of a curious mixture of Christianity, perverted mysticism and Oriental political despotism. During a period of illness following his failure to pass the government examinations, Hung Hsiu Ch'uen had visual hallucinations. He claimed that he saw God the Father and Jesus Christ the Elder Brother. Later he interpreted his dream to mean that he himself was the third person in the Trinity.

These visions caused potential rebels, later leaders of the T'ai P'ings, to accept Hung as a kind of messianic leader with supernatural insights and powers. Out of a conglomeration of religious ideas there developed an ideology which supplied the T'ai P'ings with a goal and a purpose in history which do not greatly differ from those of the Communists today. The goal of history was the Heavenly Kingdom of Great Peace which it was the purpose of the T'ai P'ings to establish. Like the Communist conception of the classless society, the period of the Great Peace would be one in which people lived together on a basis of equality. "Sharing the Property Together" was their appealing slogan. There would be no landlords, no rich people, no oppressive officials and no imperialists in this Heavenly Kingdom of Great Peace. The oppressed farmers, the poor, the disinherited followed the new leader, accepted his dictatorship, endured hardships and even faced death, all for the purpose of hastening the era of the Great Peace. The coming Great Peace, the "T'ai P'ing," was the dream, the goal, the end of history.

This religious ideology, however, was not the primary cause of the rebellion. It gave to the people of China a program and a sense of historical meaning, but behind the dream of the Great Peace were factors, already alluded to, which provided the ingredients of the revolution. The ideology provided only the formula. The ingredients consisted of the discontent of the people, the poverty, the chagrin caused by foreign imperialism, a longing for freedom, and a certain awareness of an outworn social structure which could not meet successfully the impact of the West.

Hatred for the Manchu officials, who were at that time the rulers of China, was an important factor of the revolution. The Manchus had never been accepted as Chinese, and, consequently, the people unhappily considered their rule as one of foreign domination. It was no secret, furthermore, that the Manchu officials were corrupt. Two thousand taels of silver would purchase a small officialdom, and 4,000 would buy the rulership of an entire county. Political corruption, from which follow economic distress, military weakness, breakdown of moral discipline, foreign imperialism and cultural decline, has been the primary cause of revolts and revolutions within China. The collapse of practically every dynasty has been the story of political corruption in high places.

The problem of tenancy and landlordism is closely tied to political corruption. Through the centuries there developed in China an official-landlord-scholar class, known as the gentry. This aristocratic ruling minority performed a unique function. The gentry was characterized by its scholarship, consisting mainly of a thorough knowledge of the Chinese classics. In a country where illiteracy prevailed and where there has been a deep reverence for Confucius, Mencius and all the other ancient sages, the scholars occupied a most favorable position. They were held in awe as they performed the functions of preserving and guarding the spiritual and cultural heritage of China.

The temptation of the scholar class, however, was to wield political and economic power over the nation as well as to direct the moral and spiritual life of the people. The respect in which they were held, coupled with their practical knowledge of reading, writing, Chinese laws and tradition and the use of the abacus, enabled the scholars to seize the wealth and the political machinery of the nation. The scholar lived as the ruler, the spiritual guardian and the economic tycoon of the community. This concentration of power inevitably led to landlordism and tenancy.

The statistics for tenancy may not strike the American as startling or distressful. Often the tenancy in a province is no more than 30 to 40 per cent of the population. However, in a country where one's economic security is measured completely in terms of tillable land and where the population is 80 per cent rural, such a percentage represents a disinherited population of that amount. It was estimated that more than 60 per cent of the people were landless at the time of the T'ai P'ing Rebellion. Thus more than half the population lived a marginal existence. A flood, a famine or even a poor crop could reduce them to the verge of starvation or to the possibility of becoming so involved in debt that the remainder of their lives and all their goods would have to be mortgaged to the landlord.

Another cause contributing to the rebellion was China's humiliating defeat by the British and other foreign Powers in the Opium Wars and the gradual loss of her national sovereignty to those Powers. Manchu domination was unendurable, but the humiliations suffered at the hands of the Western barbarians were even more so.

In summary, the T'ai P'ing Rebellion sprang from four factors —a new ideology, economic distress, political corruption and an imperialism which was a combination of Manchu rule plus the destruction of China's doors by the Western Powers. It is not surprising that the Chinese Communists claim the T'ai P'ing Rebellion as the beginning of the revolution for the "liberation" of the people. With slight variations these are the identical reasons for the Communist appeal and its conquest of China.

Another preparatory revolution was that of the Nationalists. It too based its appeal on the need of the masses, resentment against Western imperialism and the seeking of an ideal that would set the people free. It resulted in the overthrow of the Manchu government in 1911 and in the establishment of the Kuomintang or Nationalist Party by Sun Yat-sen. It reached its greatest political height when Chiang Kai-shek more or less unified the country in 1927, destroying the power of the war lords.

The Nationalist Revolution was much more than the handwriting on the wall, forecasting the possible triumph of Communism in China. In it were active and passionate Communists. In fact the Russians themselves contributed much toward the revolution, for after the Versailles Treaty of 1919 there were elements in China that turned toward Russia for assistance and political planning. In 1923 Sun Yat-sen himself made the statement, "We no longer look to the Western Powers. Our faces are turned toward Russia."

This wink in Russia's direction poses a puzzling question. Why was China turning her face toward Russia when before she had looked to America and Britain? Why was she beginning to look to a country she had feared most? What had Russia contributed to the betterment of China? She had built no schools or hospitals, no orphanages or leprosariums; she had contributed no funds for the relief of famine-stricken victims, no personnel for the rehabilitation of China's poverty-stricken and disease-ridden masses. Or at least her institutions and her contributions were so negligible in comparison with those of others that they can be counted as none. She had made no real cultural penetration of China. Why then was China's face turned toward Russia? The answer can be found partially in the incident giving rise to Dr. Sun's statement just quoted. When he threatened to seize the Customs at Canton because the surplus revenues were being sent, according to international agreement, to the government which had been set up in Peking, the Western Powers sent gunboats and warships to Canton. Dr. Sun then made the statement, "We no longer look to the Western Powers. Our faces are turned toward Russia."

The swing toward Russia was prompted by the belief that Russia was the enemy of imperialism and the defender of equal rights among nations. Present events reveal the fallacy of this conviction, but the early history of Chinese relations with Communist Russia encouraged the Chinese who were seeking the abolition of the unequal treaties and desired the return of territory formerly held by her as a nation.

The Versailles Peace Treaty, from which China had expected real gains in the direction of equality, only increased her humiliation as a nation by ceding to Japan the former German colony of Tsingtao and the Liaotung Peninsula on the China mainland. On entering the war against Germany, China had hoped that Wilson's principles of self-determination would be set in motion in Asia and that a start would be made toward blotting out past inequalities among nations. It is hardly surprising that the Chinese, not understanding all the difficulties and intrigues involved in making the treaty, were deeply incensed with this transfer of former Chinese territory from German hands to the expanding lap of her most feared enemy, Japan. When the news reached China, her people—especially the student group—expressed their indignation. Students paraded in protest through the streets of all the large cities. This marked the beginning of the organization of Student Unions which became so strong and played such an important part in the political and revolutionary history of China. From 1919 on, the power and influence of the student group in directing the thought of the people in political matters has been far greater than one would suppose from their numbers.

In contrast, in July, after the Versailles Treaty of April, the Russians did what appeared to the Chinese a surprising and unprecedented thing. In a speech addressed to the Chinese people, Karakhan, Assistant Commissar for Foreign Affairs for Soviet Russia, declared the willingness of Russia to renounce all her former special rights and privileges in China and to enter into a treaty of equality. The manifesto declared:

All people, no matter whether their nations are great or small, no matter where they live, no matter at what time they may have lost their independence, should have their independence and self-government and not submit to being bound by other nations.[1]

If the people of China wish to become free, like the Russian people, and be spared the lot prepared for them by the Allies at Versailles, which would make of China a second Korea or a second India, let it understand that its only ally and brother in its struggle for national freedom are the Russian workers and peasants and their Red Army.[2]

It was their desire to see China strong and freed from imperialist designs that more than any other element caused the student group, which was influential in forming the thoughts of the people, to jump on the Communist band wagon.

Moreover, the Chinese respectfully eyed Russia, for she seemed to possess a method for accomplishing a successful revolution, of attaining those things which China herself wished to attain. Russia seemed to have the "know-how" for taking the discontented masses, the working people and the frustrated intellectuals and setting them in motion on the way to freedom. She evidenced a

[1] H. B. Morse and H. F. MacNair, *Far Eastern International Relations* (Houghton Mifflin Company, 1931), p. 670.
[2] Wen Han Kiang, *The Chinese Student Movement* (King's Crown Press, 1948), p. 78.

recognition of the fact that there were two essential problems in China—that of national dignity, as I have mentioned, and that of filling the rice bowl.

After 1921 the works of Marx, Engels, Lenin, Bukharin and other revolutionists were substituted by many of the intelligentsia for the Analects of Confucius and the sayings of Mencius. Of the new books on the social sciences translated and published between 1928 and 1930, over 70 per cent dealt in some way with Marxism and dialectical materialism.

Still the Chinese intellectuals did not accept uncritically and wholeheartedly Marxian ideology. They did accept, however, as sacred and infallible a book which was greatly influenced by the Russian Revolution, as well as by Western thought. The Bible for China was the *San Min Chu I* or *The Three Principles of the People,* written by the great hero of the modern nation, Dr. Sun Yat-sen. He took as the watchwords of the revolution Nationalism, Democracy and Livelihood. These words themselves indicate the drastic difference between the problems of Asia and those of the West. "Independence" became the watchword of the American Revolution; "Liberty" that of the French; and today "Freedom" fires the imaginations of Americans to struggle against totalitarianism and dictatorships. It was "Nationalism" that fired the imagination of the Chinese, the need for a strong central government that could take its place in the respect of the nations of the world and throw off the yoke of imperialism. China's call was a call for patriotism to the nation from a people who had too long been loyal only to the family clan. Again in the watchword "Democracy" (which also includes much that is similar to the Western conception) Dr. Sun stressed the importance of the strength and freedom of the nation rather than that of the individual. In fact the individual should not have too much freedom, for his liberty rests on the recognition of his duty to sacrifice his individual interests for the general good that the nation may be strong. The final principle, "Livelihood," embodies the plea to provide for the people a decent existence, for the question of subsistence is at the heart of China's social problem. Recognizing this, under the principle of "Livelihood" Dr. Sun discussed matters relevant to the problem, such as land, food, trade and capital.

An understanding of these problems should help clarify the reasons why the Chinese people do not get too excited over our watchwords of democracy, freedom and internationalism. To the Chinese internationalism smacks of foreign imperialism; the American concept of democracy and freedom, received and misinterpreted through our secularism, implies a selfish individualism in which a man may do as he pleases with his gifts and abilities and have little concern for the welfare and livelihood of others. The Communist literature in China makes devastating attacks on the American conception of democracy. It uses as an example the American-trained Chinese who employ their technical knowledge to amass great wealth and to exploit the people. "This," cries the Communist, "is what the Americans call democracy and freedom."

In the *San Min Chu I,* with passion and religious fervor, Dr. Sun urged the people of China to put their faith in the Three Principles, for, he asserts, these principles contain the idea and the force which will save China.

What are the San Min Principles? They are, by the simplest definition, the principles of our nation's salvation. What is a principle? It is an idea, a faith, and a power. . . . Why do we say that the San Min Principles will save our nation? Because they will elevate China to an equal position among the nations, in international affairs, in government, and in economic life, so that she can permanently exist in the world. The San Min Principles are the principles of our nation's salvation; is not our China today, I ask you, in need of salvation? If so, then let us have faith in the San Min Principles and our faith will engender a mighty force that will save China.[3]

When Sun Yat-sen delivered his first lectures on the Three Principles, the effect on the nation was electrifying, although there is much in them of naïveté and untruth. China's youth, believing that they had found something which would make China strong, rallied around him.

When Dr. Sun, honored as the Father of China's Republic, died

[3] Sun Yat-sen, *San Min Chu I,* translated by F. W. Price and edited by L. T. Chen (G. E. Stechert & Company, 1927), pp. 3-4.

in March 1925, the people practically deified him. In 1928 the Nationalist government built for him an extravagant and beautiful tomb on the Purple Mountain outside Nanking. This spot became the most sacred place in all China. To it came his admirers and worshipers from every province of the land. The memory and the purpose of Dr. Sun were preserved in all Chinese schools. Before the Communist victory all students repeated his Last Will and Testament and bowed three times to his portrait in a ceremony held on Monday of each week. The first sentences of this Last Will and Testament are revealing in helping us to understand the mood of China and especially her youth.

I have served the cause of the People's Revolution for forty years, during which time my object has consistently been to secure liberty and equality for our country. From the experience of these forty years, I have come to realize that, in order to reach this object, it is necessary to awaken the masses of our people and to join hands with those countries which are prepared to treat us as equals in our fight for the common cause of humanity. *At present we have not yet completed the work of the Revolution.*[4]

Week after week, month after month, year after year for more than 20 years students have repeated the above words. The question "Why have we not completed the work of the Revolution?" tortured the mind of every thinking and determined youth. The thought that they were not treated as equals with other races tormented their souls to an extent which only the Chinese themselves, proud of their cultural past, could feel.

Under the determined leadership of Chiang Kai-shek it appeared as if the Revolution were truly in the phase of completion, but in the late twenties and early thirties certain unpleasant phenomena began to raise their deceitful heads, casting a shadow of defeat on the Nationalist government. It is natural that with the passing of time the revolutionary flame should somewhat dim and the passionate zeal among the leaders, who had reached positions of power, should subside. But these years tell an even sadder story. It is the story of a nation that had rejected its ancient traditional

---

[4] Last Will and Testament in Leonard Shihlien Hsü, comp., *Sun Yat-sen, His Political and Social Ideas* (University of Southern California Press, 1933), p. 43.

culture and spiritual heritage and was living on a borrowed American secularism and a watered-down Marxism. In other words it was a nation whose ancient soul had ceased to exist. In its place were some general principles and ideas which were not geared to action. Lacking a faith which inspires action, it merely talked of democracy, nationalism and livelihood. China had become a nation without a soul and without a faith. There remained only the desire to be strong and to be respected by the rest of the world.

John Dewey, Bertrand Russell and Julian Huxley were idealized as the saints of the scientific age. Their attack on religion encouraged the Chinese intellectuals to develop a completely agnostic position. Hu Shih, the greatest of China's literary figures, proclaimed a mechanistic philosophy which he called the "scientific view of life." Explaining his new creed, he writes:

On the basis of all our verifiable scientific knowledge, we should recognize that the universe and everything in it follow natural laws of movement and change, and that there is no need for the concept of a supernatural Ruler or Creator.

On the basis of the biological sciences, we should recognize the terrific wastefulness and brutality in the struggle for existence in the biological world, and consequently the untenability of the hypothesis of a benevolent Ruler.

On the basis of the biological, logical, and psychological sciences, we should recognize that man is only one species in the animal kingdom and differs from the other species only in degree, but not in kind.[5]

Hu Shih goes on to suggest that the highest form of religion is for man "to live for the sake of the species and for posterity," and thus all of our achievements will live on in the "larger self." This is immortality.

The idea of democracy became meaningless when the ruling bureaucracy tasted the Satanic joys of power and wealth. During the war with Japan the officials, military officers and landlords discovered an opportunity for speculation and illicit gain which the devil himself could not have conjured up. With neither Confucius nor Mencius to disturb the consciences of the rulers, the nation became a paradise for the property-holding class in black-marketeer-

[5] Wen Han Kiang, *The Chinese Student Movement*, p. 73.

ing and speculation. The spiritual and moral void had freed the
ruling class from moral restraints.

The collapse of China's moral and ethical standards, together
with the negative impact of China's religions, left the people wan-
dering about in a vacuum. Within the empty shell one could hear
only the embittered cry of a confused people who sought national
unity and desired a decent livelihood, but who daily witnessed conscripted foot soldiers suffering and dying for their country while
the sons of the gentry, never conscripted, held lucrative positions
within the government.

As early as 1934 Generalissimo Chiang recognized the empty
moral void into which China was settling. He charged the people
with deceit, frivolity and laziness. He attacked them as lacking faith
and a sense of responsibility. To revive the nation he inaugurated
the New Life Movement, which was a return to China's ancient
virtues. It was built around the four classical virtues, Li, I, Lien
and Chih—propriety, loyalty, honesty and honor. In launching it
in 1934, he said:

> The New Life Movement calls for the revival of the cardinal vir-
> tues of propriety, loyalty, honesty and honor, which have consti-
> tuted the bulwark of our national existence. Propriety safeguards
> us from cowardly behavior in times of danger. Loyalty makes us
> dare death for a cause. Integrity gives us clarity of judgment be-
> tween right and wrong. Honor impels us to erase the disgrace that
> today hovers over the fair face of our native land. Cultivate these
> qualities.[6]

In their cultivation Chiang urged the people to acquire habits
of cleanliness, simplicity, promptness, thrift, etc. In the convulsion
of a gasping and dying civilization, the hurling of moral platitudes
seemed naïve and trivial, particularly when viewed from the historical background of the war years. In 1942, only a few months
after Pearl Harbor, when China's military and political situation
was rapidly disintegrating, the government outlined a four-point
program for the nation: (1) Eradication of opium; (2) Suppres-
sion of gambling; (3) Encouragement of thrift; (4) Emphasis on
physical exercise.

[6] Wen Han Kiang, *The Chinese Student Movement*, p. 104.

When China needed a vital crusading faith, she received as a substitute a dull and harmless classroom lecture on how to be good.

The failure of the Nationalist government was due to inability to combine the great principles of the Revolution with action. Theory and practice were divorced from each other. The effort to promote action through moral lectures was hopelessly doomed. The Christians of China sensed this failure, but their numbers were too few, and the aspect of the Christian faith which aroused interest among the government officials and the intelligentsia was only the moral teachings of Jesus. China needed more than a religion of morals.

The condition of the Nationalist government was one of paralysis. The ideals and principles for a new China dangled before the eyes of the people, but the nation could not rise up to grasp and hold them. Like a bird with its wings clipped, it could not lift itself from the ground and fly. Like a person in a dream caught in a burning building, it was unable to open the door and rush to safety. The power to act, to free the people from their agony was absent. The Revolution of the Nationalists had exhausted itself, leaving only an empty vacuum.

Like a storm thundering into a low-pressure area, Communism rushed into this vacuum of a helpless and prostrated nation.

The conquest of the Communists mystified many Westerners, and even today the people are confused as to how the Communists, with their guerrilla armies, with inferior equipment, without air force or navy, without the strong industrial centers of Hankow, Mukden, Shanghai, Tientsin, Wusih, etc., without the large number of Western-trained personnel, cut off from the sources of oil and coal, and scattered in isolated bases throughout the country, could conquer the well-trained and U.S.A.-supported Nationalist armies. Until the fall of Hsuchowfu, a city 200 miles north of Nanking, the Nationalist armies had a definite preponderance of fire power. How was it possible for the inhabitants of desolate Yenan to organize a nation and defeat the motorized units of the Nationalists? This is the mystery of China's civil war, the question which demands an answer.

Communism made its first inroads into China because it extended a hand to the disinherited, the poor tenant farmers who suffered from floods, famine, landlordism and corrupt officials. It offered to the dispossessed small tracts of land which were to be their own. And, what is more important, it offered protection against landlords. Communism offered educational opportunities to all the peasants. In contrast to the very complex and highly developed educational system of the West, which had been copied by the Nationalists, the Communists initiated a system of schools which reached all ages and made education available to those of the lowest economic levels. They established half-day schools, traveling schools, night schools, short-period training schools and winter schools which opened immediately after harvest and closed just before the spring planting. From our point of view this educational system possesses one ominous and dangerous feature. It is centered around the purpose of Communist indoctrination and of furthering the class struggle. The fact remains, however, that the Communists did not ignore the peasants, but believed that in them is China's strength and the source for completing the revolution.

In the second place, Communism swept into China because it restored the sense of national dignity by the refusal of the government to crawl before the foreign Powers. This "illusory" evidence of independence captured the enthusiasm of the students and many of the intelligentsia, who through the years, as already mentioned, had been bitter in their denunciation of the former unequal treaties and the many privileges granted to foreigners. Moreover, Westerners often harbored an attitude of superiority and condescension toward the Chinese which robbed them of their national and racial self-respect. The Communist victory is a judgment upon the superior attitude of the West. The Chinese, especially the students, were filled with pride when the Communist government dared to rustle the mane of the British lion by disabling the British destroyer *Amethyst,* which was sailing down the Yangtze River. They were even more surprised at the courage of the Communists when they clipped the wings of the American eagle by arresting such diplomatic officials as Vice-Consul Olive and Consul-General Ward. The paralyzed body of China regained confidence and strength when Mao Tze-tung claimed in his speeches that the "liberation army" won its victories without foreign aid against the American-supported Nationalists.

With surprising sharpness the mood of China is revealed in the very important Chinese-Soviet Treaty of 1950, which states: "The government proved its ability to defend the state, the territorial integrity of the nation and the *national honor and dignity of the Chinese people.*"

The third factor in the Communist success is perhaps the most vital. It is the acceptance of a system of ideas which combines theory with practice. Action and belief, faith and works are combined in a strange and terrifying way. An excellent symbol of this unity is the new ideal of a teacher. The test of a good teacher is the extent to which he is willing to live a courageous and revolutionary life. In the early days of the civil war the high-school teacher often was a leader of a guerrilla band; the professor of science was the brains and the commander of a demolition squad. How startlingly different from the traditional ideal of the sedate, well-mannered and dispassionate Confucianist scholar!

By what secret are theory and action molded into an effective fighting unit? What is the inner spring which propels a person forward to act according to his convictions? Obviously there are social and economic factors. The foot soldier fights better when he knows that after the job is done he may go home to till an acre of land which belongs to him. Women rally enthusiastically to the cause which has freed them from being mere possessions of their husbands and subject to ill-tempered mothers-in-law. These are important elements in the release of social energy, but alone they cannot explain the mystery of Communist motivation.

At the center of Communist theory is the conviction that history is moving toward an inevitable goal. The Communist senses a movement in history with which he wishes to identify himself. He clings to a creed which might be stated in words such as these:

I believe that history moves forward through the class struggle to the inevitable classless society, to an era of peace and equality, where wars shall cease and oppressive governments shall vanish. With the end of the present capitalistic society, the last barrier will have been destroyed. The Communist party is the vanguard in this victorious struggle against the exploiters of mankind.

The Communist, therefore, joins in this march toward liberation. He wants to carry the ball down the field and across the goal line for a touchdown. Impelling and irresistible is the feeling that the future belongs to him. Driven by this fanatical faith in the future, and following an aggressive program of social, political and economic reform, the Communists have conquered China. The T'ai P'ings tried it and failed because they lacked intelligent leadership and the foundations for their revolution were very superficially laid. The Nationalists partially succeeded, but ten years of exhaustive war with Japan plus the disintegrating forces of cynicism, lack of faith, loss of objective and the growth of a corrupt officialdom brought defeat.

Have the Communists, then, completed the Revolution? No longer are the words of Sun Yat-sen, "The work of the Revolution has not been completed," repeated by the students on Monday morning. The slogans of today portray a new attitude as signs such as "The saving star has arisen; a new day has dawned" are painted on the city walls and school buildings. Has the era of the Great Peace finally dawned on the Asiatic stage?

In spite of Communism's successes, the people of China recognize the weakness in the movement and feel that greater agonies lie in wait for them, that the Revolution has not been completed, and that no prospect of its completion waits at the threshold. Only confusion confronts the majority of Chinese as they try to unravel the situation in an effort to find the real basis for China's agony and enslavement. Why is there confusion and doubt?

The only group which can give a really clear and intelligent answer is the Christian Church. There are many groups and individuals in China other than Christians who are opposed to Communism, but their antagonism springs from reasons which the Christians do not emphasize. There are groups which are anti-Communist because they still live in a world of semi-feudalism or of Western imperialism. Still others bitterly resent the loss of China's ancient traditions and believe that there has been a collapse of all human values in that Confucius has been cast from the pedestal. The Communists have robbed these people of the very reason for human existence.

The Christian's attitude, however, is very different. The word "anti" hardly fits. The Christian is not aroused to the hateful fervor of the Communists because of their disregard for these cultural values, which, perhaps, need to be replaced by new values, for the Christian knows there is nothing permanent in the achievements of man. He may even rejoice in the abolition of feudalism, the breakdown of a stifling legal Confucianist system and the end of Western imperialism. Many Christians, in fact, view sympathetically Communism's pretended passion for economic justice and equality, its supposed concern for the poor and the disinherited, its ostensible campaign against slavery, such as prostitution and child labor, and its attack on illicit gain made in gambling and speculation. The Christians understand that in Asia the primary problem is man's struggle for food and land. For the Chinese the "good earth" is the *summum bonum*. If one has no piece of land each anxious day casts its ghostly shadow of death, disease and hunger over the family. To fill the rice bowl the peasants of China slavishly toil through the heat of the summer and the bitter cold of the winter. The charge of laziness and inertia cannot be hurled at the common people of China, whose diligence and hard work command the respect and admiration of all foreigners who behold them. Some Christians, indeed, may even hope that the Communist economic program may help the world's hard-working people.

At the same time the Christian detects a fallacy in the clamor of the Communist for economic justice. The incessant talk of liberating the "masses" contains a very impersonal note as if the people were nothing more than a herd of dumb, driven cattle which only need to be turned loose on a fresh green pasture. This concern for humanity is well interpreted in *The Brothers Karamazov,* in which a doctor says: "I love humanity, but I wonder at myself. The more I love humanity in general, the less I love man in particular. . . . But it has always happened that the more I detest men individually the more ardent becomes my love for humanity."

The Christian detects the mystery of the human personality which the giant materialist completely ignores. It is at this point that the Christian sees the illusions and pretensions of Communism. The Communist's liberation of the people ends only in another form of enslavement, for he denies man his spiritual freedom. Recognizing man only as an economic animal, he believes that man does live by bread alone; that land, food and shelter comprise his basic needs.

The Christian detects in the claim of the Communist party to be the sole judge of human existence another dangerous illusion and pretension. The simplest Christian is able to discern the fallacy of such a claim. A Chinese coolie has succinctly stated it in the remark: "God is my Creator and Judge, and, what is more, He is the Judge of Mao Tze-tung."

Although the Christian dislikes the word "anti," he grieves over the Communist's arrogant disregard for truth and his rebellion against God. So the Christian discerns that China's days of agony are not over because the Communist tower of Babel will surely fall, bringing along with it the tragedy of millions of people. The Communist claim, "I am the truth," sounds like the most terrible of all blasphemies in the ears of the Christian who believes in the One who said, "I am the Way, the Truth and the Life."

The painful consciousness of this arrogant Communist pride is well expressed in an incident which occurred soon after the Communists took North China. A Christian woman, greatly respected in her village, was asked to attend a Communist meeting which was being held in the church. In preparation for the rally the church had been decorated with pictures of Communist heroes. Hanging directly over the communion table were pictures of Mao Tze-tung and Chu Teh, the most honored men in the party.

At the time of the meeting this Christian woman was standing at the back of the church. A Communist came forward to ask her to sit on the platform, telling her that the commissar had said, "We cannot begin the meeting until she is on the platform."

The woman replied, "I cannot do it. He must excuse me."

A few minutes passed and another Communist came to her saying, "We want you on the platform."

Again she refused.

This happened a third time. On the third occasion the woman replied, "I cannot sit up there. If I do, I shall weep."

The prospect of a woman weeping on the platform ended the attempts to persuade her.

The next day the leading commissar came to her home to ask, "Why would you not sit on the platform? We wanted to honor you, for you are greatly respected in this community."

She replied, "How could I? Hanging over the communion table

were your two human heroes. How foolish! They are human beings like you and me. They will die as you and I will die. That sanctuary is holy because it belongs to the eternal God who has conquered death through His Son Jesus Christ."

"The work of the Revolution has not been completed" means for the Christian that China has not accepted Christ. The Christian looks toward that day when every knee shall bow and every tongue confess that Christ is Lord.

But does not the Communist Revolution destroy all hope of a Christian transformation of China? Under the new Communist regime can the Church function? Is it possible for Christians to speak freely and to preach Christ?

Let us consider for a moment the situation of the Christians in China today. What has happened to their work, their churches and their freedom to testify to the truth of the Lord? From the point of view of institutional strength there have been serious setbacks, and the prospects of some institutions look very gloomy. For example, in Manchuria, which is the most rigidly governed area in China and which more than any other has come under Russian influence and the police state, only 49 of the 296 churches of Christ in China remain open. To one not acquainted with church life in China this probably sounds most discouraging, as if the Christians hold only a small beachhead on the vast plains of Manchuria. These statistics, however, are very misleading. Actually the Christians of Manchuria are boasting of the fact that today there are 49 self-supporting churches, each with its own pastor.

The Church in Manchuria illustrates a process which is taking place among the churches. It is the inevitable purging and purification of the Church. Churches too greatly dependent on foreign funds and personnel are in danger of being submerged by the Revolution. Like panning for gold, the Revolution sifts out of the Church hypocrisy, commercial gain and the love for this world, leaving the pure and faithful "colony of heaven" to bear its witness to a rebellious world. In a letter from 19 Christian leaders to the mission societies of North America and Europe, there are these words: "The Chinese Church will not emerge through this historical change unaffected. It will suffer a purge, and many of the withered branches will be amputated, but we believe that it will emerge stronger and purer in quality, a more fitting witness to the Gospel of Christ."

The Christians who fill the churches in Peking, Mukden, Nanking, Tsinan, Shanghai, Amoy, Canton, Tsingtao and the towns and villages of China are present on Sunday morning because they accept Christ as Lord and King. No longer may criticism of the Church as the arm of Western imperialism justifiably be hurled at the Chinese Christians and no longer does the scornful phrase "rice Christians" have meaning.

At the time of this writing, 18 months after the capture of Nanking, there is actually an upsurge in Sunday attendance in the churches in Central and East China. Shanghai churches at Christmastime reported the largest congregations in their history. A church north of Nanking received 50 new members at Easter. Among the 50 only one person was over 25 years of age. The reports that the youth of China are evidencing loyalty to the Church have surprised even the missionary personnel and the supporting boards, who feared above everything else that the pressure of the Communist regime would reduce the Church to an old people's fellowship. But such is not the case. Christian fellowships are sprinkled throughout the high schools, colleges and universities of China. In a county-seat town of North China the pastor of the church heard that there were more than 30 Christian students in the newly established Communist medical school. The pastor called on them and invited them to attend the church worship services on Sunday morning. The following Sunday a large number attended. When Communist authorities questioned this action, the students replied, "We are Christians and we are in the habit of worshiping on Sunday morning." The next Sunday the group was even larger and a member of the faculty, a Christian, accompanied the students to church.

If we can assume that the present policy of the Chinese Communist toward Christianity will not undergo radical change, we may expect the churches to carry on many of their Christian activities without serious and severe persecution. This does not mean that the churches will not undergo extreme difficulties, but these troubles will arise mainly from the heavy taxes on church property, the limitation on receiving funds from abroad, the un-friendly attitude of certain government officials and the lack of financial support from relatively well-to-do Christians who have either escaped from the mainland or whose incomes have been sharply reduced. Also the thousand or more Protestant mission-aries who continue to work in China will be greatly limited in their activities.

Although there is not much actual persecution of the Church today, it appears that Communist practice intends eventually to eliminate the Church and all religion. The main weapons used by the Communists for achieving this goal are controlled education and Communist indoctrination. In the secondary schools there are strict supervision of courses and restrictions on religious teaching and chapel attendance. Several courses in Communist indoctrina-tion are required, such as courses in "New Democracy" and "Dia-lectical and Historical Materialism." Textbooks interpret history according to historical materialism, and political-science books trace the growth of society according to the Marxian theory of the class struggle. Communist party members or Communist sympathizers are placed in all schools, and participation in political demonstra-tions is expected of the students. Schools, in fact, become the arsenals of Communist propaganda and the emotional centers of the movement. It is here that the children learn to shout the propa-ganda songs, perform the Communist dances and act the Com-munist dramas. All teachers and a representative from every family must also attend indoctrination classes held for them.

What is the future of the Christian Church that is faced with these restrictions and confronted with an aggressive attempt to convert all people to the Communist religion? If present policies throw hindrances before the Church, what will it do in the future if Chinese Communism follows the usual pattern of gradually increas-ing the restrictions until a full-fledged police state is in operation? Indeed, the Church is alarmed by a totalitarian system which com-pels people to attend indoctrination classes, uses Communist text-books and controls all the channels of information and propaganda. How may a defenseless church, numbering 4,000,000, protect itself against the proud Leviathan of 460,000,000 which claims for itself the right to dispense all truth and authority?

The situation today has all the appearance of that of the shepherd boy standing unarmed before the giant Goliath. The lad stands without sword and shield, without helmet and breastplate and even without shoes on his feet. In his hand he holds only a sling. The boy, controlling his fears, confidently approaches the giant, for in his hand he holds the Word of God. The defenseless Christian Church in Communist China, trusting in the Word of God, stands confidently before the great giant that has conquered all of China. Is this not a fantastic thought? Can these unarmed Christians dare to take even a step forward toward the champion gladiator who brandishes his sword and scorns the talk of mercy, love and truth? Is it not a preposterous absurdity for the Christian to believe that through his life God can melt the giant's heart of steel and direct revolutionary ways to the Cross of Christ?

Fantastic! Absurd! Unbelievable! But this is the faith of the Christian in China today. He believes that the essential problem in China is that the Communist has never really heard and understood the Gospel. He has seen religion in its superstitious garbs, its ecclesiastical ornaments and its philosophical and unattractive doctrinal statements. He has seen religion as an escapist, pious and other-worldly movement which appears to be an "opiate for the people." But the giant has never heard the proclamation of the good news of the Christ who defends the poor and extends mercy to the sinner and aid to the dispossessed, of the Christ who has conquered death and offers to man the joy of salvation. The giant has never really seen the humble, the fearless and the confident lives that are hidden in Christ.

Although these Christians realize the dangerous and precarious position of an independent fellowship within totalitarian China, they are, nevertheless, confident of success. The dominant attitude among the churches today is the one which accepts this occasion as an opportunity and challenge. The Christians live by the faith that the "Word is not bound." The Word is free and like light it seeps through the crevices and the cracks of the bamboo curtain. Consider again the situation in Manchuria. Although the majority of the churches in that area, long dominated by Communists, have been closed, the Christians are meeting in homes. Only the physical structure has been abandoned; the Christian community remains.

A guarded and conservative statement places the number of the "home churches" far beyond the number of churches which have been closed.

A certain Chinese pastor, while addressing a group of missionaries who were preparing to leave for America, said, "Tell your friends that the City of God exists in China and the gates of hell shall not prevail against it. If our churches are closed down by the government, we will worship in the homes. In place of a few large congregations there will be hundreds of small worshiping groups." Reports from all over China indicate that "the Church in your house" is a growing movement, and the very genius of China's social structure, the family-clan system, lends itself to this development, a type of growth which is most essential during a period of persecution.

The importance of "the Church in your house" is well illustrated in a vital and most fascinating indigenous Christian denomination which is known as the Family of Jesus. The strength of this denomination is greatest in those areas which have been under Communist jurisdiction for the past ten years. The growth, witness and methods of this group point to the power of the Christian faith to transcend Communist totalitarianism.

The Jesus Family is a denomination which numbers over 10,-000 members who are scattered in more than 250 families or churches. Its distinctive character is that it embodies the Christian Gospel within a form which is typically Chinese. The Jesus Family has brought a fresh, vital meaning into the heart of Chinese culture, the clan or large-family system, which rapidly was becoming a decayed and empty social structure. On joining the Jesus Family, a person sells all of his possessions, gives the money to the poor and enters penniless into the Family. Here he shares everything in common. Every member engages in productive work and all financial gains are placed in a common treasury. For example, in a town near Nanking a teacher of mathematics sells bean curd on the streets after school hours. Her income from teaching and selling bean curd is given to the Family. She considers both tasks opportunities for bearing witness to the truth of Christ.

The Jesus Family prides itself in outdoing the Communist, not only in communal living but in living a life of hardship, sacrifice and productive enterprise. The founder of the movement, Mr. Ching T'ien Ying, speaks of his denomination as "The Kingdom of Heaven's Dare-Devil Division, which seeks recruits to engage in the battle for the Kingdom of Heaven." The Jesus Family has found that love is the only method and weapon for this engagement against evil.

In the field of education also we may expect Christian heroism to find ways for the light to penetrate the curtain. For example, the principal of a Christian high school in North China received orders that religious services could not be held in school buildings. It seemed as if religious worship must cease and the students be deprived of all Christian instruction. The principal, however, leads the students each morning to the neighboring church, where they engage in morning devotions. Although attendance cannot be compulsory, practically the entire student body attends. In the evening the students, breaking up into little groups of six to ten, meet in the students' rooms, where they engage in Bible study and worship through prayer and song.

When the spirit of defeatism prevails and doubts are raised as to the future of the Church in China, it is well for us to recall the periods of persecution which have tested that church in the past. The Church was born and bred in the atmosphere of persecution. Robert Morrison instructed his Chinese friends behind barred doors and under a veil of secrecy. At a spring of water that flowed from the foot of a mountain, beyond the view of censorious and disapproving eyes, Dr. Morrison baptized the first Chinese convert, Mr. Tsai A-ko.

In the years following, conditions improved, but periodically there arose violent and vicious opposition to the Christians. The most serious of these was the Boxer Rebellion of 1900, in which hundreds of Christians were martyred. This anti-Christian upheaval occurred at a time when the Church was very weak and numbered only 200,000 Protestants. Missionaries would have doubted the possibility of the Church surviving such a violent persecution had they been able to anticipate the fury and swiftness of the rebellion. To the joy of Christendom the Church not only evidenced strength, but it emerged from the rebellion with a sense of confidence and an increased faith. For the first time in a national crisis the Christians realized that they had stood the test and were found faithful.

In 1927 an even more vicious form of persecution occurred. Although this did not take the form of the Boxer violence it was more widespread and more insidious in character. Throughout the entire nation anti-Christian campaigns and demonstrations were held. Students bearing such slogans as "Down with the Christians, a Class of Parasites!" and "Down with the Christians' Deceptive Morality!" paraded through the streets. The Christian was ridiculed and called the "running dog of the foreigner."

The persecution of 1927 increased the strength of the Church in an unforeseen way. By necessity the educational institutions were transferred to Chinese leadership. Fears were expressed that national leadership was neither prepared nor adequate to assume this responsibility and that the Christian schools were in danger of coming under the influence of the government and becoming purely secular institutions. The events of the following years proved that these fears were unjustified. In fact, out of this nationalist and anti-Christian movement there developed a vigorous and strong educated Christian leadership which had a profound influence on the entire nation.

The Church today is prepared to face the antireligious attitude of the Communists, for the Christian knows that the foundations laid by his fathers are solid. The determination to remain faithful and to carry on the traditions of the early Christians was vividly brought to my attention shortly before I left Communist China. I was worshiping in a little church which, according to American standards, was not conducive to Christian worship. The music was poor and the building was without elaborate or beautiful ecclesiastical ornaments. Yet the occasion was deeply moving, for the pastor delivered a great sermon on the text, "And if not, be it known unto thee, O King, we will not serve thy gods." You will recall that King Nebuchadnezzar had set up a golden image and had commanded the people to bow down before it. Shadrack, Meshak and Abednego, friends of Daniel, had refused to do so, saying, "Our God is able to deliver us from the fiery furnace, and if not, be it known unto thee, O King, we will not serve thy gods nor bow down before the golden image which thou hast set up."

The most lowly of the Christians in China, together with the highly gifted ones, discern a profound truth: obedience to God's will and faithfulness to Him is to be free. This freedom is beyond the power of man to contain, a freedom which neither chains nor tomb can confine; a freedom which the flames of the fiery furnace cannot consume. This is the freedom which proceeds from God's revolution!

A Japanese Story

By Tamaki Uemura

MY FATHER was a son of a Samurai, one of the 80,000 high guards of the Shogun, who was the governmental head of all Japan. When the Shogun's regime gave way to that of the Emperor in 1867, the family lost everything. My father as a small boy had then to earn the living of the family, which included my grandfather, who was not used to any trade. My father went to their old fief to cut wood and brought it to Tokyo to sell. He tended pigs and rabbits. He ran errands for traders.

The family were Shintoists to begin with, although they were all converted to Christianity later on. My father as a young boy frequented a Shinto shrine at some distance, where a popular hero of 300 years ago was enshrined, noted for sincerity, constancy and bravery. His desire was that the same noble traits should be bestowed on himself.

He swore to the Shinto god whom he worshiped that he would never partake of the flesh of any fish, if the hero-god would only help him become like the god himself in personality. Now fish was a necessary item of diet for the Japanese people of that time for its protein content, since they customarily had neither chicken nor beef nor pork. My grandmother watched her son closely and after a few months she said, "Son, I am afraid your vow is robbing you of your strength. This is no easy age, and you cannot afford to be a weakling. Moreover, to be particular about one's diet is a great nuisance to others with whom you may have to live. If you enter a good school you will have to live with other students in a dormitory, and of course you must acquire knowledge in order to live properly in the present world. The knowledge you should be in search of seems to be in the possession of those blue-eyed, red-haired Westerners who live here in Yokohama." (In the Japanese language the term "red hair" covers all that is not black. So also "blue eyes" means "not black.") "Go and study. Be not anxious. Eat fish when it is put before you. Meanwhile I myself will take over your vow and perform it. The god will consider that proper." Up to the time of her conversion five years later she never ate fish.

On my mother's side were earnest Buddhists, some of them priests of high degree. Mother was converted in Yokohama. She was one of the first pupils of Ferris Seminary, which was started by missionaries 80 years ago. Later she taught Chinese classics and calligraphy in the school and studied English in exchange.

She went home to Minabe in Wakayama prefecture for vacations and zealously bore witness there to the Christian truth. First, one of her younger sisters, already married, was converted through her influence. Mother happened to be with her when a divorce on account of her Christian belief was being pressed. My aunt firmly professed her faith before her displeased family and said she would rather accept divorce than deny her Lord. However, she died in an epidemic before the longed-for moment of baptism arrived. Nor was the divorce an accomplished fact, so swift had been her death. She was indeed a corn of wheat fallen into the ground which brought forth much fruit. Her husband and mother-in-law, marveling at this woman's conviction, began to inquire into the truth themselves. They later became pillars of the church of Tanabe.

Next the two Buddhist sons of my mother's elder sister came to argue with her. They studied the Bible in order to refute Mother's beliefs and in so doing they in their turn were converted. They expelled themselves from the Buddhist temple where their inheritance lay. Both entered Meiji Gakuin, a Protestant school for boys in Tokyo. One died before graduation. The other became quite a scholar in comparative religions and a professor in my father's theological school in his later years, after study at Auburn Theological Seminary in America.

Next in the list of conversions came my eldest uncle, who was a very rich merchant—a manufacturer of *sake* (a liquor distilled from rice). Dr. J. B. Hail, one of the early missionaries in the Kansai district, who had led my young aunt to Christianity, worked hard on the worldly-wise young fellow. This uncle of mine had been one of the strong persecutors of my Christian aunt. But the Gospel made his conscience very uncomfortable. One evening he called on Dr. Hail and hotly argued with him and left him angrily. As he galloped away on horseback along the beautiful beach of Tanabe, he thought he heard the voice of Christ commanding him to go back. He tied the horse to a pine tree and returned on foot to Dr. Hail. It was midnight, but the good missionary was overjoyed to see this young man entirely broken in his spirit. My uncle was baptized very soon afterward. The first thing he did after baptism was to give up his thriving trade in liquor, in order to study for the ministry of the Church. He was the first minister in the Lutheran Church of Japan.

The whole of Mother's large family finally became Christians.

Father entered an English school in Yokohama, established and led by Dutch Reformed missionaries. James Ballagh, Samuel R. Brown and Guido F. Verbeck were working then in Yokohama, and the great missionary doctor, James C. Hepburn, was doing his wonderful healing and literary service there. The missionaries knew that these Samurai-born boys did not care to take charity. They were wise in making a charge for tuition, which seemed like no small sum to the students. Father was proud of being able to work his way through. He was endowed with a good brain, and what he learned in the daytime he taught at night. There were many young people who were glad to receive secondhand teaching at cheap tuition rates. Grandmother herself learned English from Father, and then in turn she taught the very first steps of the language in his little night school.

The pioneer missionaries were people of great stature who understood Japanese minds correctly. They were like generals who first seize a strategic stronghold, in order to lay hold later of a whole province. The young men and women they captured were of such caliber that numbers of converts were later brought in through them. It was indeed providential that Christianity was a forbidden religion in this country at that time, since those who came to the missionaries risked some danger and did not aim at any material gain in relations with them. At first, all who came had only one aim—to learn English and Western sciences. Those young people were drawn to the noble personalities of their teachers and wondered what their secret sources of strength were. My father often said that he had been moved to the depths of his soul by the beauty of their home life. Gradually the keen, inquiring minds discerned that these teachers were worshiping neither heroes nor saints, but God the Creator of heaven and earth, the Lord of man's destiny. The truth of the Christian religion was first demonstrated through their lives, and then when the time came, it was publicly preached from their lips. No wonder there were results. What these converts received by way of teaching they already knew to a great extent through firsthand personal contact with the living example of their missionary teachers.

In 1872, when the very first church was started in Yokohama with 11 members, the police of the prefecture came to arrest them. They could not carry out their intent, however, as the prefect himself, a progressive man, interfered on behalf of the Christians. Dr. Ballagh's admonition to the young converts at that time was: "Even if you are arrested, do not hold any grudge against the State. You can run away to America, if you like, but that is not the spirit of Christ. Go with cheerful spirit wherever the law banishes you." A wise and thoroughly Christian bit of advice! Not one of the young converts left the country. Instead, the flock increased in number, and many of them dedicated themselves to the Christian ministry.

Father started his new home and his little congregation at one and the same time. Mother, Father's parents and his brother made up the membership of both. His flock increased slowly but it increased surely. The famous Professor Miyabe of Hokkaido and his family were among those who became Christians at this time through my father's influence. Father was then, along with his teachers and colleagues, engaged in the translation of the Bible. To support his family, he wrote for magazines and taught English in mission schools. Mother and Father were like the two wheels of one wagon, going toward one fixed destination, laden with the invaluable substance of the Gospel.

Since Mother and Father formed a truly Christian home, my three sisters and I naturally came into a Christian heritage. My grandparents died rather young, after their conversion. Father was especially devoted to his mother, and for the rest of his life whenever he was in any difficulty he might be heard saying, "My beloved mother with Christ in heaven is praying for us." Thus we all felt real communion with the unseen sphere in the work of the Kingdom of Christ.

Of the four daughters of my parents my next elder sister was taken out of this world at the age of four. My younger sister made up her mind to become a Christian minister while she was a student in Miss Tsuda's College. After graduation she finished the regular course in the Tokyo Theological Seminary, of which my father was the founder and principal. Later she went to the United States and entered the junior year at Hartford Theological Seminary. She did remarkably well in the regular course for the ministry, but in her senior year she was taken ill and was sent to the Presbyterian Hospital in New York for an operation. Her life could not be saved, and she died on December 15, 1920. What superabundant kindness was poured on her by Dr. and Mrs. Robert E. Speer, Mr. and Mrs. Dwight Day and many others! Her last letters from the hospital breathed only gratitude and trust in God and in friends. In one of them she said, "My education has not ended. Please do not consider that my studies are made fruitless through death. I believe that I shall be employed in a better sphere, but still for the coming of the Kingdom of Christ."

When the cabled news of her death came to my parents, they sat together for a time in silent prayer. Then they got up and went right about their work. As I knew how much they loved Keiko, this attitude of theirs awed me.

Dr. and Mrs. Speer cabled an offer to have Keiko's body interred in their own family burial plot by the side of their loved daughter. Such Christian love, which seemed to have no end, fairly overwhelmed and inspired us. It was decided, however, to have her ashes brought back to Japan.

My eldest sister was married to a man who afterward became a minister of the Church of Christ (Presbyterian), and they are still its faithful servants. My brother-in-law is a church historian and has already produced trustworthy volumes on the progress of Christianity in Japan.

I am referring to these events in my family in order to show that my Christian parentage was a dynamic influence in my life and that of my sisters. If I am a Christian, I owe it to the grace of Christ, who worked on me directly and through my parents. And they came to Christ through His messengers, the missionaries.

As a little girl, I was naughty beyond words. I was pugnacious, and my playmates were afraid of me. Even my gentle elder sister could not be quite safe when I was around. But to my lovely younger sister I was tenderness itself. I cherished her. She was my idol. If urchins in the neighborhood made this little sister unhappy, I was sure to appear on the scene and retaliate, an eye for an eye, a tooth for a tooth. I enjoyed seeing the boys scatter in fear of me. I suppose I had more bodily strength than I could rightly expend. Had my parents been wise enough then to engage me in vigorous physical exercise I might have been different. Father gave me some bodily punishments, of which I was not a whit afraid. I laughed them away. But Mother's tears and supplications were what I was afraid of. In answer to her prayer, God was good to me and something happened to change my course.

When I was ten years old, my eldest sister fell gravely ill. As days wore on without bringing recovery to her, I began to be struck with remorse. Perhaps my wickedness was the cause of her illness! Probably she was suffering vicariously! This should never be. I prayed to God to let her off and punish me instead. I reflected on all my childish sins. How terribly bad I was! Afterward this sister often showed me the tear-stained letter I wrote to her when she was lying in the hospital. It said, "O dear sister, ask God to heal you, for I shall be a good girl. I shall never, never beat you or pinch you again in my life. I ask your pardon. From your repentant younger sister." That was my childish conversion. From that time on I became a tractable little girl, thoughtful and kind, or so my mother told me later on.

In my eleventh year Mother sent me to a music teacher. Western music was a great luxury at that time, and only royalty and the peerage sent their children to such teachers. My parents wanted me to be trained in church music, and they did what they could. The other children were all dressed beautifully, especially for the recitals in which we all performed.

Some of them found it an amusing thing to ask me, "What are you going to wear at the concert?"

I always answered, "Whatever my mother has ready for me."

They would then laugh and say, "Oh, the same old stuffy thing you had on the last time!"

I felt somewhat put out and reported to Mother.

She took me to Father's bookcases and said, "Daughter, do you know that the dresses you cannot have to wear turn into these books? Father is a great minister of Christ. In order that he may preach the word of God without mistakes, he and I buy these commentaries. By wearing what we can afford to provide, you are helping him and me, and consequently you are serving Christ! You are truly very rich, are you not? Much richer than those people who have beautiful clothes!"

Then she would read from the Bible, "Blessed are ye, when men shall revile you!"

Thereupon I resolved not to care about worldly riches or to mind any unkind comments.

When I was 12 years old, I began wondering for what purpose I had been born. I greatly marveled at the evil that existed in the world and it made me sad. For one year I spoke little and ate little, to my parents' distress of mind. Then came a deliverance. In my new experiences in Joshi Gakuin, a Protestant mission school, light shone for me. The Word of God came upon me with new force. I began to feel that Jesus was very near to me. The death of one of my teachers, Emma Alexander of Maryville, Tennessee, and some childish unkindness of a classmate at about the same time drove me to a life of prayer. At 14 I professed my faith in my Lord as Saviour and was baptized by my father. Such changes took place in my outlook that I felt impelled to dedicate myself to some task for the Master. I selected what seemed most difficult for me. I went to Father and asked him to give me training for work with lepers. He knew better and admonished me to pray and wait.

On my graduation my beloved missionary teachers, Miss Elizabeth P. Milliken and Miss Elizabeth Campbell, the latter a graduate of Wellesley College, resolved that I should go to Wellesley to study. After a year's special preparation with Miss Milliken, off I went. Miss Campbell had by that time been married to a medical man in Seattle, and on my arrival at that port I was privileged to stay for two months in their home and was given a better understanding of American life.

In college, where I was the recipient of a Helen Gould Scholarship, I first made very much of zoology, not having yet given up the idea of becoming a doctor to lepers. I found out in three years that I was not meant for medicine, and that I was to make speaking and writing for the glory of God my lifework. In my junior year I went through a spiritual struggle, since the Bible instruction of my college at that time was somewhat more liberal than that to which I was accustomed. However, it all worked for the good of my own soul and to the advantage of my future service. Nothing shook my faith in the deep parts of my spirit. Even before that time I had not accepted the verbal inspiration theory, but the cardinal truths of the Bible had always been the compelling force in my spiritual life. The atoning death of the Son of God, the resurrection, the fellowship of the Holy Spirit, man's justification through faith, regeneration, growth in sanctified life, the salvation of mankind through the preaching of the Word of God, the life of the body of Christ, namely the Church—all these were to me not points of theological fencing but constituent parts of my spiritual life. Without relying on them I could not live as a Christian and of course could not bear witness to Christian faith.

My four college years gave me lifelong friendships with most beautiful Christian women. I was so impressed with the wonder of Christian character even in those who often did not claim to be Christians that I once said in a college prayer meeting that those who denied or were indifferent to Christian faith ought to be grateful for their Christian heritage and beware of the great danger of not handing down what they enjoy to the next generation, since their heritage was unmistakably generated through faith in Jesus Christ.

I had become engaged to Shuso Kawado, when I was 19 and he was 24. He was very eager to marry me, but out of a fine sense of courtesy he first came to my father before he spoke to me. My mother and father liked him and left it to me to decide.

Shuso Kawado was converted while he was still a student in the college of Yamaguchi prefecture, under the influence of his married sister, Michi Munesuye, who was an evangelist to him through correspondence.

Shuso came to Tokyo for a university education when he was 20. He entered the engineering department of the Imperial University. At the same time he joined my father's church and began teaching in the Sunday school. He lived with his mother and his younger sister Suma. His mother had been a widow since her boy was five years old. As I look back on those days of our acquaintance, I recall that she had almost no flaw in her personality—straightforward, kind, patient, with sparkling wit. She gave the impression of being almost self-sufficient in the moral sphere. Perhaps that was why she was not particularly interested in the Christian faith, although she was glad her son had it. A lady evangelist, a volunteer worker in my father's church, called on Mrs. Kawado often and read the Bible with her. Out of politeness to this friend, the elderly lady began to listen and gradually grew into a real Christian faith. Two years later she was baptized.

Shuso graduated from the Imperial University at the age of 23 and entered the Shibaura Electric Engineering Works, which had a connection with the General Electric Company of America. He went to Schenectady a year later. I had already been in Wellesley for one year and had begun to wonder whether our engagement was right, since I had not adequately understood at the time of the agreement what was involved in matrimony. I felt at that stage that I would rather we two should be good friends throughout our lives than husband and wife. I told Shuso so. He was grieved, but he was wise. As I had requested, he returned all my letters to him and accepted back the engagement ring and the letters he had written to me.

After three months he came to Wellesley to see me. By that time I had come out of my confused state, and I believed that we were meant to be husband and wife at some future time. When I told him, he was a happy man indeed and I was a happy girl. But how emaciated-looking he had become in three months!

When I came back home from Wellesley in August 1915, my fiancé and I were expecting to marry in the fall. However, Shuso was found to have a light case of tuberculosis in one lung. He

and his relatives held strongly to the idea that we should lose no
time in starting our married life, since, according to their thinking,
the joy and peace of being established in a home of his own would
help the cure. But I thought differently. He should first get cured;
it was evident that his case was only a light one. He should rest
entirely from his work, as he could not do if he had a family to
support, and live in the country in pure air without any responsibilities. He did so, although he seemed disappointed at first. He
got entirely well in less than two years. There was no tubercular
trace left in his body. So we were married on April 24, 1917.

Immediately after our marriage we commenced holding a little
worship service in our small home. My father's way was to advise
a newly married Christian couple to select for their new home a
locality where there was no church, and there to start a new congregation. On Sunday mornings we used to go to Father's church,
where we had our membership, but we always hurried back to
our home to prepare for our afternoon service. Father would come
to preach on most Sunday afternoons, but when he could not, he
would send some other minister. The congregation in our house
grew gradually and it is now a thriving church. There are nearly
20 such home churches which grew out of Father's church in this
same way.

Before Shuso and I married, we decided that we should set up
a separate home of our own instead of living with his mother. This
was contrary to the custom of the time. For ages in Japan a young
couple has been expected to live with the husband's parents or
parent and with sisters and brothers if there were any. We loved
and respected our mother, but we thought that by living separately
both sides would get more satisfaction out of the relationship. And
so it turned out.

A year later a baby girl arrived for us. Not long after that my
husband began gradually to lose his sight. We found out later that
he had cancer of the brain. When he grew ill, his mother wished to
come and live with us. Of course she was more than welcome.
I have never known such a selfless woman except my own mother!
This mother-in-law of mine acted as assistant to me and would
never take the principal place in the household. My husband, who
was blind by this time, was most filial to his mother and tried to

act as if he could see, in order to alleviate her anxiety. One day he asked me, "Please do not let Mother come to the hospital. I cannot bear having her see me get worse." But I had to let her come into his room, because she wished to. She would creep in and creep out without saying a word to him, and hence unnoticed by him. He suffered a great deal, was operated on and soon after passed away. He was a beautiful Christian character. His great trust in the Lord, his kindness and cheerful patience during his illness in the hospital testified to the truth of the Gospel. The two nurses who took care of him were baptized after his death. He said often in his delirium after the operation, "Come, O Lord Jesus! I am ready." After he passed away, my mother-in-law and I had a wonderful mutual understanding and for many years we comforted and helped each other.

A few months after his death came our baby son. Living with my two children and my precious mother-in-law, I began teaching in Mrs. Hani's School. She was an elder in my father's church. That school is "Jiyu Gakuen," the "School of Freedom." During the militaristic regime the government commanded Mrs. Hani to change the name of the school, for, they said, freedom was not the aim of the nation but rather order and obedience. She did not give in, but replied that in true freedom there is order and that is the only order worth the name. We often wonder how she got away with such a stand in those days of oppression.

There was a lonely woman among our acquaintances. She seemed to enjoy alienating people who were on intimate terms with each other. She often came to see us, and my mother-in-law was very kind to her. As I was a teacher at Jiyu Gakuen, I was naturally absent a good part of every day. The woman came in one day and found my mother-in-law sick. She perhaps wanted to comfort the old person. At any rate what she said was, "I am sorry that your daughter-in-law does not take better care of you. What an idea, to let you look after the two little children. It is too much for you!" When I came back from my work my mother-in-law said, "Daughter, will you please tell that Miss H. never to visit us again? How dare she say evil things of you in your absence, to me, your mother-in-law?" Yes, my gentle mother-in-law was angry on behalf of her daughter-in-law.

At midday, September 1, 1923, an earthquake of great magnitude shook the Kwanto District of Japan. Thousands of people perished in it. Violent tremors followed one after another every 30 seconds or so and then the intervals gradually lengthened. The earthquake lasted more than a month. My four-year-old son was ill at the time with infantile paralysis. We had taken him to a hot spring in the north and had returned to Tokyo only the day before.

On this day, at the moment of the first tremor my mother-in-law was watching the little boy playing on the veranda, and my little daughter was with me in my study. At once they all came to my room, bringing the young woman who was helping with kitchen work. We got out our thick quilts, put them on top of tables and chairs. Then I had everybody creep under the biggest table. When the kitchen assistant made a move to crawl out again to help me put barricades around us, Machiko, my five-year-old daughter, whispered to her, "Don't! Didn't Mother tell us to be quiet? Mother is safe if we pray for her. Let us be praying to God!" So they all prayed under the table, and I finished the barricading. An hour later we were out of doors in open space, called out by kind neighbors. We carried heavy quilts, a bucket of water, a large bowl of rice, a kettle, a pan and a few other things from the shaking house. The quakes brought down trees, walls, roofs and steeples onto the streets, and made walking extremely dangerous for anyone. Fire came from all sides. Refugees streamed ahead of the pursuing flames.

We hurried first to my father's house, a few blocks away, to fetch my mother out. She had nearly been crushed under the falling books and bookcases. The aged mothers, the two children, my kitchen helper and I then ran for our lives. People were kind. They made way for us, saying, "Let the old folks and the children pass!" In the face of calamity, people became extremely unselfish and shared what they had with those who had not. God drew out the milk of human kindness from the hearts of men in an amazing way. We stayed for three days in the grounds of the palace of the Crown Prince (the present Emperor). Since the war it has been converted into a national library.

Meanwhile my father got back from Korea, where he had been

on a preaching tour with another minister. They had walked many miles, as trains were not running. He found his house, but it was empty. He started out in search of his family, not knowing which way to go. All communications were disrupted. There was no transportation. Confusion reigned. He finally located us all at the house of his assistant, who had rescued us from the palace grounds on the fourth day and taken us to his home, which the fire had not reached. My father's traveling companion was not so fortunate. He also set out to search for his family, but found only the bodies of his wife and five children, burned to death in Honjo ward.

We were able to come back ten days later to our own homes; the roofs leaked; the winds rushed in; but the houses were standing. It was very strange that my father's house was not burned, standing as it did in the midst of a big tract of burned-out ground. The very precious historical documents of the church survived.

Father and I began relief work at once. We went hunting for missing persons and took relief material to the homeless. His church and his seminary had been swept away by the fire. A barrack type of building was straightway put up for the use of both. We never missed even one Sunday service after we came back. We met in the dilapidated house of a member. How true to our experience sounded Martin Luther's hymn from the Forty-sixth Psalm, "Therefore will not we fear . . . though the mountains shake!"

People came to the services on foot from great distances. As I look back, it seems Japan was a better country then and the Japanese were better people. How grateful we were to the countries which sent us such abundant relief material, and especially to our neighbors across the Pacific! If we had gone on in that direction of simplicity and humility we would not have done what we did later to Manchuria, China, other Asiatic countries, and to America.

My little daughter became ill with dysentery during the quakes, and we used up most of our castor oil, which was the only medicine at hand. When the younger child fell into the same condition, what remained of the oil was not enough for his need. He grew worse. On the second morning my father turned to me and said, "The boy is dying!"

Suddenly the child cried, "Mammie, is Jesus really here?"

"Though you cannot see Jesus, He is very near you," I assured him. I prayed for him aloud, "O Jesus come and take Ha Chan to you! He loves you."

The little one said "Amen" and threw himself into my arms. There he passed away.

I think my father's health had begun even then to fail, partly through all his extra exertion because of the earthquake, including the erection of new buildings for church and seminary. He told me one day, "My life may not last for more than a year or so. I have so much to do for Japan. May God grant me a little more time!" But we knew by then that his body was sorely stricken. He had kidney trouble and a bad case of asthma.

My good mother-in-law had been with us since the death of my husband, but about this time she said she would like to spend the rest of her life in Iwakuni in the south of Japan, where she was greatly loved by the countryfolk. After her departure I went to my parents' house to live. I was glad that I could serve them in their old age, although they were not really old in years, both of them being only 67.

My father's death occurred on January 8, 1925, while he, my six-year-old daughter and I were eating a supper which he himself had prepared for us. In those days I was looking after my mother, who was down with pneumonia, and so sometimes Father did the cooking.

As we ate, Father asked Machiko, his granddaughter, "Is it good?"

She answered, "Very good, Grandpa!"

Then he took up his own fork, but suddenly he laid it on the table and with a little moan leaned on my shoulder. A heart attack had seized him and he never regained consciousness.

Father's death made me think that perhaps I should resume my maiden name, as the only way of having the name of Uemura carried on, there being no son in our family. I became therefore a Uemura again. But my daughter, as was proper, kept her father's name, Kawado. For years after that, little Machiko often complained of her surname, not understanding why it was different from mine.

Father's death made a sad gap in the Church in Japan. He left behind him the largest single church in the country, the most influential Christian weekly and a strong theological college.

Mother and I talked much about the situation. I remember her words: "Daughter, do you not wish to do something your father would be doing if he were alive? Go anywhere you choose to study. You can use the money the church and our friends gave us at your father's death. I will look after your child. I know God will take care of me, although I am little better than an invalid."

Off I went to Scotland and entered New College Theological School in Edinburgh. My father was always a champion of women's ministry. He was the person who at the Synod of 1905 introduced the action providing for women's eldership, which was passed in the same year. That is how it happened that to become a minister of the Gospel was no strange idea to me. My younger sister would have been one before me, had she not died.

Before I left Japan, Mother said to me, "Do not come home, even though you should get word that I am seriously ill. For I have a promise of God that I shall live until you come back. Remember, you are on the Lord's business. You cannot leave it half finished. This is your only chance for preparation for your ministry.

In my second year at Edinburgh word came from my brother-in-law that Mother was critically ill and that I should come home. I was torn between my longing to go to her and my desire to follow her expressed wish. But remembering her admonition for just such a situation, I stayed on. A second cable came a week later, which told me that Mother was going to live! When she recovered and found out what my brother-in-law had done, she chided him and said, "Do you not believe in the promise of God?"

In Scotland I enjoyed my life and my theological studies. Dr. H. R. McIntosh, Dr. W. P. Paterson, Dr. Adam Welch and Dr. William McGregor were the professors who influenced me most, at three institutions: the New College Theological School of Edinburgh, the Divinity Hall of Edinburgh University and the United Free Church College in Glasgow. They grounded my faith in strong foundations.

While in Edinburgh I lived in the United Free Church Women's

Missionary College for four years and associated with women missionaries going out and coming back for furlough. I did not take any studies in this college, but while staying there I heard many lectures about conditions in different countries. Through fellowship with those lovely people I became greatly interested in China, India and Africa. I became friendly with Miss Guli Medora, a doctor of medicine who was a Parsee from India. Through her I gained some knowledge of Zoroastrianism. Though she was not a convert to Christianity, she was permitted to live at the Women's Missionary College during her period of study and she was of much assistance to her fellow students in giving them an understanding of her race.

The warm fellowship I had with the Ashland H. Barbours (the youngest son, Robert, married Dr. Robert E. Speer's daughter, Constance) was very beneficial to me. Dr. and Mrs. Barbour were great internationalists. Their drawing room was frequented by many different races and nationalities. They had understanding and sympathy ready for them all. Dr. Barbour was a great friend of Henry Drummond's. At the latter's deathbed Dr. Barbour was the physician in charge. Dr. Drummond asked Dr. Barbour to be with him as much as possible, "for I feel Christ very near when you are around." Whenever I sat with Dr. Barbour, I also felt vividly the presence of Christ.

Mrs. Barbour had gone about the country during the first World War making speeches on the attitude one should take toward the people of the nation against which one's country was fighting. She said that many of the reports they were hearing about German atrocities were not true. War should not blind their eyes to facts. In thus correcting their misunderstandings and blunders Mrs. Barbour necessarily met with misunderstanding herself on the part of her fellow countrymen. She was rather a sad woman when I saw her in 1925, but her sadness had peace and hope in it.

Another great friend in Scotland was Mrs. Constance Greenfield, who was about 77 at the time I was there. She was afflicted with arthritis which had crippled her joints, but she had risen above this physical handicap and had consecrated her life to Christ. She would listen to the unfortunate people who came to her and ungrudgingly give them advice and comfort. As I was leaving Scotland after my graduation, this mother of many missionaries said to me, "Now, my Japanese daughter, I feel as if I myself were being sent to Japan as a missionary. You have told me so much of the country that I feel as if I really know the people. Be brave, my daughter! The Lord be with you! My prayers are with you always." After my return to Japan, I heard from her every week. It was wonderful help to have her speak to me across the ocean. At last one week she did not write, and that was the time when she peacefully passed out of this world.

I feel those Scottish friends of mine, together with my parents are praying for me.

I came home in December 1929 and found my invalid mother faithfully waiting as she had promised, and my little daughter grown to 11 years of age. My mother was really seriously ill with cancer. For the next six months she failed rapidly, but she gave me many invaluable pieces of advice for my life as a pastor. When the time came for her to "cross over Jordan," she said, "Daughter, I have prayed to God that He might spare me to assist you in your pastor life. But God seems to need me elsewhere. Know that when you pray to Christ, I am very near you, for I am with Christ."

She left me a number of Japanese poems of her own composition, which became my treasures. Most of them were burned to ashes in 1945, but I have managed to save some of them. They tell of a life of devotion without a desire for recompense, of humility which unconsciously fills the atmosphere with lovely fragrance, and of courage that counts not its cost. She is ever my inspiration in my evangelistic life.

Shortly before she died I was ordained to the ministry. When I began my work on October 1, 1930, with a Bible class, my mother was present in spirit in my small room. I knew that! The first inquirer who came to me was a university student who brought another the next week. The numbers grew, and in the autumn of the year 1931 my congregation was recognized as a church, having 20 baptized members and ten inquirers.

One characteristic of our little church was that we welcomed Koreans and Formosans among us. We started a dormitory for Formosan men students near my house, and in addition six or seven Formosan girls always lived with me. We tasted the joy of real fellowship regardless of racial differences. Both sides received benefits from the contact. Formosans are musical people. I can never forget their dawn choir on Christmas, which we heard from our beds, dreaming of the angelic "In Excelsis." My Formosan dormitory was backed by the Women's Board of Missions of the Japanese Church of Christ, which was started in 1906, the same year that women's eldership was recognized in our synod. This board supported ministers of four different fields in Japan. It was also greatly interested in Christian work in Formosa, Manchuria and China.

From September 1930 to June 1936 I taught at the Tokyo Women's Christian College and at the Tokyo Shingakusha, the theological seminary of which my father was founder and first principal. Later this school and certain other seminaries joined together and after some other changes the present Tokyo Theological College of the Kyodan came into being. I taught also at the Seikyo Gakuin, a women's Bible school of the Evangelical Church of Christ. The teaching was mainly for financial reasons; nevertheless teaching religious poetry and the New Testament was a great joy to me.

My mother-in-law passed away in her old age in the Christmas month of 1934 at Iwakuni, the town she loved. One of her three daughters was with her and she was surrounded by friends.

The entry of Japan into Manchuria was often up for discussion. It is true there were many shameful deeds on the Japanese side. The Lytton report at the time it came out was a great shock to everybody. But still most of us, even Christians, believed in our government and thought that we were defending ourselves against a Russian inroad. Had Christians only been keener on international affairs instead of just arguing theological questions! The Japanese Christians were too wary of being drawn into political affairs.

Yet even in those years there were some Christians who were awake to political justice. One was Mr. Nihei, a Congregational minister with great social consciousness. My personal relationship with him was such that he treated me as his colleague in his work against national injustice. He often remonstrated with the premiers and war ministers, and he let me sign my name to such documents of protest. These were handed to the premiers, one after another, for the ten years before "Pearl Harbor." Premier Konoye paid attention to us, but alas, his good will was too weak! The articles which Mr. Nihei wrote against the Japanese inroad into Manchuria, the invasion of North China and later against the Japanese attitude toward other nations were many and fiery. They ought to be translated into other languages and made public internationally. He sometimes was called up to the police and to the procurators' office, was fined, and his magazines were suppressed. Why they did not imprison him, I often wondered. He said repeatedly, "They do not listen to us, but our remonstrances will serve to remind them later that opportunities for repentance were offered to them." I myself was writing for the Y.W.C.A. magazine articles which advised the Japanese to turn the other way, but those were suppressed.

My connection with the Y.W.C.A. through the years has brought me many rich and varied experiences, especially through attendance at conferences that have taken me all over the world. While studying in Scotland I attended the Oxford and Budapest conferences of the World Y.W.C.A. What a blessing it was to get to know those Christian women of different countries—of Europe, of Asia, of Africa and of the two Americas! I saw many outstanding Christians of various types, and I admired them.

On a trip to Europe in 1928 I was privileged to visit Eisenach, Luther's town, and to stay at Haus Heinstein, where German young men were combining study and labor. Wartburg Castle was near by, and some of the extremely musical among those boys would slip out on a moonlight night with their violins, cellos, saxophones and flutes to the point nearest the castle and would break out into singing, "Ein' Feste Burg ist unser Gott" and other Luther hymns, to the accompaniment of their instruments. Some of the boys would shed tears of joy. Here I came across a piety which I had not known before. The rigid Protestant piety of Japan would do well to learn a bit of this spontaneous and romantic expression of emotion. I went up to Wartburg Castle every day for a week, the better to breathe in more of Luther's faith.

In 1936 a World Y.W.C.A. Regional Conference took me and a Japanese friend to Colombo, Ceylon. A delegate from Korea and four representatives from China were there among many other Asiatics and delegates from Europe, Canada, Australia and America. One morning the Korean, one of the Chinese and I shared the platform. That was a daring combination of nationalities at the moment. My colleagues were very outspoken about the deeds of Japan. Their poignant words gave great pain to my soul. I spoke in fear and trembling. What could atone for the sins of my country? I felt so abject that after going back to my room I cried and cried. I felt a soft touch on my shoulder, and my tear-filled eyes met those of Miss Emma Kaufman, my good Canadian friend. She mourned with me. That was a great comfort.

After the Ceylon Conference we attended the Indian Y.W.C.A. Conference at Kandi; from there I went on to Madras to the school of my Scottish friend, Helen Greenfield, and thence to Bombay to see another Scottish friend, Elizabeth Hewat, professor of history at Wilson College. She was a woman of high scholarship and great devotion, a graduate of New College, who held a B.D. degree from Edinburgh University. Her application for ordination had not been granted, just because she was a woman. She fought valiantly for the privilege from 1927 on, but without success!

The Hindus and the Mohammedans were fighting each other on the streets of Bombay in those days. What do such religious animosities mean? I had to meditate on this.

On my way from Bombay to Calcutta I saw Nehru, who was on the same train with me. At every important station he got off, and people cheered and carried him on their shoulders to a temporary platform where he had to speak. What popularity! They would run ahead of him in their flowing robes, strewing flowers and what looked like palm leaves on the road, like the crowd that followed Jesus from Bethany to Jerusalem. What were they shouting? I wondered. Nehru, too, might experience the fickleness of a crowd.

At Calcutta I met Emma Kaufman by appointment, and we both went to Darjeeling. I was overwhelmed at the sight of Mount Kanchenjunga. I understood the psychology of the children of Israel at the foot of Mount Sinai. The mountain was supersublime, and I nearly cried out, "I shall die, for I see thy Glory!" I often tell my own people, "Before you see other countries, do not think that your nation has a monopoly on the beauty of nature!" It is the same with other things. Our Japanese insularity, our childishness and our narrow-minded arrogance are the cause of our tragedy!

On my way home in December 1936, I stopped at Formosa. There I found that I was needed as principal of the Presbyterian Girls' School in the city of Tainan, since the militaristic government was threatening the very existence of the school. But first I went on home to Japan.

After taking a couple of weeks to get the affairs of my Kashiwagi church in shape for my absence, I left for Formosa and arrived in Tainan on January 11, 1937. There I met some very fine English missionaries who were working in the girls' school, the boys' school, the theological college and the mission hospital. Two of them, Miss Mackintosh and Miss Livingstone, passed away later on, during their internment in the Philippines. How extreme the privation and malnutrition during that period of confinement must have been!

Besides the regular duties of the principal, my work in Tainan lay mostly in negotiation with the government. I also taught the Bible. I sometimes preached in Japanese churches in Tainan and elsewhere and sometimes in Formosan churches. I dearly loved the Formosans. The government officials did not appreciate what our school did, since it had too much individuality and did not move along the rails laid down by the government. At any rate I was fortunate in securing government recognition, which permitted the school to go on, and also in finding a successor for the principalship. Therefore I felt free to leave Formosa in August of the same year. I was sad about going, but I thought I could work for the Formosans back in Tokyo.

By this time the militarists had me on their black list on account of my friendly relationship with the Formosans. Of course a few Formosans would sometimes get involved in an independence movement, and I would have to petition the police for their release. At about the time of the "North China incident," a great friend of mine, a Formosan intellectual, wrote a book on what China and Japan should be like in their relationship. He was put in prison, and some of his Japanese friends were called up for questioning, myself included. Some were detained by the police. One had to escape to China, where he stayed to the end of the Pacific War. He is today a member of my church. We shudder now when we talk together of the experiences of those days. This man came near being killed by the Japanese army in Shanghai for refusing to work as a spy. He was always upright and dauntless and spoke boldly what was in his mind.

I was called up frequently by the Tokyo police for several years. Sometimes anonymous letters would come, saying such things as "You will be killed on the street before such and such a day." They were written only to intimidate me. My Formosan girls and my daughter would often say to one another, "Let us give Mother something especially good to eat before she goes out today, for we know not what may happen to her!"

Searle Bates came from Nanking and reported to us the atrocities done there by the Japanese army. Nobody in Japan had known of them, since the militarists took great pains to give the public only such information as they wanted it to have. We could hardly believe the report.

The noble Samurai warriors of old, steeped in the Japanese code of ethics, were supposed to be terrible to the arrogant and unyielding, but kind and benevolent to the weak and vanquished. They regarded it beneath their standard of conduct to abuse the helpless.

In the sixteenth century, Kenshin Uesugi, Lord of Echigo, is said to have sent much salt to his foe, Shingen Takeda, Lord of Koshu, while the two were engaged in a deadly struggle. The latter's country was shut off from access to the sea by hills, and for lack of salt the soldiers and citizens of his province were suffering physically. Kenshin did not wish to fight against an army of sickly men.

Had Japanese soldiers entirely lost those ancient standards of chivalry? Could our countrymen in China do such things, so filthy and cruel? It was hard to believe, but I became convinced of the truth of the report, and we began talking about it. Very soon the police came to my house and searched it. All the documents concerning the "Nanking incident" and some 30 books on peace and international good will were confiscated. A comical thing was that they took away also many of my European and American victrola records, saying, "These records savor too much of Western freedom. We need no freedom in this country save freedom from the possibility of indignity inflicted by a foreign country." Poor things! They were suffering from a phobia.

Since Mme. Chiang Kai-shek was a Wellesley graduate and I too, the Foreign Office of the Japanese government asked me to speak to her for peace on the radio. I said to them, "If you will not interfere with what I intend to say, I will do it. But if you are to interfere with or dictate what I am to say, I will not undertake the task." The idea was dropped summarily.

The militarists wanted to put an end to Christian churches and Christian organizations. Many of the denominations and the Salvation Army were threatened with disbandment. Many Christian ministers were put in jail, and some died there in the course of time.

The government, being altogether too busy with external affairs, wished to simplify internal matters. It thought of coercing the many sects of Buddhism to join in one body, those of Shintoism to do the same, and all denominations of Christianity and all Christian organizations, such as the Y.M.C.A., Y.W.C.A. and the Salvation Army, to come together in one united Christian Church called the "Kyodan." Perhaps some government people who were not quite so militaristic as others pushed the idea in order to protect Christians. Needless to say, we Christians had to get together in order to survive. Hence we united—34 denominations and some other Christian organizations—on November 24, 1940. Although the union was somewhat unnatural, we came together with fervent prayers that we should sometime truly be one Church of Christ in Japan.

Then occurred the nightmare of the Pearl Harbor attack! How wily the militarists were to get the navy into it like that! Poor Admiral Yamamoto knew that such a war had no excuse and consequently would plunge the country into ruin. But he was drawn into it. The nation was deceived by a gross misrepresentation on the part of the army. It was told, until it believed, how proud and intolerable were American demands. Thus it became foolishly and hotly incensed. The Japanese people at large had had no training in the use of their own judgment but had always been forced at every turn simply to listen and to obey. It is almost impossible to break a habit like that.

The next four years were a terrible period in every phase of Japanese life. But I found a little happiness in going over to China in the spring of 1942 to negotiate with the Japanese government in Shanghai for the security of the Chinese Y.W.C.A. buildings. Somehow we succeeded. Miss Shizue Hikaru, the general secretary of the Japanese Y.W.C.A., was with me. I was the president of the Japanese Y.W.C.A. by that time, having been elected in 1939. I was also one of the vice-presidents of the World Y.W.C.A. It was a great sorrow that we women could do nothing to stop the course of the war. Since it was going on, we simply had to do anything we could to lighten the evil.

It was heart-rending to know that the missionaries in Japan were interned and suffering privations. They do not talk about their experiences, but we know that they suffered much. We shudder at the things that were done to missionaries in the Philippines. There are no words to describe how shocked we feel over what befell those great friends of Japan, the Covells, Baptist missionaries who were caught there. Their small son was killed with them. We never suspected our countrymen of such cruelty as to murder a little boy. But they did this and much more. No wonder some people of the world cannot yet reconcile themselves to the idea of associating with the Japanese.

The churches had to be very wary of pitfalls, often deliberately set before them by militarists. The ministers had to be prepared to meet unkind and impossible questions. Some failed to dodge them and were put in jail.

At me they shot sneering remarks like "You will betray our country sometime." Of course I tried to say as few words as possible in reply. They were not so hard on women, it seemed, because of their disdainful attitude toward our sex. So long as I did not say a word about the war the police could not touch me, although they did command me to speak in public in praise of the Japanese army and navy—a thing which, of course, I could not do.

The government made a rule that at the beginning of every public meeting a bow must be made in the direction of the Imperial

Palace, and silent prayers offered to the gods for Their Majesties and the soldiers. Since, in the Japanese way of thinking, the Emperor was divine in origin but not a god to be prayed to, what was required of the people was first to bow to their Emperor and next to pray to their gods for the Japanese soldiers. The Christian churches received no exemption from this command. In my church I had my people assemble five minutes before the regular worship. We would turn in the proper direction and make a deep bow, which was funny, perhaps, but not sinful. Of course after this formal bow we prayed to the true God for the restoration of peace, for the forgiveness of our sins and for spiritual solace for any and all who were on the battlefields of the world.

Then after this five-minute interval the organ would announce the beginning of our church service. The government wished the bowing to take place during the service itself, but to this we never acceded. One Sunday a procession of people carrying an urn containing the ashes of a soldier passed the gate of our church. The service was just over, and the congregation was coming out of the building. The young girls who were in the lead did not notice what sort of procession it was, and unconcernedly they went on talking to one another, whereas the proper etiquette on such an occasion was to stop and in silence bow to the urn. So my church was reported to the police for such behavior.

At another time a girl who lived in our house did not cover the light in her room fully for a blackout and I was reported. For ordinary persons such small incidents would have brought only slight reprimands, but for us Christians they served to deepen the suspicion the militarists had of us.

One day a policeman came to my house and ordered me to appear at the police station at a certain time. I was made to sit before four police officers who had pencils and paper in front of them. They jotted down what was said. One of them stated that he had been in the congregation at my church on the preceding Sunday and had heard me pray for the souls of the Emperor and the Empress and for all the wounded on the battlefields of the world.

"Do you admit that you have prayed in this way?" was the first question I was asked.

"Yes, I admit it."

"What do you mean by praying for the souls of the Emperor and the Empress as if they were common people like you?"

I answered, "You do not understand the spiritual meaning of the blessings of God. The Imperial Household are in need of guidance and sustenance from God, the Creator of Heaven and Earth. I believe it is a very patriotic act for us to pray to God on behalf of our Emperor and Empress."

No reply. Just note taking. Then they said, "What did you mean by praying for our enemies on the battlefields, when you said 'all the wounded' and did not specify Japanese only?"

I could only reply, "I meant precisely what I said. If we were so selfish as to pray only for the Japanese wounded, God would not be pleased and would not answer such a prayer. Do you not wish our wounded to be blessed by God?"

The next question was "What do you mean by praying 'forgive the sins of the nation'? You were heard to say these words on this same day and also on another Sunday."

"I meant just what I said. Again you do not understand what Christians mean by 'sin.' I will explain, if you will be patient enough to listen."

They were not at all inclined to be patient enough to hear me out. One broke in, exclaiming, "Japanese people have no sin!"

"Yes, they have," I replied. "You are a sinner and I am a sinner. Americans are sinners and Chinese are sinners. All men are sinners. Do you not agree that we the Japanese are neither so truthful nor so merciful nor so wise as we aspire to be? That is to be sinful! God sees a sin which we do not see in ourselves."

They next tackled me with this: "Which is greater, your God or our Emperor, and which is more important, the Imperial Edict or the Bible?"

"Oh, the Emperor and God belong in entirely different categories. God is the Lord of heaven and earth, and our Emperor is the head of the country. So also different are the Imperial Edict and the Bible. The Bible is the word of the Creator of the universe and the Imperial Edicts are commands of the Emperor. It is as wrong to compare these two which are so different, as it is foolish to compare air and earth."

I was kept there for seven hours. I was called for three more sittings at the police station on consecutive days, once for two hours, the next for three hours, and the last for one hour at the procurator's office. They threatened that if I should go on in the same way, I should certainly be imprisoned. But I continued preaching and praying without change, except that instead of saying "sinful" I said "wide of the mark," or " rebellious to the Lord of our souls," since "sinful" seems to mean to the Japanese "legally wrong."

I was called up often afterward for saying this or that, but somehow I was let off every time. I just had to bear very discourteous, scornful words from the civil police and sometimes from the military police as well.

The events of the war heaped up the sense of guilt on our consciences. At times we Christians said among ourselves, "Shall we go to the army and tell them that we are positively against the war and be executed as a consequence?" Then we said, "No, we must live in order to make a better world. We must be preserved! The militarists would not change their program in any case. Japan will go on to the end of this disastrous road, and then she will have to wake up, perchance to be saved. We are in the same boat as the nation at large, although we do disagree with it." Such was our psychology. Was it defeatism? Was there anything we could have done?

In the meanwhile Japan went on committing atrocious acts and deepening her guilt. She was heavily punished, though nothing really could atone.

On May 25, 1945, Kashiwagi Cho, our section of the city of Tokyo, came under incendiary bombing. As we expected all our cities to be bombed, we just accepted our turn. A dear girl, a teacher who had lived with me for seven years, was killed at Joshi Gakuin that night, having stayed on guard duty at the mission school. We hunted for her body in the neighborhood for four days. When we finally found it, we had to cremate it ourselves in the open, building the fire of what wood we could pick up, and watching to the end. Later we tenderly put the ashes into a proper box and sent them to her mother by a messenger, all the way to the distant southern island of Kyushu. Ashes are always carried by hand.

In this same raid our church and my home were burned down. After that we held our services in the house of one of our members. At first we were few in number, but gradually people found out where we were meeting, by the signs we posted near the old site. Those who had scattered to the outskirts for safety came miles on foot, electric trains and trolleys having been destroyed. When air raids overtook them on the way, they scrambled into the nearest dugouts. Later we had to give up meeting in this home because our increased numbers broke the floor down.

On June 1, 1945, a friend of mine, Mrs. Haruye Miyagi, and I went to Sendai to prepare for the opening of an orphanage under the auspices of the United Church of Christ. The number of war orphans was increasing at a terrible rate. There we underwent a severe bombing on July 10, 1945, during which all the furnishings and equipment we had planned to use were destroyed. So we had to come back to Tokyo, but not until we had cremated the body of a friend of ours who was killed that night. Public crematories had disappeared long before this.

The afternoon of August 6, I was calling on a lady member of my church. Her husband suddenly stepped into the parlor. He was pale. Never before had he said a word to me, since he had never forgiven the Christians for converting his wife. But he spoke to me on that day. "A strange bomb fell this morning on Hiroshima. It must have been an atomic bomb. We shall have to stop the war."

It was a staggering piece of news, but at least I was glad at the prospect of an end to the fighting. The atomic attack on Nagasaki a few days later decided everything with finality.

At noon on August 15 the Emperor's voice came over the radio. His declaration of the ending of the war came as a thunderbolt to some, but to me it was long-expected news. I wept in mingled emotions which I cannot describe. I loved the Emperor a thousand times more for his heroism in having fought the problem out for himself and in standing firmly against the Prime Minister and others who insisted on continuing the conflict.

Some disturbances naturally ensued in army circles. My nephew, who was an electrical engineer, was teaching in a school for air pilots. The principal, a colonel, said that they were all to commit "harakiri" together, out of a sense of shame over the defeat of

Japan. By a few days later this colonel had thought better of it, and my nephew came back safe. The war mentality was indeed a strange and terrible thing.

The landing of General MacArthur and his army in Japan was conducted on a high and honorable plane. He really glorified God in the magnanimity of his bearing and in his attitude toward the vanquished. As they marched through Yokohama, the American soldiers seemed solemn—as if paying respect to the demolished city; so the observers remarked.

On that day a young Japanese was hiding behind a door in the New Grand Hotel in Yokohama, waiting for General MacArthur's entrance. He was resolved to kill the general, when he should come within shooting distance. But the moment he saw the general's face he was struck with the nobility, benevolence and dignity reflected in it. "He is no cruel conqueror, this man," murmured the young fellow to himself. Powerless, his raised hand holding the weapon dropped to his side. The young man came to me later and confessed this unaccomplished crime. He has recently gone out of his mind, so I have no means of knowing whether he fabricated the story or not. In any case, the fact of the impression General MacArthur made on him remains.

One Matsuzaki, an artist and a worker in lacquer from Wakamatsu, was greatly struck by the attitude of General MacArthur's combat troops when they came to occupy the town. The Japanese had been afraid of the Americans. But these soldiers were kind to children and had lovable traits. Matsuzaki concluded that the commander of the whole army was surely a great man to be leading such troops. He resolved to show his appreciation to General MacArthur through some work of art in his own line. Yes, he would make a box for his Bible. Now Matsuzaki was not a Christion, but he rightly traced the noble leader's integrity and kindness to their divine origin, his God, revealed in the Bible.

He made a rarely beautiful box, with a figure of one of Fra Angelico's angels on top of the lid, and on the inside of the cover he painted three galloping horses full of dashing spirit and power. The box was accepted in the spirit in which it was given, not for its material value, though it had intrinsic worth, but as a symbol of the real appreciation and gratitude that were wrought into the craftsmanship and the paintings. I think Matsuzaki will one day be a Christian, for he is a serious and honest thinker. He is a true Japanese artist, devoid of greed and desire for easy success, dedicated to the pursuit of truth and beauty.

The coming of four American churchmen, Dr. Walter W. Van Kirk, Dr. Douglas Horton, Bishop James C. Baker and Dr. Luman J. Shafer in November 1945 gave the churchmen of Japan and the Japanese church at large the great assurance of the unchanged friendship of our American Christian friends who had forgiven us and promised us their assistance in evangelizing our country. I can never forget the first moment of our meeting with them. They could not speak for emotion. Neither could we. They gave great encouragement to many congregations. Our abject churches came to feel they might rise again with surging hopes.

Such men as Russell Durgin and William C. Kerr, who came out as civilians with the Occupation six months before missionaries as such were permitted to re-enter Japan, did more good to the Japanese people than they themselves admit or than the Japanese people really are conscious of. How generous and how understanding they always were! Withal they were very just and wise in their judgments. They did not come to spoil the Japanese but to show them right paths. Russell Durgin has contracted a serious disease as a result of his long and arduous labors for the Japanese. He became honorary general secretary of the Y.M.C.A. in Japan after his term of service with the Occupation was over.

William C. Kerr is working still as Protestant adviser in the Religious Section of the Occupation. We owe to him and his co-workers many reforms in regulations concerning Japanese religions. It was through a directive from their office that state and religion were separated and the strangle hold of State Shinto and shrine worship on the people was broken. Religious freedom was not only declared, it was guaranteed as a reality.

The Emperor's declaration to the nation in the papers of January 1, 1946, that he was not divine but only a human being oriented many Japanese hearts in the right direction. He himself had never thought of himself as divine.

Since the spring of 1946 many missionaries have come back or come anew to us. As Y.W.C.A. president, I cannot pass over

Miss Mildred Roe, who almost slaved for us from December 1946 to February 1948. We often wonder how such limitless kindness could be possible.

One day early in 1946 Charles Iglehart, a Methodist missionary, returned to visit us. He gave such a beautiful message of good will that all those grim heroes of the United Church of Christ began to shed tears. They had been almost stoic in their resolution to live or die with the Kyodan, but the warmth of the love of this American friend melted their hearts and they felt they could relax at last and be their natural selves again.

I cannot resist a digression at this point in my narrative, to refer to my daughter's life, since she and I are knit together in every way. When I came back from Scotland, she was still in primary school. For the four years of my absence she was very strictly brought up by my mother, who was like a Samurai's mother to the end of her life. Nevertheless, I was glad to find the little one mirthful and keen in spite of the discipline. Her joy seemed to lie in serving people. She entered Mrs. Hani's School of Freedom in 1931 and graduated in 1938. Under the inspiration of Mrs. Hani the class in which she graduated resolved to start a boarding school in Peking for Chinese girls of the middle and lower strata of society. Machiko and one other were selected from the class to go as pioneers, headed by three other young women who had graduated eight years before.

This project seems to have been a success. They all lived together, slept and ate together—Chinese girls and Japanese teachers. They all joined in worship every morning. The Chinese girls learned the Japanese language and were taught weaving, dyeing and other handwork. They were learning to lead worth-while lives. The school motto was:

> "We learn language together.
> We learn life together.
> We learn arts together."

Many Chinese girls came to Tokyo to study after they had finished this "School of Life" as they called it. When the war ended, the Peking school was taken over by the Chinese themselves with friendly feelings, and it was still thriving the last we heard. Machiko, having known Formosans, could talk to Chinese girls easily. She was learning very quickly to speak the Peking dialect when I sent for her to come back. I had applied for a scholarship for her in a junior college in Canada, to prepare her for Toronto University. I had all the arrangements made. Her passport, her berth, her trunks were all ready.

Machiko arrived at Tokyo Station on August 18. She was welcomed by Mrs. Hani and a large group of her friends. They said she had grown into a young woman. My mother eyes, however, saw weariness in her gait. When she was examined by a doctor, he shook his head and said, "You cannot go abroad. Go to bed and stay here." She had a hemorrhage of the lungs shortly after, and that settled the question. She lay very still in her bed for months and then went into a sanitarium where she stayed for three years.

In 1936, when she was 18, she had become engaged to a brilliant young college student, Yoshitake Oishi, who had been converted to Christianity and was under parental disfavor because of his new faith. He was working his way through college, headed toward a course in philosophy in the Imperial University. He said he felt called to the ministry. These two loved each other dearly, and I approved of the match. But when she was pronounced a consumptive, he was advised from all sides to break the engagement. His answer was that he would wait for any number of years. Then a term of intensive study in philosophy turned this young man into a thorough skeptic. He continued to come to church, but there was no more any radiance in his countenance; he spoke very little to anybody, although he was affectionate toward Machiko. She waited patiently in her sickbed for his rediscovery of the truth. It took Machiko 12 years to recover health. It also took 12 years for that young man to regain spiritual health.

He was graduated from the Philosophy Department of the Imperial University in March 1941 and was drafted into the army in January 1942, after teaching for nine months in a middle school. He was sent to Manchuria, but fortunately he was not faced with the necessity of killing people. He was taken prisoner and sent to Siberia. He has not talked much of the experiences of those days—

it is too unpleasant a period in his life. But he had completely regained his faith before he was repatriated on December 2, 1949.

Machiko went to the port of Maizuru and met him. One of the first sentences he uttered to her was spoken vehemently: "I am not a Communist!"

So they were married on March 2, 1950. At his request they live in the same house with me, naturally divided into two apartments, with a common dining room.

Machiko's name means "a child of waiting." My father gave it to her, saying, "Waiting is the heroic and positive attitude of one who trusts in the Lord." She waited for me in her childhood; waited for the recovery of her own health; waited for the return and spiritual recovery of her fiancé. Now all the waiting has changed into fulfillment and great joy. However, she has to wait still—for the coming of the Kingdom of God, especially to this land where people seem to be growing materialistic and crass. She, her husband and I will toil on with our colaborers. "Wait upon the Lord, O my soul!" will be Machiko's watchword to the end of her life.

Dr. Luman Shafer brought to me in November 1945 an invitation from the Presbyterian women in America to attend their Quadrennial Meeting the next spring. From that point on, lively negotiations went on between the Presbyterian women and the State Department in Washington and the Occupation in Tokyo. Finally I left Japan on April 2, 1946, by boat. Mr. Durgin and some other friends helped make it possible for me to leave Japan— the first citizen of my country to go abroad since the beginning of the war. It was many months before the necessary procedure was regularized and others were allowed to go.

Thrilling and life-changing experiences began with May 12, 1946, when I was met at the Grand Rapids airfield by Mary Mc-Donald and Virginia McKenzie. Mary had been my lifelong friend, and it was with great longing that I had thought of her during the war years.

The Women's Quadrennial was a marvelous revelation to me of the hearts of the American Christian women. They gave me a prayerful welcome. I was happy to be the bearer of a little gold lacquer box from the Empress of Japan, a small gift but neverthe-less filled with her good will. Mrs. Paul Moser, the outgoing chair-man of the Presbyterian women's council, Mrs. John Irvine, the incoming chairman, Mrs. Harper Sibley, the chairman of the women's council of all denominations, and all the other women of the American Church made me feel that I was truly being reinstated after Japan's failure and fall through the war.

The General Assembly of the Presbyterian Church in the U.S.A., summer conferences of women, of girls, of students, of "caravans" and different synodicals, the Chautauqua in New York State and a meeting of the women's interdenominational council, all emphasized the impressions I had received at the women's as-sembly in May. I was gradually getting back my strength, mentally and physically.

In September started the speaking trip called the East Asia Fel-lowship Mission. It was made up of three of us from the Orient—Dr. Josefa Ilano of the Philippines, Miss Foh-Mei Hsiang of Shanghai and I—with Mrs. William C. Kerr, our American leader. It must have been hard for Dr. Ilano and Miss Hsiang to speak on the same platform with me, for I was a countrywoman of those soldiers who had committed hateful atrocities in their lands. I cannot forget that during the progress of our tour Dr. Ilano, out of consideration for me, gradually changed and softened the strong, virile words she had been using to describe certain events of which she had been an eyewitness during the Japanese invasion of the Philippines. Nor was that all. When I was present she eliminated entirely from her speeches certain high points of dra-matic interest, because these very stories focused the attention of the audience on acts of the Japanese army, the relating of which was devastating in its effects on me. Is there any more sacrificial thing that one public speaker can do for another? It was through the grace of God and the loving and sympathetic atmosphere with which Mrs. Kerr surrounded us that our hearts were reconciled from their depths, that I was forgiven and was treated by the others as if I were their sister. Dr. Ilano and I, Miss Hsiang and I did indeed meet in America as true sisters.

After Mrs. Kerr left us at the end of October in order to join her husband in Tokyo, Mrs. Hugh Bousman became our leader. She knew the Japanese atrocities in the Philippines only too well, having been in an internment camp during the war. She and Mr. Bousman were so utterly unconscious of my being a member of the enemy nation that I was grateful with all my heart.

On November 3, President Truman granted the three of us an interview and placed me on his right hand when a picture was taken. This honor made a deep impression on the Japanese people.

At the conference of the council of all Protestant Church women in North America later in November, Mrs. Harper Sibley was chairman. At one meeting there was a procession of people from about 20 countries dressed in their differing costumes, bearing their national flags. The line extended from the entrance of the church down the center aisle to the platform, on which about 20 representative delegates were to make three-minute speeches. I was almost overcome to see, so soon after the end of the war, a huge "rising sun" flag of Japan ready for me, with a stalwart young man to carry it. Nor was that all. As an escort there were 15 American women dressed in kimono and obi, waiting to march down the aisle with me.

This was of a piece with Mrs. Sibley's stalwart championship of Negro people. Upon my return to Tokyo I took great pride in broadcasting all over Japan the story of her part in the selection of a Negro woman as the "American Mother" of 1946. May Japanese Christian womanhood one day reach that stage of broad-minded Christlikeness!

In January I went to Geneva for a World Y.W.C.A. executive meeting. There I was freshly struck with the world consciousness of Christians. I called at the office of the World Council of Churches and was filled with joy to know that the Japanese church was to be included in the fellowship of the international church family.

After I returned to the United States from Geneva I attended many church gatherings. I was enabled to go to Washington again to meet Ambassador Grew and different officials of the government in their departments. Ambassador Grew's words to me were reported by me to the Japanese public and gave them hope and cheer. He did a tremendous service to the country which had given him great sorrow!

Toward the end of February the Bible which the Presbyterian women had been preparing as their gift to the Empress was ready to be handed to me as their messenger. It was a superbly beautiful piece of craftsmanship.

The ceremony in which it was presented to me, and the communion service that followed, I have shared with my Japanese friends both publicly and privately, and especially with the Empress. It all was a most exquisite expression of Christian love to the soul of the Empress and through her to the Japanese nation.

I was invited to attend a meeting of the Japan Committee of the Foreign Missions Conference of North America, where they discussed reconstruction projects and their evangelistic programs for Japan. I was deeply impressed by their great earnestness. Dr. Karl Reischauer and Dr. Luman Shafer knew what to advise from their intimate relationships with Japanese Christians.

On my way across the continent from east to west I enjoyed the great honor of having the degree of LL.D. conferred on me by the College of Wooster, Ohio, on March 8, 1947. I was again grateful for such extraordinary kindness.

I came back to Japan in April 1947. Since then I have been the minister of Kashiwagi Church, which has been rebuilt. My work as president of the Y.W.C.A. of Japan is quite heavy. Two and a half years ago I was made one of the five National Public Safety Commissioners—the only woman on the commission. We are a policy-making and advisory board for the police system of the nation. I do much public speaking and writing for papers and magazines.

The Empress and her daughters are studying the Bible. The invitation to help them with their study came to me as an outcome of the gift of the Bible from America. This is a great step for the Japanese Imperial Household, and it may have far-reaching results if Christians abroad will co-operate in prayer with us Japanese Christians.

Japan is changing, and for the better in many respects. However, unless she is given faith in Christ, the liberty which she has received gratuitously will degenerate into license, and she will be enslaved by gross misinterpretations of the ideas of justice and equality. The Christians of Japan are wide-awake, but how difficult is the task ahead!

India and Pakistan— The Price of Their Freedom

9

By Rajah B. Manikam

"WE BELIEVE that it is the inalienable right of the Indian people, as of any other people, to have freedom and to enjoy the fruits of their toil and have the necessities of life, so that they may have full opportunities of growth." These were the opening words of the Independence Pledge the Indian nation took on January 26, 1930, under the leadership of the Indian National Congress. On August 15, 1947, Great Britain of her own accord decided to grant freedom to India as the culmination of a series of steps she has taken during her rule to equip India for self-government. Exactly 20 years after the Independence Pledge, the new Republic of India was born. Timeless in her tradition, hoary in her history, and yet adventurous in her spirit, this young republic has launched on a new career in her political history. Kings and emperors, knights and warriors have sat on the imperial throne in Delhi, but today a son of this land, enthroned as its President, presides over her destiny, supported by a cabinet of ministers who through their memorable sacrifice and service have brought luster to her fair name. Truly, every son and daughter of Mother India can with pardonable pride say:

A day, an hour of virtuous liberty
Is worth a whole eternity in bondage.

The freedom of India and Pakistan is no small event in world history. Containing as they do over 400,000,000 people, their freedom means the liberation of one fifth of mankind. And the liberation has been brought about without any recourse to arms or shedding of blood, but through peaceful negotiations. This in itself is a great tribute to the statesmanship and political sagacity of Great Britain.

As a result of the partition India lost 30 per cent of her area and 22 per cent of her population. While she occupies 2.5 per cent of the world's land area, her population is a little over 16 per cent of the world's population. With about 350,000,000 people, she is one of the large republics of the world. Her population is predominantly Hindu; about eight to ten per cent is Moslem and two per cent Christian.

Pakistan is the largest Moslem state in the world, with the largest Christian church in any Moslem state. While India has declared herself to be a secular democratic republic, Pakistan stresses the fact that she is an Islamic democratic state.

Partition of a land may seem an easy answer to a political problem, but it brings no lasting solution. As in Korea and in Germany, so also in India partition brought in its wake terrible tumult, turmoil and tribulations. Inhabitants of several districts in both countries were brutally robbed or injured or massacred, their houses burned to ashes, and their women forcibly abducted. Thousands were subjected to forcible conversions by riotous mobs. Both India and Pakistan stood bewildered, shocked and staggered. All principles of decent human living were thrown to the winds, and the moral standards gave way to madness and frenzy. It must be said to the credit of these two young independent countries that their governments did remarkably well in bringing order out of chaos and allaying human suffering and communal tyranny. Though communal riots have been quelled and the refugee problem is being solved, the relation between the two states is not yet happy. Even three years after the partition there is no through train communication from one state to the other. Both are firm in their belief that they have come to stay, and are zealous of their freedom and prestige in the eyes of the world. It is to be hoped that when the Kashmir issue is settled amicably, an era of enduring peace and sympathetic understanding will dawn in these states which have today a common history and a common heritage.

What has freedom brought to India and Pakistan? Three years are but a brief moment in their history, and a final judgment cannot be given until many years hence. Nevertheless, enough has happened in these three years to enable us to sense the direction in which we are going and to assess our progress so far.

The common man in India and Pakistan feels that he no longer belongs to a subject race but is a citizen of a free country and that the country is his, and its future lies with him and others like him. Has freedom meant anything more than this welcome self-respect and patriotism?

India and Pakistan may point out with pride that their governments were able to tackle successfully the problems resulting from the world's largest migration of population from one country to another—10,000,000 in all. Many had wondered at the beginning of the partition whether Pakistan could continue a stable independent state. Most of the civil servants, bank clerks and businessmen were Hindus and they had migrated to India. Would Pakistan be able to run her civil government with a predominantly new and inexperienced Moslem staff? This was the question in the minds of many. With only a few industries, with but two decent seaports, with a distance of hundreds of miles dividing Pakistan into East and West, and with no great mineral resources such as coal and iron, would not Pakistan crumble like a house of cards? Pakistan has defied all such dismal prophecies; she has ended the first years of her independence with a credit balance. She has fought inflation successfully, and suffers from no food shortage as India does. Her people are united and contented and are hopeful of a bright future.

India has today achieved a new solidarity which she had never known in all her history. The Indian states—and there were 566 of them—have been integrated with the Indian Union, some by merger, some by being taken over for central administration and some by becoming units within a federation or union of states. All this has happened within the short space of three years, while a century and more of foreign rule had failed to achieve it. Social reforms in some states, such as prohibition, abolition of landlordism, revision of the Hindu social code, statutory abolition of untouchability, etc., have been effected, and generally public opinion has been back of them. The *Panchayat* system (village administration) has been revised; social education of adult illiterates vigorously pushed in several states; compulsory primary education extended to new areas; a new fillip given to aviation and broadcasting; defense forces have been trained and strengthened; and nationalization of railways, irrigation, mines and electric developments completed.

Since August 15, 1947, when India became the mistress of her own destinies in the sphere of industry, the main tasks before the government have been to increase production, control the distribution of essential items in short supply and to plan the development of Indian industry in order to raise the people's standard of living and to achieve self-sufficiency in important materials. Many schemes for the industrialization of this country and greater production in food and industrial output have been worked out and are awaiting implementation. The serious hindrance has been the lack of adequate finance.

India became independent within two years after the war. Politically she was stable; industrially she was the seventh leading industrial country in the world; all her external debt had been wiped off, and she emerged from the war a creditor country; her internal debt was comparatively small, but well invested in railways, hydroelectric schemes, etc. Britain left her with Rupees (Rs.) 3,800,000,000 when she gave up her rule over India.

However, the partition of the country broke up its economic unity and created many problems. India spent millions on relief for the refugees and their rehabilitation; Kashmir has accounted for much military expenditure. Inflation assumed alarming proportions. The cost of central administration leaped from Rs. 390,-000,000 in 1938-1939 to Rs. 1,650,000,000 in 1948-1949, while provincial civil expenditure rose from Rs. 800,000,000 to Rs. 2,750,000,000. The defense expenditure today is 40 per cent of the total revenues of the country. Costly reforms, such as the abolition of landlordism in some states, have deprived the government of valuable revenues which could have been utilized for more urgent nation-building activities, such as education, scientific agriculture, sanitation, etc. Ill-advised threats of nationalization and vague pronouncements regarding industrialization have made private capital go very shy. The pre-independence Reserve Bank balance of Rs. 3,800,000,000 has dwindled to Rs. 1,500,000-000. The Treasury bills of Rs. 10,000,000 have swollen to Rs.

3,800,000,000. The sterling credit of Rs. 14,000,000,000 has now come down to Rs. 8,000,000,000. Therefore India's budget for development has had to be drastically cut. The Calcutta Indian Chamber of Commerce computes that 87 per cent of the population earn below Rs. 2,000 annually and pay only 13 per cent of the tax revenues, while 13 per cent of the population which earn more than Rs. 2,000 annually pay 87 per cent of the taxes. So this small well-to-do class pays most of the taxes, and hence the capacity of Indians to contribute to government loans has been considerably crippled.

The effect of all this on the man in the street has been tragic. If he does not have a house to dwell in or a roof over his head, if his food is strictly rationed and he does not get enough to eat, if the cost of living has gone very high, disproportionate to the wages he receives today, he surely is most discontented and cares little whether New Delhi or London rules him. He desires freedom from hunger and destitution. While the per capita national annual income in the U.S.A. is Rs. 7,600, and the United Kingdom Rs. 3,100, that in India and Pakistan is only Rs. 150.

It is true that the largeness of population in India and Pakistan tends to lower the standard of living. When the first census was taken in 1872, undivided India had a population of 265,000,000. But in 1941 she had about 400,000,000. The population of India and Pakistan increases at the rate of 50,000,000 in every ten years. Economists agree, however, that increase in the production and consumption of food has kept pace with the increase in population. Some believe that India and Pakistan are overpopulated and some do not, but all are agreed that an increase in population implies a decrease in the standard of living. To offset this, they need to increase the purchasing power of their people. They need to absorb and apply in agriculture and industry the techniques of organization and mechanization. The wooden plow, the spinning wheel and the handloom, which had been for years the symbols of India's struggle for independence and still are symbols of her solidarity, must not be allowed to impede India's economic advance. The first task of Indian and Pakistani statesmanship must be to superimpose the best of Western industrial technique on the best of India's and Pakistan's social and cultural traditions, without damage to either.

If what has been called "the Economic Man" has to be educated and uplifted, what about his body? What about his health? It is well to remind ourselves of the World Health Organization's definition: "Health is a state of complete physical, mental and social well-being, and not merely the absence of disease or infirmity." No one can be truly proud of the health of the Indian or Pakistani people. Since Independence, the scarcity of foodstuffs and the rising cost of living have added to the problem. The mortality rate for India and Pakistan is 22.5 per 100—twice that of the United States and the highest in the world, barring Egypt. Malaria accounts for 2,000,000 deaths annually and tuberculosis for 500,-000. Life expectancy in India and Pakistan is 26.9 years as against 58.24 in the United Kingdom. In view of malnutrition, insanitary rural and urban conditions, habits and superstitious beliefs, lack of milk and milk products, absence of pure water supply in many areas, inadequacy of medical and preventive health organizations, etc., how can we expect the health of India and Pakistan to be any better?

The inadequacy of the health programs of India and Pakistan may be judged from the following facts:

India and Pakistan have 5,700 doctors, *i.e.,* one for 6,300; while Britain has one for 1,000.
India and Pakistan have 8,500 nurses, *i.e.,* one for 43,000; while Britain has one for 300.
India and Pakistan have 6,000 midwives, *i.e.,* one for 60,000; while Britain has one for 618.
India and Pakistan have only 900 health visitors, 90 qualified pharmacists and 1,250 qualified dentists.

These figures give some idea of the magnitude of the task to be accomplished in increasing trained personnel of various kinds.

Of the many tasks which faced India and Pakistan after the advent of Independence, perhaps the foremost was that of providing education for their teeming millions. The percentage of literacy in pre-independent India and Pakistan was only 14.6. An estimate of the government of India for the year 1949 gives the figure for literacy as 18 per cent. This shows an increase of 3.4, and considering the huge population of India it is no small increase. Among the states, Delhi stands first with 31.6, Coorg second with 30.5. For the former Indian states figures for 1949 are not available; but according to the 1941 census the Madhya Pradesh (central India) states with 4.8 had the lowest literacy, while Travancore with 56.1 had the highest, Cochin coming second with 41.7.

It is conceded by all that any improvement in the economic status of the people demands the prior eradication of ignorance. It is not an easy task to educate the population of India and Pakistan, for it means the education of one fifth of mankind. To do it successfully huge sums of money and a vast army of teachers are necessary, and India and Pakistan do not possess either of these prerequisites to any large extent. If these two nations are to take their rightful places in a commonwealth of nations, they must be literate, and hence their governments must tackle the question of universal compulsory education for the children of school-going age. While the education of children is important for the future welfare of a state, the education of adults is equally essential for the very existence of these young democracies.

During the first years after Independence blueprints of the new educational edifice had been prepared. While the pre-independence Sargent Scheme of Education of India and Pakistan envisaged a 40-year period, within which universal primary education could be accomplished for all of India and Pakistan, the Kher Committee recommendations indicated the introduction of universal compulsory basic education all over India within a period of 16 years by means of two five-year plans and one six-year plan. It was recommended that 70 per cent of the expenditure should be borne by the states and 30 per cent by the Center.

Another committee under the chairmanship of the Honorable M. L. Saxena has suggested methods of solving the problem of adult illiterates. It has recommended the immediate launching of social education for making literate 50 per cent of the people in the age group 12-40 in the course of the next five years, the expenses thereof to be shared equally by the states and the Center.

The economic situation in the country deteriorated during the second half of 1948, and this compelled the revision of the educational program and the curtailment of educational expansion. Nevertheless, the educational situation is better today than it was in the pre-independence period. Then the educational budget of the Center was Rs. 20,000,000, but for 1949-1950 it stands at Rs. 52,000,000 for India alone. The states have equally increased their expenditure on education.

The year 1949 has seen a steady progress in basic and social education in several states, notably Delhi, Assam, Bihar, Bombay, Madras, Madhya Pradesh and Uttar Pradesh. However, the fact that 82 persons out of 100 in India, and a greater number in Pakistan, cannot read or write their names is appalling. Adult suffrage under these conditions is fraught with danger. No improvement in either the economic or the health realms can succeed with masses which are illiterate. Therefore India and Pakistan must devise ways and means whereby political freedom may go hand in hand with freedom from ignorance.

The advent of a secular constitutional democracy in India, hailed as a signal national event, has a direct bearing on the moral and religious life of the nation. Subjection to foreign rule for a long time, however good that rule may be, is not conducive to the growth of the rugged and manly virtues of a human being—such as courage, hope, self-reliance and love of truth at any cost—and at best produces the passive virtues of long-suffering, patience and humility. Liberty which does not lapse into license is invigorating and calls for the best in an individual. Evidences in this direction are discernible even within this short period. However, the new-found freedom does tend to lower the standards of efficiency and success in many walks of life, and there is great need to call attention to the standards which Gandhi, the Father of the nation, set before it. India's becoming a secular state does not imply religious animosity, but only religious neutrality. Religious freedom is guaranteed in the constitution, and the state is said to be founded on the principles of justice, liberty, equality and fraternity, though it remains to be seen how far these ideals embodied in the constitution will be implemented in the day-to-day life of the nation. Contemporary nationalism in India is already expressing itself in the revival of a culture which is predominantly Hindu, and in the cry for a Hindustan. In Pakistan nationalism demands an Islamic state based on *Shari'at* or the religious law of Islam, though there is a significant minority which demands a secular state. However, it is significant to note that in both countries there is increasingly less identification of Christianity with imperialism or Western civilization.

The repeated emphasis on India being a secular state undergirds the secularism that is now sweeping the country. The fabric of society in Hindu India has until now rested on village life, the caste system and a code of religious beliefs. But these bulwarks of stability are less secure today. The acids of modernity in the form of education, industrial development and scientific advancement have eaten into the bases of the old order, and the result is that a new humanism has begun to express itself in its insistence on remaking society by the use and control of human and natural forces, without reckoning with the real nature of the ethical problem. Secularism is also manifesting itself in a materialism in which religious values are denied or ignored.

In its most dynamic form this secularistic materialism blossoms forth as Marxian Communism. In Assam, Bengal, Hyderabad and Travancore it has assumed ugly proportions, and it aims at creating chaos and at bringing about social justice through violent methods. Strangely enough Communism has not made so much progress in Pakistan as it has in India. Perhaps the Moslem brotherhood in Pakistan is a bulwark against its assaults. In its ideological aspects it captures the attention of the intellectual classes. It has taken root among industrial and agrarian laborers and student groups. Widespread poverty in India proves a fertile soil for Communism. Also the corruption and injustice prevalent in India further its growth. It condemns the capitalistic society and the feudal landlordism and proclaims the dawn of a classless society. It does not hesitate to use violence and sabotage, believing, as it does, that the end justifies the means. India has tried so far to check it by imprisoning those of its leaders who resort to violence, but the ideals of Communism still continue to have a strong appeal to certain classes, augmented to a large extent by the success of Communism abroad. While it appeals successfully to youth to demand social and economic justice and to live sacrificially and dangerously, it seeks to achieve these ends at the cost of regard for human personality, social security and orderly development. In its materialistic and atheistic aspects it comes into violent conflict with Christianity.

In marked contrast to this atheistic materialism and secularism stands another distinctive development in Indian thought, which for lack of better expression we shall characterize as "religious universalism." Mahatma Gandhi was its prophet, and Sir Sarvepalli Radhakrishnan is its chief exponent. It emphasizes the similarities in all religions. All religions are the same in their ultimate objectives. Just as all rivers flow into the same ocean and all doors open into the same temple, so also all religions lead to the one and the same God. The Real is one, by whatever name it may be called. This religious universalism is proud that it has no exclusive spirit and no hampering dogmas. It is not concerned with historical events, for "there is not much meeting ground among followers of different religions who adopt different historical events as their religious bases." [1] It is eclectic in that it bases its spiritual fraternity on the common features of all religions, and thus it obscures the distinctions among religions in their historical development and in their teachings regarding God, man and society. This religious indifference and complacency cannot but undermine not only religious but also social values and personal integrity.

In Pakistan this religious universalism is not so prevalent as in India. Islam, it must not be forgotten, is a missionary religion after all and it does not yield place to any other religion, as it is deeply conscious of its own mission in the world. But in Pakistan one notices a cultural revival which embodies in it some of the aspects of religious universalism. The educated Moslem hovers between two worlds. The materialism implicit in his education and evident in all aspects of modern life drives him to consider all moral standards relative and moral values fleeting. He, like the Hindu also, seeks security in the past and revives his old culture and religious traditions by pouring new wine into old bottles.

In an independent India, predominantly Hindu, a new aggressiveness of Hinduism is discernible in that it claims that the problems of humanity may be solved by the universal application of Hinduism. It emphasizes Hindu spiritual values in contrast to

[1] Report of the University Education Commission, I, 298.

Western materialism. This aggressiveness has led to the formation of organized movements, such as *Rakshya Seva Sangh,* which demands absolute obedience from its Hindu followers. Popular Hinduism in its crude forms of idol worship and animal sacrifice still persists. Though legally untouchability has been abolished, caste in its rigorous forms remains unbroken, especially in rural areas. The burden of daily existence for millions desperately poor and despicably ignorant is met with the Hindu doctrines of transmigration, *Karma* and *Samsara.* Release from this burden is offered in pilgrimages, festivals, astrology, etc. In opposition to Vedantic monism, *bhakti* cults have come into existence. They demonstrate the truth that mere intellectual apprehension of the divine is not enough, but that there should be a spontaneous release of the soul and mind in an ardent abandon to the object of worship.

Since national Independence, attempts have been made to do away with the distinction between the Hindus and the animists, of whom there are about 20,000,000 among the hill tribes (Adibasis). Politically efforts are made to separate the Christian and the non-Christian Adibasis, and to discriminate against the former. The advance of modern civilization and the impact of other cultures have brought about marked changes in their traditional tribal outlook and life. The state has done little as yet for the Adibasi animists except to incorporate them into the political structure.

Moslems in Pakistan feel a new sense of power and mission in life. They do not hesitate to declare dogmatically and proudly that Islam is adequate to meet all the needs of the world. Though their brotherhood is limited to the faithful, yet they desire to widen its application. Minorities have been assured of their civil rights and their religious freedom.

While all this is true, one notices also a certain restlessness among liberal Moslems as to the implications of an Islamic theocratic state. On the other hand, the orthodox Moslems are bent on setting up an Islamic order in Pakistan, and therefore there is noticeable a certain amount of tension and cleavage among religious Moslems in Pakistan. This tension is being increased by the discontent of the refugee Moslems who resent the power and influence of the older residents in Pakistan. On the other hand the

young Moslem is disillusioned and becomes a cynic when he hears
of the proud claims of Islam to establish a state where righteousness and truth shall prevail, while corruption and nepotism are
openly practiced everywhere.

In marked contrast to all this, the Moslems in India exhibit a
different frame of mind. Having had to flee for their lives in certain cases, and being in many places an unwanted minority, they
have lost their confident belief in the efficacy and all-sufficiency of
Islam. Hinduism holds no attraction for them because of their
recent experiences and certain Hindu attitudes and habits. There
is therefore clearly noticeable among them a new attitude of open-
mindedness and willingness to hear the Christian message.

The Sikhs have gone through a terrible ordeal recently because
of the partition. They were a well-to-do people, owning rich agricultural lands in the old undivided Punjab. After partition they
were uprooted by the million, many losing all their wealth, and
quite a number their lives. They are now pushed into the relatively
barren areas of Eastern Punjab. They are a much disillusioned and
disappointed people. They too have believed in a political theocratic
state which will usher in the golden age. Their religious beliefs
are a curious mixture of Hinduism and Islam. Some are more
Hindu than others, and some violently repudiate their Hindu heritage. Factionalism is destroying their unity. Sikhism is no longer
the militant missionary religion it was a decade ago.

Against all these changes and developments, what has been the
place and role of the Church in India and Pakistan? There have
been Christians in India ever since the first century of the Christian
era. Indeed the tradition is that Saint Thomas came to India in the
first century A.D. and suffered martyrdom in A.D. 56, and the place
of his burial is said to be Saint Thomas Mount, near Madras.
Whether this tradition is true or not, there is no doubt that a
church of Thomas Christians has been in South West India for
a very long time.

The first Europeans to settle in India were the Portuguese,
and their most famous missionary, Saint Francis Xavier, came in
1541. The Catholic Church began with the conversion by Xavier
of the fishermen of the Coromandal coast; the Goanese community
of Bombay State is also his legacy. Robert de Nobili and Brito

nurtured the plant Xavier had planted. Today the Catholic Church in India and Pakistan numbers about 5,000,000 adherents.

The first Protestant mission in India was founded, strange to say, under the patronage of a king of Denmark in 1706. The Protestant community arose as the result of the work of the Protestant missionary movement in the eighteenth and nineteenth centuries. The Danish, German, British, Scandinavian, Swiss and American missions each had areas to evangelize and a church to establish. Today the non-Roman Christians in India and Pakistan number about 5,000,000.

A church of about 10,000,000 has taken firm root in India and Pakistan, and it will survive even if persecuted. In Pakistan it is about 500,000 strong, and it is the largest church of any Moslem state. The Church in India is the largest church on the Asiatic continent and second largest in the Orient. It is larger than the entire population of such countries as Sweden, Norway, Denmark or Holland, and is equal to that of Canada or Australia. Hence, while its numerical strength compared with India's vast population may be small, it is a significant smallness. It is a living, witnessing, growing church, growing faster than many churches in other parts of the world.

Religious freedom has been assured in the Constitution of the Indian Republic. The fundamental rights mentioned in the Constitution guarantee that "all persons are equally entitled to freedom of conscience and the right freely to profess, practice and propagate religion. Every religious denomination shall have the right to establish and maintain institutions for religious and charitable purposes; to manage its own affairs in matters of religion; and to administer such property in accordance with law. . . . No person shall be compelled to pay any taxes, the proceeds of which are specifically appropriated in payment of expenses for the promotion or maintenance of any particular religion or religious denomination. . . . All minorities, whether based on religion or language, shall have the right to establish and administer educational institutions of their choice. The state shall not, in granting aid to educational institutions, discriminate against any educational institution on the ground that it is under the management of a minority, whether based on religion or language."

These rights are judicable rights, and the right of appeal to the Supreme Court is possible in case of their violation. Religious communities in India rejoice that religious freedom has been guaranteed to them in the Constitution, and they hope that it will be equally guaranteed in daily life. The Pakistan draft Constitution omits the right to "propagate" religion, while it makes mention of the right to "profess" and "practice" religion. However, conversions are taking place in Pakistan, and the Christian community is not encountering any serious opposition.

The non-Roman church in India and Pakistan is a poor church, poor spiritually, educationally and economically. There are about 11,000 organized Protestant congregations in India and Pakistan, and 10,000 groups of Christians; for these 21,000 groups there are only 3,500 ordained ministers, Indian, Pakistani and foreign. An educated ministry, much larger in number, is a dire need. Educationally, too, the Church is backward. Only 25 per cent of the Christians in these two countries are literate, and that means that 75 per cent of the Christians do not know how to read their Bible! How can a strong church be built up under these conditions? Econonomcially the Church is poor, since 90 per cent of its members come from the depressed classes.

Though the Church is poor in these respects, yet by the grace of God it has been able to make a significant contribution to the life of India and Pakistan. In the struggle for the independence of India, Christians played a worthy part. They were not communal-minded and they asked for no special safeguards. Rather they pressed for religious freedom for all. By trusting the majority community they blazed the trail for other minorities to follow.

Enabled by help from sister churches in other parts of the world, through finance and personnel, the Christian missions and churches in India and Pakistan have ministered not only to the souls of men but also to their minds and bodies. In a country very backward educationally they have regarded it as one of their primary duties to impart education and spread enlightenment. The very framework of the educational system in India and Pakistan had been built with the aid of missionary educators. The non-Roman agencies in these countries maintain roughly 15,000 elementary schools, 500 middle schools and 300 high schools. The Roman Catholic

Church runs 5,000 elementary schools, 600 middle schools and 400 high schools. Christian organizations have been pioneers in the field of education for women. All over the country Christian schools for girls, especially convents, have reached a particularly high standard of education, and are very popular.

Here is a remarkable piece of testimony given by Dr. A. Lakshmanaswami Mudaliar, the Vice-Chancellor of the University of Madras, who, speaking at the Silver Jubilee celebration of the Loyola College at Madras in October 1950, said:

There are 58 colleges of arts and sciences in the Madras State, of which 23 are under the management of missionary agencies. The total number of students studying in these 58 institutions in the year 1950-51 is 35,000, out of which 14,500 are reading in Christian colleges. Out of these 58 colleges, no less than 24 were started within the last eight years, of which seven had been started by missionary agencies.

The part played by missionary societies cannot but be stressed on such an occasion as this and I venture to state that, but for the help given by these institutions in the earlier years, South India would not have made the remarkable progress it has in the sphere of higher education.

This testimony refers, however, to South India only. In all India and Pakistan there are today 50 Protestant colleges with 21,802 students, and 38 Catholic colleges with about 20,000 students. There are 30 teacher-training institutions run by Catholics and 65 by Protestants. Thousands of adult-education centers and night schools for illiterates are being set up and literacy charts and literature and magazines for semiliterates are being produced under Christian auspices. Notable therefore has been the contribution of Christian churches and missions toward the education of India.

In no sphere has the Christian spirit of service been more nobly shown than in the skilled treatment of the sick and in the struggle against disease. The Christian missions and churches have rightly stressed the ministry of healing. There are today 260 Christian hospitals and 580 dispensaries run by Protestants, in which work 240 foreign doctors and 435 national doctors, 275 foreign nurses and 1,200 national nurses. The treatments given in these institutions amount to 6,500,000 annually. There are eight Protestant Christian tuberculosis sanatoria in India and Pakistan, three medical schools and one medical college. The Christian missions have taken by far the greatest share in the treatment of leprosy. About 80 per cent of all the nurses in India and Pakistan are Christians, and about 70 per cent of them have been trained in Christian hospitals. This is only half of the story. The Roman Catholic Church is making an equally great contribution in the realm of healing.

The Christian mission has rightly stressed the importance of the economic basis of life in India and Pakistan. We cannot fight Communism only on the ideological level, leaving out the economic. The passion for economic and social justice which animates many a Communist must be the passionate concern of the Christian also. The Christian missions have therefore established individual, co-operative and professional institutions all over India and Pakistan. There are 80 agricultural settlements and 50 co-operative societies under Protestant auspices alone. Over the country are scattered 165 industrial schools and 50 printing presses run by Protestants. A like number is being maintained by the Catholics.

Mention must be made also of the social and welfare work done in these two countries by the Young Men's Christian Association and the Young Women's Christian Association. Numerous Y.M.C.A.'s dot these lands; they not only provide boys and adults with healthy recreation but also afford them abundant opportunities for training in social service. There are a number of rural uplift centers run by the Y.M.C.A. The Y.W.C.A. has ministered effectively to the women of India and Pakistan by providing them with homes and group activities. It maintains today a College of Social Service in Delhi, leading to a university degree.

When our motherland was unhappily partitioned and, as an aftermath, we faced a terrible refugee problem both in India and Pakistan, the relief service rendered by the Christian missions and churches was truly remarkable. They supplied 25 Christian doctors, 80 nurses and 95 social workers in the refugee camps in India alone. They also trained women in these camps in useful occupations and assisted in the rescue of abducted women from both countries. Through the help of their fellow Christians abroad they brought into India and Pakistan milk powder, clothing, costly drugs, vitamin tablets, cereals, wheat and rice—worth in all Rs.

4,000,000—and these they distributed freely among the refugees without any consideration of caste or creed. The record of their refugee work in Kashmir and in the two Bengals is equally striking.

From this narrative of the contributions that Christianity in India and Pakistan has made to the life of the nations, it must be clear that their service has been significant and that it has been rendered in the spirit of the Master who said that He came to minister and not to be ministered unto. Christianity in India and Pakistan is no longer confused with foreign rule and is therefore given a new kind of attention. Christian social-service standards have been accepted by the nation, though not publicly acknowledged as such. It is not uncommon to hear non-Christians speak unconsciously of their "Christian duty," and quite often leaders in public life exhort the people to undertake social service and rural uplift with "missionary zeal." There is an awakening of a new social conscience and an awareness of human personality and inner worth, exemplified in such social legislative measures as the abolition of bigamy, drink, absentee landlordism, dowry and untouchability.

There is profound wisdom in the words of the poet:

> Ill fares the land, to hastening ills a prey,
> Where wealth accumulates, and men decay.[2]

That was why Egypt fell, Greece fell, Macedonia fell, Rome fell—in fact any nation will surely fall if wealth accumulates and men decay. Righteousness alone exalteth a nation. The cry everywhere in India and Pakistan today is for men of character and integrity. Is there a better agency in these two countries, and for that matter anywhere else in the world, which works for justice and mercy, truth and righteousness, than the Church of Jesus Christ? Christians in India rejoice that, in spite of the fact that they are a small minority, they have contributed two members to the Central Cabinet, two Ministers of State—in Assam and Madras—and one Governor of the large State of Bombay. A number of Christians in humbler roles of public life are today serving their country and

[2] Oliver Goldsmith, "The Deserted Village."

God, and on them rests a heavy responsibility which they must needs discharge.

In September 1947 a remarkable development took place in the Church in India, which we regard as one of the most outstanding events in the life of the Church since the Reformation. At that time the Church of South India with its membership of 1,000,000 came into existence, bringing into organic union for the first time in Christian history the churches of the Anglican, Congregational, Reformed and Methodist persuasions. This union was not the result of a hasty decision but of long negotiations extending over a period of 28 years.

In North India the conversations on church union are progressing well, and it may be that it will not take another 18 years to bring about a United Church of North India. The Church in India is therefore blazing the trail for church union. It need hardly be emphasized that in a non-Christian country like India, Christian agreement in a united church is of paramount importance.

While it is true that the Church in India and Pakistan has taken root and is the largest church in East Asia, one must not forget the vast dimensions of the unfinished task still before her. Ninety-eight per cent of India and Pakistan remain non-Christian, and that in spite of the fact that Christianity is older in India than in some countries of the West. There are still areas in this land, with 1,000,000 and 2,000,000 and even 5,000,000 inhabitants where there is no church and Christian faith is not preached. There are also many unreached classes—the high castes, Parsis, Jains, Sikhs and Moslems. There are whole unevangelized realms of life. India's social system with all the ramifications of caste, Islam's *purdah* and *kismet,* the industrial life with its slums and strikes, the exploitation of cheap human labor, etc., has to be brought into captivity for Christ and revolutionized by the application of Christian principles.

The Church in India and Pakistan needs to be evangelized from within also. There is great need for a religious revival, the strengthening of inner life and a recapture of the zeal of the first-generation Christians. Urban congregations must become centers of Christian life and service, helping the rural churches and radiating a powerful Christian influence. A new self-governing India and Pakistan will look askance at a church so little self-supporting and so dependent on foreign help. Christian giving must increase and go hand in hand with the Christian teaching and example. Literature for evangelism as well as for devotional life must be produced in greater abundance. A better educated ministry must be recruited and trained. A theology, vital and pertinent to India and Pakistan, must be worked out. We have to tackle the problem of communicating the given eternal truths of the Christian religion in terms intelligible to the common man. If the state takes over the social services hitherto rendered by the Church, she must pioneer in other fields of service—such as the care and nurture of the young, the mentally defective and the physically handicapped; newer ways of demonstrating social justice; radio evangelism; audio-visual education; personality adjustments, etc. In rendering service in these realms, the Church's one objective must however be to testify or give evidence that Christ is the Lord of all life, and not merely to practice a social gospel.

The scandal of a divided church must be removed. Our unhappy divisions must be bridged over or healed so that there shall be an effective instrument for one Lord. United planning and closer cooperation in Christian service must characterize the relationship among the organizations more markedly than hitherto. With the "older churches" of the West, the Church in this land must enter into a new partnership and live an ecumenical life, undertaking in obedience the evangelization of India and Pakistan.

The Christian Gospel affirms that, in Jesus Christ, God has taken decisive action to deliver man from sin. It proclaims the creative power of Christ for the individual and society. Therefore, it has the answer to the ills of India and Pakistan, and it is their one hope of salvation.

Up to 1947 nationalism in this land provided the Hindu and the Moslem, the Parsee and the Jain with self-confidence in their struggle against foreign rule. But now that freedom has come, the same nationalism is baffled when it sees everywhere corruption, moral degradation, black-marketing and nepotism. The desire of India to construct a secular state without communalism in politics is not inconsistent with true Christian citizenship. Christians must support the state in its endeavor to maintain religious neutrality, but they must ever be vigilant to guard against a so-called "secular" outlook which will make religion a superfluous appendage or which, under the guise of religious neutrality, will impart non-Christian or syncretic beliefs.

India and Pakistan desire to be democracies. One wonders whether a country can be truly democratic without Christianity and its teaching about God and man. Respect for human personality and brotherly love for one's neighbor issue from the realization that every person is precious in God's sight, and that for each of us Christ died. It is the man who renders unto God the things that are God's who will render unto Caesar the things that are Caesar's. So in India and Pakistan the full recognition of human worth, which is the basis of a true democracy, is possible only when the Christian teaching of God, man and society is fully understood.

India and Pakistan, which are predominantly rural, offer to the Christian wonderful opportunities to proclaim Christian truth as fully relevant to rural life, assuring the villagers that in God's plan they too count, and thus saving them from frustration and failure. There is wide scope for the Christian to promote modern methods of agriculture, adult literacy, rural sanitation and hygiene, and other forms of service which will remake rural society.

In the cities and towns also the Church has an important part to play. The two countries are becoming rapidly industrialized and are now among the first ten industrial countries of the world. But they need to be saved from the four harmful effects of Western industrialization—(1) unemployment; (2) urban squalor; (3) malnutrition; and (4) total war. The Christian should fearlessly battle to eradicate the selfish profit that results in bad housing, unjust wages and exploitation of cheap labor. There is great need in these two countries to establish "Christian cells" in the urban community which will leaven the group from within. There is also a place for work of the "settlement" type.

The Christian cannot meet the challenge of Communism by merely trying to defend all the existing conditions of life. Tutored in the teachings of the Old Testament prophets and the New Testament, he must be the severest critic of social and economic injustice. But he will recognize it to be the result of sinful nature and not ascribe it to any particular class. He will therefore not seek an easy solution through adopting ruthless methods which violate the moral law, but by seeking a Redeemer who can save men from sin. Following as he does a Saviour who was moved with compassion when He saw the multitudes, the Christian will do all in his power to bring about economic and social justice, but he will not forget at the same time that man does not live by bread alone. It is Christianity which teaches men that history has a Lord and a Judge, and so, while recognizing the importance of action in history, it looks beyond history to the Saviour of men.

The true answer to the religious universalism which is today sweeping the land is found in the fact that the Christian Gospel as the revelation of God in a Person has to deal with historical facts and events. Jesus Christ is not a stage in religious evolution. In His life, death and resurrection particular events happened, whose importance the two countries can ignore only at their peril. "The Word was made flesh, and dwelt among us, and we beheld His glory." Therefore all paths cannot lead to the same goal. The different religions of India and Pakistan do propound their teachings of God, man and society from quite different premises, and their differences therefore cannot be ignored. True universalism does not consist in making an amalgam of good found in every religion, but is seen in God's search for man everywhere, and His showing him the way, the truth and the life.

Christianity is not just the crown of liberal Hinduism or popular Hinduism, Animism or Islam or Sikhism. It is both their fulfillment and their judge. The way to combat corruption and moral degradation is not through reliance on man's own natural ability but in the power of God revealed through Christ. The impact of Christianity upon Hinduism is most evident among those who have suffered most under the injustices of the caste system. The Christian love for the outcaste emerges from the fact that God's unmerited favor is bestowed on all alike, and that He came to redeem all mankind.

In applying the Christian faith to Islam—especially in Pakistan —individuals must be shown the faith in transformed lives of Christians as demonstrated in words and deeds. It must be shown that the ideal of a theocratic state finds its fulfillment in the Kingdom of God which Jesus expounded. Just as Judaism needed this reminder in the days of Jesus, Islam needs it today. The Christian must show that loving service is universal and is not limited only to the faithful, that in the fellowship of the Church the equalitarian ideal of Moslem brotherhood can be transcended, and that in the life lived with God in and through the Holy Spirit even the most mystic Moslem can find his complete satisfaction.

Today, more than ever before, the Sikhs are looking for the promised "Sinless Guru" and are awaiting an authoritative word. We believe the Christian Gospel has that word. The Sikhs are casting about to find some foundation on which to build a new nation. The Christian conception of the Kingdom of God is the authoritative word that can now be uttered with effect. The fellowship of the Church can be held out to the Sikhs who have lost the fellowship of the Panth through its internal factions. Today they are smarting under a deep sense of loss and betrayal. The Christian Gospel, however, calls them to repentance and assures them of peace of mind, as God forgives them through Jesus Christ and as they in turn forgive those who trespass against them.

Before our very eyes a new India and a new Pakistan have been born. We have witnessed the birth pangs. We have tried to assess objectively the gains and losses that political freedom has brought to the two new republics. To win political freedom men and women in this ancient land long endured imprisonment, suffered punishment and courted martyrdom. Finally the day of political emancipation dawned on August 15, 1947. For almost four years now we have basked in the sunshine of Independence. How far has political freedom really set us free? How far have we really made progress? According to Western ideas progress is often difficult to reconcile with the social and religious customs of our peoples. The caste system, the persistence of unhygienic habits, the extravagant expenditure on social and religious ceremonies, the purdah system, the serfdom to moneylenders, idolatrous worship—these still prevail, though not in all places or to the same degree. They are deplored and discouraged by enlightened public opinion. But it cannot be denied that they are a part of an ancient social structure which has religious sanctions. As long as they remain, they are bound to depress the social level and accentuate the poverty of those who practice them.

The Indian scene is baffling in its complexity. Communal strife, a widening gulf between the rich and the poor, the threat of Communism, rising prices and falling production, labor strikes, repeated failure of the monsoon and consequent famine conditions in some parts of the land, abject poverty of the many and the fabulous riches of the few, secularism, illiteracy, disease—these depress one almost to despair. There is no denying the fact that there is a close correlation among a nation's standard of living, its degree of education, its level of public health and its philosophy of life. On the other side there are powerful factors to dispel the encircling gloom—India's and Pakistan's ancient wisdom and culture, the administrative talents of their leaders, their self-sacrificial and indeed selfless service, their political sagacity not only in the councils of the nation but also in the United Nations, the natural reserves of mineral wealth and the superabundance of man power. No doubt there are still charms in this ancient land that hold the hearts of those who visit her, and those who name her as their mother. It is the charm of a mighty land, of rich and rare diversity, with a noble and heroic past. There is therefore no cause for despair, but there is reason for close heart-searching. Can political freedom be an end in itself for India and Pakistan? Is freedom from foreign domination enough? Should not one seek freedom from sin—from "missing the mark"—and all that gives birth to fear and want?

Here we come to grips with the real meaning of freedom from the Christian point of view. It is the freedom of the whole man that is required, and not just his political emancipation. Political freedom is not to be decried; it is good, it is needed, it is to be sought after. But we cannot stop there. It is easier to gain freedom than it is to retain it. The freedom of the whole man implies his salvation, his redemption, not only from political subjection, but also from the shackles of his own limitations.

If India and Pakistan are really to be free, in the highest sense of that term, they must know the truth of Christ which alone can make men free. Judged by this truth, they are far from free. In a great measure the same verdict is applicable also to other countries which are only nominally Christian and yet boast of a Christian civilization. It is true of nations, as it is true of individuals who make up a nation, that unless they are "born again," they cannot be free.

Latin America Tomorrow

By W. Stanley Rycroft

FIESTA, siesta and *mañana* are three Spanish words commonly known among English-speaking people. They have helped movie-goers get the false idea that life "south of the border" is all fun and frolic and nobody bothers about time. Anyway, who wants to be a slave of time like the North Americans? One often hears the phrase "lands of *mañana*," the implication being that in Latin America people mostly do not do today what they can put off till tomorrow.

With a delightful Latin-American touch of humor, Quintanilla, the outstanding Mexican diplomat and writer, describes the Hollywood version of Latin-American life, and particularly that "highly fantastic musical extravaganza known in the U.S.A. as *fiesta.*" "Then at the climax of the *fiesta*," he says, "enters the villain. Ah, the villain! An honest-to-goodness North American gangster would walk in, pull his gun, shout, 'Stick 'em up' and then quietly carry on his routine job of raiding the place. Not Pancho, the Latin-American bandit; he is always suave and affected; in fact, quite a man of the world. Then, whereas a Yankee gangster goes for the safe and money, Pancho—God bless his soul!—goes for señoritas. With the unerring instinct of a true connoisseur he singles out the most glamorous specimen and immediately starts wooing her, preferably with a song or a dance or both. Small wonder Main Street movie-goers are convinced that 'south of the border' everything is fun and crazy; that life down there is just a blissful succession of siestas and *fiestas* today, *mañana* and again after *mañana.*" [1]

In another sense the 20 Latin-American countries, some big and some quite small, *are* lands of *mañana*. . . . Larger than Europe and the United States combined, they are the lands of

---

[1] Luis Quintanilla, *A Latin American Speaks* (The Macmillan Company, 1943), p. 29.

great promise, young, vigorous and forward-looking. They are rich in natural resources, as well as in the more intangible wealth of mind and heart. Since their political independence from European Powers, gained over a period beginning more than 100 years ago and ending with the liberation of Cuba and Puerto Rico at the end of the century, the Latin-American countries have made great progress. While in many interior regions primitive savages still roam the forests, and in the more inaccessible mountain areas life is very backward, yet modern civilization is making a tremendous impact and centuries are being bridged in a few decades. The expression "from oxcart to airplane" applies. Many places can now be reached by airplane that are not accessible by either railroad or motor vehicles. A network of airplane systems circles the continent and crosses it at a number of points. In some countries roads are bringing remote places into touch with the outside world while North American movies penetrate inland towns and villages wherever there is electric power.

Argentina, Brazil, Chile and Mexico are rapidly becoming industrialized—that is, more and more of the small industries are being established in urban centers and in some places huge steel mills are in operation. A recent book bears the title *Industrial Revolution in Mexico*. Industry is viewed by many as the magic rod by which they may escape from economic colonialism and almost complete dependence on foreign markets in a world of fluctuating prices for raw materials.

In many parts of Latin America there is a consequent exodus or migration of people from the rural areas to the urban centers, with serious possibilities for the future. In Santiago, for example, live one fifth of the total Chilean population of 5,000,000 people. In some of the capitals the expansion in new housing projects and buildings of all kinds has been astounding in recent years. São Paulo in Brazil is the fastest-growing city in the world. Nowhere else can be found such beautiful cities as Buenos Aires, Rio de Janeiro, São Paulo, Belo Horizonte, Santiago, Lima, Mexico City, Montevideo and Havana.

In the foreseeable future great progress and development will take place in education, engineering, industry and agriculture. The people of Latin America are still largely related to the soil, at least 70 per cent deriving their livelihood from it, and yet scientific agriculture is practically unknown. The United States government and some private agencies like International Basic Economy Corporation and the Rockefeller Foundation, it is true, are beginning to do something in this field, as well as in education and health, co-operating with local governments.

The population of Latin America is almost equal to that of the United States, but its rate of growth is much greater, due not only to immigration but also to natural increase. Recent studies by demographers have revealed that the population is growing at a faster rate than that of any other major area in the world. Between 1920 and 1940 it increased by 40,000,000 people or, by 41 per cent, a rate double that of the world as a whole.

While Spanish, Portuguese, Indian and mestizo types predominate, all races and cultures are represented. Race prejudice does not exist as in other parts of the world—South Africa and the United States, for example. With a mingling and growing together of all types there is slowly evolving what has been called the "cosmic race."

Then there are the resources of mind and heart. What traveler has not been captivated and thrilled by the charm, generosity, courtesy and idealism of the typical Latin Americans? Their whole-hearted support of the League of Nations and, later, of the United Nations, together with their brilliant participation in these organizations, has opened the eyes of many to the contribution they can make in the world of tomorrow in the concert of nations.

Up to now the picture we have tried to draw has been bright and full of promise. Latin America *is* the land of *mañana* . . . and yet most, if not all, students would agree that many grave problems remain unsolved.

Latin America is one of those areas of the world where the vast majority are still underprivileged people, lacking the essentials that make up the good life—health and sanitary conditions, food of the right kind and quantity, decent clothing and attractive homes, education, freedom from want. Development has just begun. The three enemies of the people, recognized by many liberal Latin-American writers, are landlordism, militarism and clericalism. These have a strangle hold on the people and often represent the forces of reaction which impede progress and the development of a free and democratic society. Nowhere in the world is there a greater longing for freedom and democracy, and nowhere are there more elaborate constitutions that are less observed in practice. This gap between intention and performance stems partly from the idealism of the Latin Americans and partly from the general lack of moral righteousness and justice.

It is evident that there has been one fundamental error in the thinking of the people—the belief that a perfect political constitution can produce good government, stability and justice. There is a complete contrast in Latin-American life between form and reality, theory and experience. Simón Bolívar foresaw this when, in 1812, he wrote, "The codes consulted by our lawgivers were not such as could instruct them in the practical science of government, but rather the inventions of well-meaning visionaries, who, thinking in terms of ideal republics, sought to attain political perfection on the supposition of the perfectibility of the human race."

How can Latin America achieve that greatness and happiness which so many dream about, sing about and long for? How can the great social evils and injustices that hold millions in semiserfdom be eradicated? How can these countries become real democracies, lands of freedom?

Before offering any kind of answer to these questions, let us examine more closely the situation as it exists. The pattern is not the same in all countries, since there are diversified factors arising out of differences of racial texture, topography and agrarian reform.

We have referred to landlordism as one of the obstacles to progress. In many countries ownership of large tracts is more of an aristocratic obsession than an economic necessity or obligation. The landowner is an absentee in a large city and has a manager who tries to get as much as possible out of the farm for himself and the owner, with cheap labor and a minimum of expenditure for improvements. Agriculture under these conditions is primitive and unscientific. Feudalism keeps the cultivable land in the hands of a small group, while the millions eke out a bare existence. Agrarian reform is long overdue in many sections, but the results of Mexican social revolution in the last 40 years have demonstrated that basic though land reform may be, it alone is not a panacea, sufficient to uplift the people.

However, the basic fact must be faced of the poverty and consequently low purchasing power of the masses. It is estimated that about one per cent of the population own 40 per cent of the wealth. In *A Latin American Speaks* we read: "The naked truth is that of the 126,000,000 Latin Americans certainly no fewer than 85,000,-000 are actually starving. They have no houses, no beds, no shoes." [2]

William Vogt in *The Road to Survival* [3] deals with the serious problem of soil erosion and refers to the millions of acres that have already been eroded under destructive agricultural practices. The conservation of natural resources, particularly of soil, is of great importance to the future of the population. Vogt notes the difficulties in the situation—the cultural lag and the exploitation by foreign interests. One of the great weaknesses of the countries is the corruption and incompetence of national governments, comparable, Vogt says, to the "shambles of corruption, incompetence, waste and misery" in local government in the United States.

In Latin America so much public money is stolen and payrolls are so padded that governments cannot afford competent employees. A man with a government job knows that he may not have it for long. He justifies his graft and corruption by claiming that his salary is too small. Vogt cites the case of a government that set up a fund of $250,000 for an erosion-control campaign and put an American expert at the head of it. He actually received $1,300, a mule and a typewriter without a ribbon. Vogt then quotes a Latin-American scientist who observed that the number-one problem is not soil erosion but moral erosion, because you cannot solve the former problem until you have solved the latter.

Morality is the cement which holds the ideal society together; all problems in society have a moral aspect or basis. The term credit, used so much in business, is one of moral values. The fulfillment or nonfulfillment of promises made and accepted in everyday

[2] *Ibid.*, p. 81.
[3] William Sloane, Associates, 1948.

contacts determines the stability of social, political and economic life. Sometimes graft and corruption in Latin America are at the expense of the North American taxpayer.

In one of his books Carleton Beals tells the story of the building during World War II of the part of the Inter-American highway which goes through Nicaragua. The construction did not come up to specifications and actually deviated from the surveyed and planned route in order to service one of the dictator's estates. Mr. Beals met a Nicaraguan employee going along the road in a fine car. He was a well-paid spark-plug inspector. When he had nothing else to do he took his family out for a spin; of course he looked over some cars and trucks and changed some plugs (at least in his report), but in substance he sold new plugs.

Militarism is a cancer which eats into the life of the Latin-American countries. It goes along with extreme nationalism, on which it feeds, and the selfish ambition of a few individuals or groups. Badly trained armies, in some countries composed mostly of poor, ignorant, conscripted Indians, are a burden on the economy, and pawns in the hands of power-hungry generals and colonels. Outmoded tanks, guns and airplanes are sold to some countries and used by dictators to keep the people down. In more progressive nations the armed forces are better equipped and trained.

Clericalism also is a block to progress, an upholder of reaction and obscurantism and often an ally of the powerful landowner and the tyrannical dictator. To understand this phenomenon one would have to study the history of Spain and go even farther back. When Constantine accepted Christianity, it became the religion of the state, but history has shown that the state captured Christianity rather than the reverse. The relation of the Christian to God took on the nature of that of the Roman citizen to the Emperor, and arbitrary law took the place of strength of moral character in the individual. Down the centuries Church and State became one and the same, and so the Spanish conquest of America has been termed the "Last Crusade." It occurred as the Spaniards emerged from seven centuries of bitter struggle against the Moors who had occupied their country, and thus the Catholicism they brought to the New World was most fanatical, dogmatic and intolerant.

Priests and friars took part along with conquistadors in the subjugation of the native population whom they misnamed Indians, and the process was attended by much cruelty, violence and robbery. Not all the friars were aggressive exploiters; some were capable of amazing feats of bravery and endurance, especially in the mountains and jungles of the interior. Later on the Roman Catholic Church became the principal vehicle of a culture that was superimposed on the pre-Colombian cultures of the Incas, Mayas, Aztecs and others.

The tragedy that began with Constantine has continued until today. Roman Catholicism in Latin America is an ecclesiastical system which is upheld by a priesthood, clerical power in political life and widespread superstition and medieval magic, all of which are contrary to the mind of Christ. The establishment of a Roman Catholic monopoly, following the introduction of a dechristianized form of religion, accounts for what has been termed the great betrayal of Christianity. Instead of the transforming power of the Risen Christ and the knowledge of the richness of His earthly life and teachings, we find a dead Christ on a Cross and a triumphant Virgin Mary, crowned Queen of the Americas, together with an appalling ignorance of the Scriptures. Fetishism, image worship, superstitious practices and pagan ritualism have taken the place of spiritual, vitalizing force that can change men's lives.

In *The Other Spanish Christ* John Alexander Mackay expresses the relative position of Christ and the Virgin Mary according to Roman Catholic teaching:

A Christ known in life as an infant and in death as a corpse, over whose helpless childhood and tragic fate the Virgin Mother presides; a Christ who became man in the interest of eschatology, whose permanent reality resides in a magic wafer bestowing immortality, a Virgin Mother who by not tasting death, becomes the Queen of Life—that is the Christ and that the Virgin who came to America! He came as Lord of Death and of the life that is to be; she came as sovereign Lady of the life that now is.[4]

There seems no doubt at all that these conditions account for the almost complete lack of moral foundations on which to build a free society.

[4] John A. Mackay, *The Other Spanish Christ* (The Macmillan Company, 1933), p. 102.

The consequences of this betrayal of Christianity are too numerous and complex to be described in detail. I shall refer briefly and in general to some of them. The first is the almost complete secularization of society. This may come as a surprise to those who are accustomed to thinking of these countries as entirely Roman Catholic.

The number of priests is quite insufficient for the total population. In Guatemala, for instance, there is one priest for every 25,000 people, in Paraguay one for every 13,000 people, compared with the United States figure of one for every 3,611 people, taking the total population in each case. So serious is the situation that the Roman Catholic Church is sending missionaries to Latin America from the United States. Official reports give the number as over 1,100 priests and nuns. I got into conversation with a Maryknoll father on a plane journey to Peru and asked how many missionaries his society had in South America. "Oh, we do not call ourselves missionaries," he said; "we are here just to help out." The Lima papers next morning had a piece with the title "Llegada de misioneros Norteamericanos" (Arrival of North American Missionaries).

It is true the Church has political power and as such has to be reckoned with by politicians and dictators, but millions of people are estranged from it. Education has gone secular and in many cases educational institutions are anticlerical. Universities, including that of San Marcos in Lima, the oldest in the Western Hemisphere, were early founded by the Church, but they have become so completely secularized that new Roman Catholic universities have been established. Millions have no faith of any kind and university students are mostly agnostic and anticlerical.

Thomas Jefferson said, "History, I believe, furnishes no example of a priest-ridden people maintaining free civil government."

The second grave consequence of the betrayal of Christianity is that the way has been opened for the spread of Communism. Masses in Latin America, as in Asia and Africa, are diseased, ill-fed, illiterate and without hope. They eke out an existence in a grinding poverty from which there seems no escape. This is the soil of despair and frustration that nurtures political extremes, whether Fascism or Communism. It is to the landless, the hungry and the exploited that Communism makes its appeal with success. But it appeals not only to them, but also to the more radical sections of the population, and in particular to the university students, who in their idealistic youth side with the exploited underdog.

It is my belief that the next great area of the world where Communism will seek to advance is Latin America. Time is fast running out. After all, the stage is set, for conditions exist there similar to those found in Russia in 1917—the great mass of the people landless, hopeless, illiterate, underfed, poor; a wealthy church, a landowning church, nearly always on the side of the rich and powerful, using political power and influence for its own ends; an ecclesiastical system devoid of spiritual power, mostly opposed to progress and social betterment, because to uplift the masses would threaten its own position, its very existence.

Communism tends to spread as a violent reaction to ecclesiastical authoritarianism. Many Latin Americans are tired of, if not angered by, the continual intervention of the clergy in politics and they often swing to the other extreme.

Roman Catholicism has failed to uplift the people or to produce a social dynamic that would break the shackles of feudalism and tyranny. It has failed to give a faith and a spiritual power that inspire men to work and to sacrifice themselves for the good of the community. Its "social work" is largely confined to a few charitable institutions, such as orphanages, homes for the aged and so on. Some of these give commendable service.

What is it the Latin Americans desire? They want freedom, or shall we say the four freedoms we heard about during the war? They want justice and democracy, a decent living standard.

As Bolívar said nearly a century and a half ago, Latin Americans have made the mistake of believing in the perfectibility of the human race, that all you need is a good political constitution, good laws and an army to keep order. A prosperous nation where the majority at least enjoy enough to satisfy their needs is not built without hard work and without certain moral foundations. It is difficult to speak about these things and make a comparison with the United States without seeming smug, and without evoking criticism of our country for its gangsterism, its race tracks and gambling, its political corruption. However, our population is very large and the percentage of gangsters is infinitesimal; the number of corrupt politicians is small compared with the number of honest ones. The greatness of the United States is due largely to the character of the early colonists; they were religious men, and their religious living, stern though it may seem to our modern way of thinking, was woven into the fabric of national life. The Pilgrims came over as families, Christian families, and they were escaping from religious restriction and tyranny. The Spanish conquistadors left their families in Spain and came as adventurers seeking gold and wealth with which to return, or with which to live in luxury while the native Indians did the hard work. There were very few Christian homes where virtues were taught and practiced, because the Spaniards mostly just took the native women as they needed them. They kept a large section of the native population in virtual slavery on the plantations and in the mines. It is therefore not surprising that as a rule there is practically no middle class, and this is a serious obstacle to democracy in any country.

The sweeping social changes taking place in Latin America are part of the world social revolution. Modern science and technology are penetrating into all parts of the globe; new ideas and patterns of life are moving swiftly into backward areas; hitherto inaccessible districts are being brought within the reach of civilization.

Let us take a typical case. Here is a remote village, whose inhabitants have never been farther afield than a journey of a day or two on foot. Now a railroad is being built up the valley, and a plant to supply power and light. Soon the engineers will want young men who can read and write and who have some education. Perhaps airplanes will land on an airstrip near the village. Years ago when the villagers first saw an airplane they burned candles to the Virgin; the savages in the forest shot arrows at it. Now all accept airplanes as a commonplace. Old ways and customs give place to new. In remote towns and villages where there is electricity, one is struck by posters announcing well-known Hollywood stars in a movie.

Sleepy, humble places in the West Indies that have remained isolated and backward for hundreds of years suddenly find themselves in the main thoroughfare of everyday air travel.

Not that all Latin Americans are now traveling by air; far from it. The common people still travel largely on foot or by donkey; sometimes by rickety bus, if there is one. Transportation by air is for the benefit of mining companies and other industrial concerns. Muscle is still cheaper than metal, and the Indian goes on using his llama or his mule—or his own back. In Haiti the women use their heads.

Several years ago I took a plane from Guayaquil to a remote spot in the southern, mountainous part of Ecuador. The journey by station wagon from the airport to the drowsy interior town took longer than the plane flight, but still it was the plane that made it accessible. I then took a journey into the country and climbed a hill in order to witness an Indian *fiesta*. Accompanied by a man of good repute in the neighborhood, I entered an Indian hut, where members of several families had gathered to chat, eat and dance. It was a one-room, thatched hut with no windows. I could scarcely see, for, besides the darkness, the air was laden with smoke from a fire on which a meal was being prepared. The owner came and sat beside me. He wanted to know where I had come from, and he seemed to have heard about the United States. He wanted to hear me say something in English. He asked how much it would cost to go to the United States and whether I thought his son could get a scholarship. That was during the war, when the United States government was more liberal with scholarships.

Ideas are penetrating into remote places. Roads have been built into the interior and these have facilitated motor-vehicle transportation. Some years ago the Peruvian government organized a big fair in Lima, the capital, with the attendance of Indians and mestizos from the distant hinterland as a distinctive feature. Thousands came in by truck to see the fair and the sights of the great city. The increased mobility is one factor in the rapidly growing exodus from the rural areas to the towns in search of more gainful employment.

There is a hunger to learn and to know. In out-of-the-way places people who can read will read anything that they can find in print. Missionaries as they travel in their cars along the road let religious tracts fly out the window. They are invariably picked up and read with avidity.

Children eagerly seek education in schools. Young men and

women throng the universities in search of knowledge. Labor unions are in touch with similar organizations in other countries and they too seek the path of progress.

In Latin America today there is a great upsurge of life, a questing and a questioning. People are asking why their countries are backward while other countries have progressed so much. They are seeking a better life and an escape from, or a solution of, the age-old evils of mankind—poverty, ignorance and disease.

A Latin-American woman from a family of privilege and wealth was asked how things were in her land. "Very bad," she said. "Why, even the cooks want to send their sons to the university these days!"

All over the world the same thing is happening. The underprivileged, the poor and downtrodden are awakening out of a long, deep slumber or stupor. They are demanding changes, reforms and better conditions. We would make a great mistake if we labeled all such demands Communistic. There would probably have been a social revolution on a world scale even if we had never heard of Communism. This is one of the great creative periods in world history, and Latin America is one of the areas deeply affected by it. The ignorant and uninformed call the change Communism when often it is not, though Communists are trying to take advantage of it. In a small South American town a housewife beat her Indian servant with a broom. The servant protested and told the woman that she had no right to beat her. Thereupon the woman slapped her face. The housewife, relating this incident to a neighbor, said: "And to think that I have a Communist servant in the house!" Those who rebel against intolerable conditions are often mistakenly called Communists.

Perhaps the most significant social change is the pressure due to the rapid growth of industrialization in certain areas. In many countries labor is now a considerable force. Even Fascist-type conservative governments have attempted to offset the increasing demands for social reform and better conditions by introducing legislation calculated to satisfy, though in reality merely palliative.

The laboring groups, by and large, have drifted away from organized Christianity. The dominant church has preached a form of quietism which consists of telling the workers that, though their lot on earth is often hard, things will be better once they get to heaven. At the same time the rich are encouraged to be charitable to the poor and to give to the Church's eleemosynary institutions.

Millions of workers are not only estranged from the Roman Catholic Church, but are actively opposed to it, because, while it should have preached social justice and championed the cause of the oppressed, in reality it has placed itself on the side of the rich and powerful. Said a North American monsignor, "The trouble with our Church in Chile is that it is largely in the hands of a few wealthy families; we have lost the workers." The working classes in Latin America are largely against organized religion and are marching toward social and economic justice under non-Christian banners.

Latin America is an ideological battleground today; totalitarian systems and ideologies of the Right and of the Left are contending for its soul. On the Right there are antidemocratic forces of conservatism and reaction, nationalism, militarism and clerical Fascism. Their argument is based on the need to preserve society against threats from the Left, and an appeal is made to maintain cultural unity around the idea of Hispanidad emanating from Franco Spain and spiritual uniformity under Roman Catholicism. Usually these forces favor a strong-man government backed by the military and the clergy.

When Perón was seeking to become the dominant power in Argentina political life a few years ago a North American Roman Catholic layman wrote an article in *Harper's Magazine* under the title "The Cross and The Sword." He said that a group of young active Catholics were advocating an authoritarian hierarchical type of society in which the choice of a form of government must be left to the good, the rich and the wise—that is, to the aristocracy, the men of property and the churchmen. Democracy, they said, is not suited to a Christian society, because the ordinary man is ignorant and unlettered and thus incapable of assuming political responsibility. "The Fascist-type society is Christian, and the state should, if necessary, employ violence to bring about a complete harmonization in society."

It is undoubtedly true that many Roman Catholics consider their church the only bulwark against the advance of the Communist philosophy or ideology. It threatens their faith (as it does all Christian faith) and their way of life. In Latin America it threatens also their wealth and privilege. They believe that the status quo can and should be strictly preserved. They do not understand that the more the masses of the people are suppressed, and the more rigid the controls to stem the tide of social reform, the greater will be the explosive reaction. The common man is on the march. The workers' unions in Latin America are growing in numbers and power in some countries and Communist influence is manifest in them. This does not mean that all union members are Communists, but it does mean that Communists, whether party members or not, are in some key positions.

We can indicate only briefly the serious possibilities of such a situation. In World War II, Russia was our ally and we were able to secure the maximum co-operation from the Latin-American workers, especially for the production and transportation of strategic war matériel. For the war effort 44 per cent of the strategic materials came from Latin America ; 80 per cent of our manganese and 80 per cent of our copper were among these. If the United States were involved in a war with Russia we would need once again to look to Latin America for much of our strategic matériels, but the sympathies of labor would not be the same. The Communists in Chile boast that they could tie up the transportation of all copper to the United States. Communist strength is greatest in Brazil, Cuba and Chile. On June 14, 1948, *Newsweek* reported that there were about 1,000,000 Communists in all Latin America, of whom 500,000 are in Brazil, 150,000 in Cuba, 90,000 in Chile and 25,000 in Mexico.

Somewhere in between the repression by the Right and the penetration from the Left lies the tender plant of democracy based on freedom and justice for all.

One bright hope is the love of freedom which is ingrained deeply in the minds and hearts of the Latin-American people, both the intellectuals and the ignorant peasants. Liberty is a word that occurs over and over again in the national anthems. It seems to express the deepest aspiration, and yet it is rather pathetic to see people longing for freedom, struggling to achieve it, and yet not knowing how it is obtained. The Latin Americans fought—and it was a glorious, epic struggle—for freedom during the first quarter of the nineteenth century. But it was political liberty that was achieved, freedom from foreign domination. In the modern world freedom is perhaps what people seek most and least understand. They think of freedom as just being able to do as one pleases, and there are certain areas of individual and family life where one does just that, but such areas are very limited. Since man lives in a society absolute freedom is impossible, because it leads to anarchy and violence.

I well remember the revolution of August 1930 in Peru when Leguia, who had been dictator for 11 years, was overthrown. All the pent-up feeling caused by years of repression burst forth like a swollen river overflowing its banks. The newspapers were plastered with the word freedom; now the people were going to be free, the dictator was in jail and he could no longer exercise his tyranny over them. But this liberty very soon degenerated into license, lawlessness and violence.

Human freedom can exist only when there is moral control. In order to be really free an individual living in a society must be under moral compulsion of some kind; he must be bound to a higher law. He must accept a higher sanction than his own will. Neither the Latin-American soul nor any other will ever be free until it is surrendered to Jesus Christ. The Protestant movement presents and represents this kind of freedom.

The tragedy of Latin America is that for centuries the Reformation never reached its shores. The freedom of the Gospel of Jesus Christ is now breaking in on hearts and lives with all the freshness of springtime. It comes with power and brings release, a sense of liberation. Many Latin Americans are at last going through a Reformation experience.

Take the case of Adolfo Martinez, a barefooted Indian from Guatemala. His wife had died, leaving him with four little children. In his desperation, off he went into the jungle, determined to end his life. He flung himself on the ground, took a drink of liquor, bent his head over the muzzle of his gun and reached for the trigger with the big toe of his left foot. Somehow the toe refused to do his bidding. He decided that it was the fault of the liquor and that he would wait until the next morning.

On the morrow a new impulse caused him to forget the idea of taking his life. He made his way to the little Protestant church, entered the crowded hall and sat well forward. The pastor was talking about sin. Yes, Adolfo knew what that was and that he himself was a sinner. But was the salvation the preacher promised only something in the distant future? He wanted something that could save him here and now from his drinking habits, his loneliness and his sorrow. He began to listen more closely. "God is your Father. Jesus Christ is your Saviour. He triumphed over sin and death and is alive today. He is near each one of you." Adolfo couldn't see anyone sitting beside him on the bench and yet the preacher seemed an honest man. He listened to him again. Now he was talking more about this Jesus. As the preacher continued Adolfo felt there was warmth and strength in the One who said He was the Saviour of the world. At the close of the service Adolfo went up the aisle to learn more.

As the days went by, he was seen more and more in the preacher's company and he also spent much of his leisure time reading the Bible, time he used to spend in the saloon, drinking with his friends. His former friends now began to mock him, calling him a woman and inviting him to come and drink with them and be a man. Adolfo found new strength in the Gospel he had accepted, and new patience and forbearance. Liquor no longer tempted him and he was gentle with those who mocked and scorned him while he told them about Jesus.

Adolfo went into the jungle, but this time he took his Bible instead of his rifle. He journeyed through the western part of Guatemala, preaching to many about the new way of life. Feeling the need of definite training, he enrolled in the Bible Institute for Indian workers, and later he was ordained a Protestant pastor.

Today Adolfo Martinez is the moderator of a Protestant synod of Guatemala and a leader among his people, a striking figure as he walks up and down barefoot on the speaker's platform, telling crowded audiences of the One who transformed his life and made all things new.

This story, with variations, is being repeated many times in Latin America. It is the story of a power making new creatures out of wretched, fearful, sinful men and women. It is the power of the

Gospel to uplift a man and make him a great influence for good among his own people.

Many businessmen, lawyers, doctors, teachers and army officers have become evangelical Christians and have carried their faith into all walks of life. In Mexico a number of generals have become evangelicals. In many places young Christian doctors are giving their time free in some Protestant clinic or hospital. Two brothers, second-generation Protestants in Mexico, started a furniture business a quarter of a century ago and decided right from the beginning, as they put it, "to make God their third partner." They would honor Him in all their business dealings and in their contacts with their employees; they would share their profits with Him. Many a worthy cause has been helped by these upright Christian men. A few years ago they celebrated the twenty-fifth anniversary of the founding of their business with a special religious service in a large Protestant church in Mexico City. At the appointed hour a large number of friends were waiting in the church, but the front pews were vacant. Then 60 employees and the members of their families from the furniture store walked up the aisle to take their places in those pews.

A well-known businessman is in charge of one of the Protestant churches in Santiago, Chile. Through his influence in business and his ministry in the church he is leading educated people and university students to Protestant Christianity. In Brazil outstanding Protestant scientists, lawyers and doctors occupy positions of prestige and responsibility.

Some years ago a bill to establish capital punishment was introduced in the Congress of Nicaragua. One deputy who opposed the bill cited the commandment, "Thou shalt not kill"; thereupon another countered by citing other laws of Moses establishing the death penalty for various crimes. A lively discussion ensued as to what the Bible really taught. A member claimed that no one in the Congress was competent to say what it meant and that if they really wanted to know they would have to go to the Protestant church to find out. Two deputies volunteered to go. The next Sunday they were in the men's Bible class and became so interested that they stayed for the church service. Later on both became members of the Church. One of them was a general. On his return to his home town he made generous gifts to his church. Someone asked what had happened to the general to make him so liberal all of a sudden. The reply was that he had been studying his Bible.

The building of a new Latin America will be done largely through men of this caliber, if it is going to be done at all. The Kingdom of God is not "prefabricated," it is built brick by brick, but they must be real bricks which will make solid foundations. There the metaphor ends, because one life alone sometimes exercises an influence that reaches hundreds of others, or is that leaven in society of which Jesus spoke.

Evangelical Christianity is not only bringing newness of life to individuals and to households in Latin America, but also is influencing whole communities and even governments. Let me cite one incident, with important implications.

Señor Arnechino is a Protestant and a deputy in the Chilean Congress. He took part in a heated debate on an important question. After he had spoken another deputy arose and said, "But after all, you are only an Evangelical." This was too much for Arnechino. He jumped to his feet and said in a firm voice, "Thank you very much for that comment. After all, I *am* only an Evangelical, but it is the greatest honor one may have and in the majesty of this Congress I wish to witness to my faith. If it wasn't for my faith I would still be a down-and-out, worthless individual, a homeless drunk, a menace to my fellow men and a disgrace to my country. Thanks to the Gospel of Jesus Christ I am here, occupying a seat in this parliament." Silence fell on those present. No one else spoke. The session ended, but the words that had been spoken continued far beyond.

Protestantism has stood for two important emphases that have had a profound influence on the development of evangelical Christianity and the progress of Latin America, namely the diffusion of the Scriptures and the development of education. Most of Latin America has not known the Bible, the book that has done more to inspire and guide the human race than any other. The well-known Argentine writer Sarmiento wrote that "it is the Bible which fertilizes the roots of democracy." Protestant agencies, such as the American Bible Society and the British and Foreign Bible Society, in recent years have distributed millions of Bibles, New

Testaments and other portions in Latin America. In 1948 the Bible Society of Brazil was inaugurated and is now printing Bibles in Portuguese. The demand far outstrips the supply.

As for education, there are about 900 schools under Protestant auspices: kindergartens, primary, secondary and commercial schools, vocational schools, agricultural schools, normal schools and liberal-arts colleges. Some of the best leaders are coming out of these institutions. In many aspects of education, such as commercial training for girls, domestic science and co-education, the evangelical schools have pioneered. In most cases the standards have been high and their range of influence wide.

In his outstanding 562-page volume,[5] recently translated into English, Azevedo pays a great tribute to the contribution of Protestant schools to the culture of Brazil. He describes how the education introduced by the Jesuits in the early development of Brazil was based on the underlying principles of the Counter Reformation —dogma, authority and discipline—and that the education introduced by the Protestants was founded on the principle of the Reformation—that is, on free examination and the freedom of the human personality. If free examination, the spirit of analysis and criticism and the love of research and adventure had been introduced earlier, says Azevedo, it would have broadened the mental horizon and enriched the culture of Brazil in the philosophical field. The Protestants have been passionately interested in liberty and in the reading of the Bible as a means of spiritual development, so that the propagation of Protestant ideas has been accompanied by an intellectual movement.

The growing demand for education in Latin America is so great that governments usually cannot supply enough schools and teachers to take care of all the children and young people. That is one reason why Protestant schools are so important and as a rule are well regarded by both the authorities and the public in general. Moreover, some of the governments have honored missionaries with special decorations in appreciation of their outstanding services in education. This recognition was given not merely because they had imparted knowledge and information, important as this

---

[5] Fernando de Azevedo, *Brazilian Culture,* translated by W. R. Crawford (The Macmillan Company, 1950).

is, but rather because they had inspired great principles of moral living and by their personal lives made a spiritual impact on many young people.

The basic Reformation principle of freedom of interpretation struck a blow at dogmatic authoritarianism and ushered in a new era of freedom of thought, not only in the spiritual realm but also the cultural and the scientific. Protestantism is a spirit and it is a movement. It means the development of free unfettered personalities, a dynamic social consciousness and progress, human betterment and the uplifting of the downtrodden masses.

Protestantism does not emanate from any one country. It is a spirit which if communicated takes root in any soil and produces its own fruit. It is true that missionaries from the United States, Britain and Canada took certain forms of worship and church government to Latin America, but it is also true that these were merely vehicles of expression through which Christian faith might be communicated. The Protestants found no hymnology and practically no Christian literature in Latin America because evangelical Christianity, which produces these, was absent; it was only natural that the missionaries should draw on the store of hymns and books in the English language.

Evangelical Christianity is deeply and securely planted in Latin America. In some countries there are strong national Protestant churches under the direction of the people. This is particularly true in Brazil. Mexico, Argentina, Cuba, Puerto Rico and Chile, where virile indigenous leadership has been developed. It is estimated that there are between 3,000,000 and 4,000,000 Protestants. The number is increasing at a faster rate than in any other section of the world.

Unfortunately, denominational traditions have been transferred to these countries and there are almost tragic divisions, just as you find them in North America. Yet one of the most significant trends is the drawing together of the divergent groups. The urgency and complexity of the world situation is unifying the evangelical sects. They are coming to realize that Christians of different persuasions who hold varying viewpoints may work together on many phases of their program and may be mutually helpful because they are bound together by a fundamental loyalty to Christ. The formation of national evangelical councils in a dozen or more countries is evidence of this drawing together in closer co-operation. The tendency to proliferation which developed as a result of the Reformation principle of freedom of interpretation is being transcended by the overarching loyalty. There are some who believe that absolute uniformity in doctrine and practice are prerequisite to any interdenominational co-operation. There is abundant evidence to show this is not necessary at all.

In July 1949 the First Latin-American Evangelical Conference met in Buenos Aires. Other notable conferences of an international and interdenominational character had been held in previous years, in Panama (1916), in Montevideo (1925) and in Havana (1929). These were milestones in the development of Protestantism in Latin America. At first the leadership in the conferences was predominantly missionary and North American. It is interesting to note, however, the way in which Latin-American evangelicals took a greater and greater share in the leadership. The Buenos Aires Conference represented an important stage in this progress. The sponsoring bodies were the national evangelical councils and the Committee on Co-operation in Latin America. The large majority of the delegates were Latin Americans.

The Buenos Aires Conference demonstrated eloquently the increasing ability of evangelical Christians of different denominations to work together and yet retain their own denominational loyalties and even their doctrinal divergencies. The reason for this is that, as in the great ecumenical conferences in Edinburgh, Jerusalem and Madras, the central place was given to the person of Jesus Christ as a unifying power.

Protestantism in Latin America is determined to preach, uphold and live by the principle of religious freedom. The Roman Catholic Church claims to be the one and only Christian Church and assumes that governments in countries where it predominates have a right to suppress non-Roman denominations. All this has been officially stated for the Roman Catholic Church in *Freedom of Worship—the Catholic Position*, by Francis J. Connell:

The (Catholics) believe that the Catholic Church is the only organization authorized by God to teach religious truth and to conduct public worship. . . . The very existence of any other Church is opposed to the command of Christ that all men should join His one church. . . . If the country is distinctively Catholic . . . the civil rulers can consider themselves justified in restricting or preventing denominational activities hostile to the Catholic religion.[6]

The implications of this are more evident in Latin America than anywhere else in the world, except perhaps in Spain itself.

Protestant groups continually suffer persecution in Mexico, Colombia, Peru, Brazil, Bolivia and Ecuador. In Colombia, for instance, violence and persecution have reached unprecedented limits. It takes many forms: personal insults, intimidations, violent attacks on individuals, searching of homes of pastors and church members, confiscation of property, destruction of churches, imprisonment for preaching even in private homes or for distributing tracts, general interference with religious services. Most of these violent acts are carried out by the police, but it is common knowledge in Colombia that the Roman Catholic hierarchy is back of the whole campaign. Some of the more outspoken priests have declared that it is the intention of the Roman Catholic Church to stamp out Protestantism.

Persecuted Protestant nationals and missionaries are displaying remarkable steadfastness and courage in the face of personal danger. Their spiritual life has been deepened by their experiences. It is the old story: "the blood of the martyrs is the seed of the church." Furthermore, many liberal-minded people, seeing the unshakable faith and courage of the evangelicals, have become more vocal in their advocacy of religious freedom.

Protestantism in Latin America is growing in social consciousness. It is only natural that the main stress has been on personal religion. Protestants have been and still are a small minority. Their continual challenge is to present the claims of Christ to others. Evangelism, in the pulpit, in the street and the market place, over the radio and through literature, remains the primary task of the Church. Increasingly, however, local church groups and young people's societies are more and more concerned about social conditions in urban centers. Protestants are leaders in the campaigns against

[6] The Paulist Press, 1944, pp. 4, 10.

alcoholism, gambling and other social evils. The Chilean government put a Protestant at the head of its own campaign against alcoholism, giving him funds to travel up and down the country.

A strong element in Protestantism today is youth. We are told that 70 per cent of the new members of the Protestant churches in Brazil are young people. Most churches have active groups. Most of the countries have national evangelical youth organizations. These have joined in an international conference which has held, so far, two important meetings—one in Lima (1941) and the other in Havana (1946).

We believe evangelical Christianity to be the creative force which will give spiritual power, new life, moral direction and social dynamic to the Latin-American people. It has penetrated into the very heart of Latin America. The evangelical Church has taken root. It is vigorous and forward-looking and its influence is felt in all aspects of life, even though it is still a minority of some 4,000,000 in a total population of 140,000,000.

The great task of the personal and social evangelization of Latin America, in a sense, has just begun. The young churches there will need the help of the older churches in North America and Great Britain for a long time to come. The delegates to the evangelical conference in Buenos Aires urged the sending of more well-qualified missionaries to their lands. The important question now is how to formulate an ecumenical strategy which will meet the needs of the situation and fulfill the overwhelming demands of the hour. The titanic struggle against the forces of evil and materialism gains in intensity all over the world, but in no area is it more crucial to the future of the world than in Latin America. Those who believe in freedom and righteousness cannot stand idly by. There is a terrifying possibility of "too little and too late."

The Latin America of tomorrow is being made today!

Literacy—The Problem and Its Challenge

11

By FRANK C. LAUBACH

ELEVEN hundred million people, almost two thirds of the world, are voiceless, for they cannot read or write; they cannot vote. In Asia and Africa over 1,000,000,000 are illiterate, over half the human race. This cold print cannot tell you what that means. You may think it is a pity they cannot read, but the real tragedy is that they cannot speak. They are the silent victims, the forgotten men, driven like animals, who have mutely submitted in every age before and since the pyramids were built. During the past decade we have been in agony at the suffering of the oppressed Jews, and we have felt deeply for our displaced and destitute fellow Christians. *They* had a voice to speak for them. But we have little indignation about 1,000,000,000 illiterates. Why? It is a human weakness not to realize suffering unless we hear a cry. The illiterate majority of the human race do not know how to make their cry reach us. For centuries they have suffered in obscurity.

The Christian Gospel declares, "The spirit of the Lord is upon me . . . to set at liberty them that are bruised." The most bruised people on this planet, the hungry, the fallen among thieves, the sick with fear, the imprisoned in mind, are these illiterates.

That is no exaggeration. I know them intimately; I have watched their minds at work. They are virtual slaves in one way or another. There are 325,000,000 in India alone; and almost every one of them is in debt all his life, he and his children and his children's children. He does not know how much his debt is or whether the interest is figured correctly. The moneylender takes all the interest he can get and still leave his victim alive—for it would be silly to kill the animal that makes you rich. The debtors never get surplus flesh; moneylenders see to that. In one form or another this is the black sorrow of nearly all the illiterates in the world.

They do not know enough to live without some leader to whom they are enslaved. More than half the human race are in slavery today; they are hungry, driven, diseased, afraid of their masters in this world, and of the demons in the next.

They can be set free. I have seen these people across Asia and Africa, and have sat beside many of them and taught them one by one; I have seen a new light kindle in their eyes, love and hope dawn as they begin to step out of blindness.

They have their appeal—those voiceless men and women. The sheer vastness of their numbers stirs us with the sense of something stupendous. It strikes hard because it is new. Few people know that 80 per cent of China, over 80 per cent of India, 95 per cent of the East Indies, 95 per cent of non-Christian Africa, Afghanistan, Iran, Iraq, Pakistan, Turkestan, Arabia, cannot read. Few know that among the followers of the greatest non-Christian religions, the Hindus, Buddhists, Mohammedans, Confucianists, Animists, over 90 per cent are illiterate.

The astounding new development of our day is that this silent billion will probably become literate in the next century. The Church must take the leadership, for whoever teaches this billion can win their hearts. The most direct way I know to lead a man to Christianity is to sit down beside him with a heart full of love and patiently teach him to read. Humility draws a man who is obsessed with a sense of inferiority; and it opens his ear and his heart. If you make good your first promise to teach him, you have his confidence as well as his love.

The Christian Church is challenged by the swiftest and the most dangerous, the most titanic educational upsurge in history.

It began in 1920, right after World War I. James Yen proved how quickly people could learn, and he has now taught 50,000,000 Chinese to read. Lenin understood the educational value of literacy and saw to it that 100,000,000 in Russia became literate. In the rest of the world other millions are learning. The total is over 250,000,000 literates in the past 30 years. Now 1,200,000,000 more in the vast illiterate areas of Asia, Africa and Latin America are on the march to literacy at the rate of some 20,000,000 a year.

Every nation realizes that ignorance is "enemy number one" as far as its progress is concerned. Nations now know that they can make men and women literate swiftly, easily and cheaply by using the latest simplified methods, and they are requesting each literate citizen as a patriotic duty to teach one illiterate a year. Since Christians throughout the world are more literate than their neighbors, they are the object of special appeals to teach. This is a perfect opportunity for Christian faith, as it offers endless occasions in which a Christian may interpret Christ to a friend while he is teaching him to read. The illiterates of the world are fast coming to the state where they want to read as much as a blind man wants to see. They know now that they are poor, sick, exploited, *because* they are ignorant. They don't want our doles; they want us to help them help themselves to better ways of living. When a Christian sits down beside an illiterate and teaches him, he is meeting that man's greatest of all felt needs. Given half a chance the illiterate will love his new friend, believe what he says, read what he gives him. Such a man has seen Christian love in action, and the door of his mind is open.

As soon as the new literate can pronounce simple words in Christian literacy campaigns he is given the second reader, *The Story of Jesus,* which increases reading speed while telling the Gospel stories. His next readers are graded Scripture portions, arranged in easy, medium and advanced stages. His graduation present and "permanent reader," a few months later, is a copy of the New Testament which he may read in his own language.

Because of its years of experience in this kind of adult teaching, the Committee on World Literacy and Christian Literature (of the Division of Foreign Missions of the National Council of Churches of Christ) finds itself caught up in the grand adventure of helping the Christian Church gear literacy into its mission programs. In personal visits to rural areas all over the world, and in volumes of correspondence, its representatives produce easy lessons, organize church and government-sponsored campaigns; and, as funds are provided, aid is given to missions and their allied churches in the printing not only of lessons and graded reading materials, but of other forms of needed Christian literature.

If the Christian Church does not respond the governments of the world will teach this rising tide of illiterates anyway in the next 20 years; whoever works hard and fast may win their loyalty.

Where governments operate literacy campaigns alone, without church co-operation, there is always the danger that knowledge will grow without morals or character to guide it, giving subversive movements fertile fields in which to plant the seeds of atheistic materialism.

Lecomte du Noüy's *Human Destiny,* one of the great books of the century, declares: "The conflict between pure intelligence and moral values has become a matter of life and death. Intelligence alone, not subject to moral values, has led to monstrosities." [1] General Douglas MacArthur puts it simply: "It must be of the spirit, if we are to save the flesh."

Today we see educated men without Christian faith sowing the world with lies, suspicion, murder, chaos. Do we want a world like that, or a world full of the spirit of Christ? Christians have the talent to teach the silent millions to read. They have the means to supply adequate literature to feed the hungry minds. Each of us first needs to learn a great deal more about the yearning in the hearts of the "silent billion," and the efforts now being made to satisfy it!

As millions become literate there looms the staggering task of providing them with enough good literature. Literacy campaigns may well double the world's readers in a generation. In India, a mighty tide has begun to rise. Millions will be literate soon—before India is ready! In China eight out of ten are illiterate. But the tide is rising there too. Millions will soon be reading—before China is ready. Ninety-seven out of 100 Africans are still illiterate. But we have found that it is astonishingly easy to begin campaigns there. The tide will be rising—before Africa is ready. Over half the human race will be surging in upon us like a tidal wave—before we are ready. Who is going to give them books? Clean books or rotten books? Will the new literates be flooded with the teachings of Christ or with atheism? Will they read love or hate? Whatsoever is sown in their minds the world will reap. What will happen when this majority speaks after the silence of the centuries?

In Asia and Africa hardly any of the simple reading matter these people need for Christian living has yet been written. It is

[1] Pierre Lecomte du Noüy, *Human Destiny* (Longmans, Green & Company, 1947).

290 WORLD FAITH IN ACTION

terrifying to see what is being circulated against the Christian
religion. All the workers in one Indian press are compelled by
the local union to subscribe to a Tamil Communist paper with a
picture of Stalin on the cover. Week by week thousands of agents
throughout the world are busy sowing tares, yet the churches and
missions delay action.

At the Tambaram Christian Missionary Conference (Madras,
1938) the report on literature stated: "The fact that we acknowledge importance and neglect action is an *anomaly.*" A *blindness*
would have been less polite but more accurate. That report contains
pages about literature for young people, and rightly; pages about
literature for educated classes, and rightly; but only six lines about
material for semiliterate adults! The curve of literacy, which has
been nearly stationary in Asia and Africa since the dawn of man, is
now sweeping upward. The present trend of the curve indicates
that we may expect within 50 years that over 500,000,000 new
readers will step out of the silent ranks—and speak for the first
time. This is perhaps the most stupendous, the most arresting, the
most ominous fact of our time. Nothing can stop it now. Many
self-seeking agencies are already flooding the vast multitude with
reading matter—everybody, it would seem, but the Church. Our
New Testament, originally written in simple colloquial Greek, has
been translated for the most part into the classical languages of
Asia, too difficult for new literates to comprehend.

One feels such a responsibility to God and to the world that one
trembles. It is every Christian's responsibility. We must remember
three facts to open the door which God is swinging open for us
to evangelize the whole non-Christian world. When the city of
Ephesus welcomed Paul, he wrote: "A wide door for effectual
work has been opened for me, and there are many adversaries."
One city! One wide door! I speak now of a door as big as half the
world, which has just swung open for us; and there are indeed
many adversaries.

The first fact is the new passion of two thirds of the human
race to learn to read. Multitudes are ready to believe in the Christian Gospel when a Christian teaches them and lives what he
teaches. Hundreds of Christian missionaries have for years been

working with teaching as a method of evangelizing. Now we know enough to speak with some authority.

Together we have made many essential discoveries. We have discovered that in most languages—except English, of course—teaching people to read does not require years, but may be done in hours, or days or weeks. It can be a short, easy and delightful process.

We have discovered that where non-Christians will not listen to straight preaching, they welcome us if we teach them, because they want to learn to read. Literacy is the entering wedge. I first discovered this for myself among the Moros of the Philippine Islands. They were violently prejudiced against Christianity, just as the people in Arabia still are. For 15 years we made sporadic attempts to start religious services, but no Moros would come. Then we began teaching them to read. They used only 16 sounds and our lessons were easy.

Now came the stunning surprise. Nobody at all would come to our religious service; but dozens, then hundreds, then thousands came to learn to read. We were thronged. We had 400 volunteer teachers who brought in as many as 1,000 names a month of people they had taught to read. Our second surprise was that people liked to teach one another at home if we furnished the cheap little four-page primers.

Our next discovery was that everybody we taught became a friend. When we first went to Lanao we did not feel it safe to venture out of the village without soldiers. But within a year the whole province became friendly. The Moros, including the highest chiefs, began to come to our religious services. When young Moros joined our church there was no open opposition even from priests. Where direct preaching had failed for 15 years to win friends, our literacy campaign paved the way for the Christian message.

The rest of the Philippines heard about this so-called miracle of Lanao. The secretary of the National Christian Council invited me to prepare similar lessons in other Philippine dialects, and all the Philippine languages proved just as easy as Moro. The women's clubs and the Philippine government adopted our method, and the news of it spread. Then letters began to come from other countries, asking us to exchange experiences with other missionaries. Scores were making the same discoveries around the world.

Daniel Fleming's book, *The Marks of a World Christian,*[2] fell into my hands with the startling statement that two thirds of the world were still illiterate. When I told my Moros, they clucked their tongues with delight: "We can teach the world."

On our next furlough we came home by way of Asia and tried our method in seven countries. It worked, but each language group presented peculiar difficulties. Clearly we would need the pooled wisdom of the whole world to get the maximum results. For the past 15 years I have worked with missionaries and governments in 61 countries in over 200 languages. Together we missionaries have developed a technique which we are convinced presents the Christian Church with the best opportunity in 2,000 years to go out and make disciples of all nations.

For while we have been learning how to teach and win, the world has been getting ready for us. A vast change has taken place in the attitude of the unlettered billion. For ages they suffered in unresisting despair. But in the past 30 years they have come awake. Automobiles, tourists, soldiers, vast military supplies, airplanes, motion pictures, radios, tell them that some people have abundance, full stomachs, healthy bodies.

Now the Communists have come and told the "voiceless" that they need not stay down. Across the scores of countries where I have worked I have seen these millions churning with immense longings that have never so stirred the masses since the world began. The illiterates' determination to rise increases every year—to rise and give their children the chance they never had. They will take the hand of anybody who reaches to help them. They will rise the Communist way or the Christian way, taking whichever hand reaches them first.

They hear two voices. One says: "You are in poverty because the rich have kept you poor. Revolt!" The other voice says: "Knowledge is power." The multitudes are willing to try either way.

Whenever or wherever we offer to teach them, they jump at the chance as the Moros did in Mindanao. I have been surrounded by

[2] Association Press, 1919.

crowds in Latin America, in Africa, in Asia and in the islands of the Pacific. Last year before 1,000 Moslems in Nigeria our group taught 100 Moslems to read the first lesson. Then to our amazement they all fell on their faces before us and began to repeat a Moslem prayer. I was as shocked as Paul in Lystra and said: "Get up. I want to shake hands with you in the good old American way." When we announced we had to leave Leopoldville, a large crowd of women students shrieked in disappointment, for they had not yet been taught.

In May 1949 it was arranged for my son Bob, Phil Gray the artist and me to visit the wildest remaining area on this globe, the immense island of New Guinea. Missionaries have converted people on the coast, but the interior is still swarming with cannibals; nobody knows how many. We prepared lessons in 13 languages at Lae, on the north coast, and then flew with 750 primers in Medlpa to a section of the interior where a Lutheran missionary has a beachhead and where the people haven't been cannibals for 15 years. As we approached the airfield we saw thousands of people as thick as flies, and had to circle around several times while they were chased off. When we landed they surrounded us, a people without a written language wanting to learn to read! In a half hour we had our chart out teaching them, and we kept it up morning, noon and night for a week. It was bedlam, not a school, for everybody wanted to learn first. At the end of a week we had taught 36 the first book. On Sunday we gave 36 diplomas in the church service, as we always do when the first book is finished. We showed them how to teach, then everybody went outside where about 16,-000 people had gathered. All day Sunday hordes of wild folk painted as hideously as the very devil danced and shouted and jumped in celebration.

"This is the greatest event in our history," they said. "You have done more for us than anybody who ever lived. We like your religion because it does so much for us. We want to be Christians. So we have voted to ask you to baptize everybody right away."

"Sixteen thousand" sounds like a large number. But 60,000 times that many, 1,000,000,000 people, are willing to say "Baptize us right away" if we will come and teach them to read. Of course no such mass baptism would be wise or fair, but people do turn eagerly and desperately to that which will take them beyond dark despair, and the harvest of true converts is immense.

A foolish man asked me how I made the illiterates want to learn. I replied, "That isn't our problem. Our problem is how to chase them home at night when we are tired out." Here is "a tide in the affairs of men which, taken at the flood," may lead millions to Christian faith. It won't run beyond this century, for every nation is determined to read, and if Christians don't teach them, others will.

In January 1950 we landed at the Firestone airfield in Liberia. There were 60,000 employees ready to learn. Then we went on to Monrovia, where the President of Liberia launched a nation-wide literacy campaign in co-operation with all the missions. His government wants 2,000,000 people to learn as fast as possible to read and it wants us to help make them Christians.

Here is good news. Every government we have helped has welcomed us and afterward officially expressed its appreciation. Not one government has thus far prevented us from teaching illiterates in their homes and telling of Christ while we teach. Governments sometime forbid our teaching religion in schools, but not at home in our "one-by-one" teaching.

When we offer to teach at home without salaries, without building new schools, governments see that this is a cheap, swift way to make their countries literate. Many of them would be delighted if we could do the job completely. This public service makes them appreciate the value of the Christian spirit. They are ready to believe that evangelical Christianity is the inspiration of universal education. When we tell them that Protestant countries are over 95 per cent literate while most of the other countries are 90 per cent illiterate, they see the reason.

When we teach because we love people, our actions tell them that Christian compassion and determination to help are necessities for their country. One deed of compassionate service is worth a million words.

All the governments outside the "iron curtain" are afraid of the whisper campaigns fomented by the Communists, afraid of conspiracies to overthrow them. In order to survive, the Communists have forced them to be on good behavior. The people want education and their governments want to please them. This is the main reason, I think, why so many governments since the war have invited us and even paid our expenses to come and help them. The officials know we are Christian missionaries; I am working with Christian churchmen and missionaries all week and on Sunday. I have never been warned to soft-pedal my religion and I never do. These governments do not fear Christianity; it is conspiracies organized by Communists that they fear. UNESCO calls literacy its number-one educational project. God moves in His mysterious way!

In 1949 we went to Thailand by government invitation. In fact it offered to pay the way of three of us by air. UNESCO had recommended us. The Thai government was afraid of the Communists' influence among the masses and needed us to give the citizens more education. Christians and Buddhists worked side by side and loved one another.

The new government of India nearly killed us with hard work and kindness in April 1949. It proposes to give all illiterates the franchise. It wants them to learn to read, more than anything else in the world. So in Calcutta, Allahabad, Jubbulpore, Nagpur and Madras the teachers and government officials hardly gave us time to rest, day or night. New Delhi, the capital, was the worst of all. On Sunday, our last day, the Governor General of India invited us to dinner. I told him the Minister of Education had already asked us. Then he said to come for tea, but the Methodist church had us speaking at that hour. So he waited in the great government building Sunday night until seven-thirty and talked with us about literacy in India until we had to run off to catch the train for Pakistan.

I was glad to escape to Pakistan in hope of a rest, but I found it just as desperate as India. The Moslems forgot all about our religious differences while they sought help in their enormous problem. I loved them as brothers—it is inevitable when one works with them to achieve literacy. Here is the soft spot in Islam. The people of Islam are 95 per cent illiterate, and yet the first page of the Koran tells them to read.

In June 1949 we found the South Korean government extremely eager to prove its concern for the citizens. The United States government was working very hard to hold the friendship of the Koreans. The American Embassy paid for our lessons when we had them prepared, out of appropriations from our War Department. The President of South Korea told me that he would do everything in his power to promote our campaign because the people are eager for education. And the Minister of Education stood up before a large group at the Embassy and in a fiery speech said, "This is what the people want. I will move heaven and earth to give it to them."

We are not having trouble with governments, but we are having trouble with some missionaries. Too many fall into ruts, get overburdened with routine which bears little fruit, and are slow to adopt new ways of evangelism. Teach those missionaries our literacy techniques, and they will march straight into the hearts of the people and lead many to Christian faith.

Here is our strategy. In the non-Christian regions we have about 12,000,000 active, evangelical Christians, scattered among 1,200,-000,000 non-Christian illiterates. That is one Christian for every 100 non-Christian illiterates. We must train each of those 12,000,-000 Christians to teach one in his own home and win him. There are about 120,000 churches with an average of 100 members. We must organize those churches into a teaching, evangelizing army. The techniques we have worked out during the past few years must be taught to each church. It is like this:

Lessons are prepared and then printed in adequate quantities. Then to each church go enough lessons for each literate member to have a copy. On Sunday morning the missionary or literacy leader goes to the church and tells the members that each one is to teach and win one non-Christian neighbor at home. He asks each member prayerfully to write down the name of the neighbor he will undertake to teach. Then the method of teaching is demonstrated. We have made the lessons easy to teach; the teacher follows the text, and prays as he teaches.

He is taught how to testify for Christ while teaching. Thank God simple people can bear Christian witness as effectively as seminary graduates! Often the teaching and witnessing are so potent that after a few days a student will ask to be a Christian. One trained person can supervise such a congregational project.

When the first primer has been taught (in a week or two) students are brought to the church for a graduation ceremony. As they march forward to receive their diplomas, the officers of the church give them a hearty handshake. It is the first time these students ever were in that church. Then they start studying *The Story of Jesus*. When that is finished in any phonetic language—and most are phonetic—they can read the Gospels.

This sort of campaign can be repeated by the congregation several times a year. There is no reason why a church should not double its membership in 12 months. In many places the rate is now faster than that, as it was at Pentecost. I visited an area in India where 10,000 a year had been baptized for three consecutive years.

How can we organize and train 12,000,000 Christians in 120,-000 churches? Here is our proposal. Let us train 12,000 missionaries, one missionary for every 100 churches, so that he in turn may go out and train those churches. These 12,000 missionaries require careful training, for this is an art and its success depends upon the thoroughness with which it is taught. The Committee on World Literacy and Christian Literature will undertake to train the missionaries with denominational co-operation.

Let each mission board select the most efficient, evangelistic missionary in the denomination for us to train for a year. He must have a passion for his job. After he has finished his training, he will begin training the missionaries of his own group. In the most suitable center he will teach some as they return from abroad and the new missionaries before they go abroad. Some missionaries will get training at interdenominational centers (there are two schools now—the Kennedy School of Missions, Hartford, Connecticut, and Scarritt College, Nashville, Tennessee) ; others in denominational camps and schools. Centers are already being set up abroad to train on the field. The aim is not to let one missionary escape without this training.

I do not mean 12,000 *new* missionaries. America alone has about 15,000 in the field already. We can train them during their furloughs. All new ones may be instructed before they leave for the field. This program is well within our reach. It can begin right away and reach its maximum efficiency in five years. I propose a five-year plan of "teach and win one" in every mission field.

This does not mean that 12,000 missionaries should drop what they are now doing. It means that they should organize and direct this work in addition to what they are doing. It means that Christian literacy should have high priority for the next five years. Ordained evangelistic missionaries should make this their major method of evangelizing; wives of missionaries should be trained to organize and direct "each one teach and win one" churches; deaconesses and Bible women should be trained to use this more effective way of teaching; missionary teachers should be trained to organize their students into teaching bands; doctors and nurses should be trained to have patients in hospitals taught or teaching.

Every active missionary is influential in one or more national churches. In each he can direct and advise while it organizes to teach.

Literacy promises to multiply our efficiency in the major job of the Church, which is to win men to Jesus Christ.

What an adventure to train 12,000 missionaries who will train 12,000,000 Christians of many nations to teach and win 1,200,-000,000 non-Christian illiterates!

A second door opens: Christian nationals and missionaries must be trained to write simply and fascinatingly to meet the hungry minds of new readers, who can read only simple stories slowly. Nearly all the Christian literature now being produced is over their heads. It will be many years before they can read and understand what we have been printing.

When William Randolph Hearst employed a new reporter he would say: "If you ever use over 17 words in a sentence, I'll know why." Yet the Hearst readers were one notch above our new literates. Ten or a dozen words are enough for them. They read so slowly that they cannot hold long sentences in mind. They must read words which they already speak. This means that we must create a new simplified literature and a new body of writers to produce it.

The Communists have learned to do this and they are succeeding in an impressive way. In Calcutta I read a newspaper article by the Red leader of China, Mao Tse-tung. He said that China has an army of writers who go down among the laborers, peasants, soldiers and shopkeepers and study their language. They play on their passions and try to meet their needs.

In Korea I called the Christian writers together and told them that they must write simply like the Communists. The best of them said: "If we wrote that way, the educated people would despise us. Besides, we don't know how." In every language of Latin America and Asia we Christians speak and write above the masses, and in most languages the Bible is too difficult for the new literates to read.

So we face the truly colossal task of preparing writers for the 150,000,000 who have learned to read in the past 15 years, and the millions who are learning every year. Since certain governments have taken up literacy, the campaigns have got out of hand so far as printed literature is concerned. But we are not dismayed. Our strategy calls for the preparation of some of the 12,000 missionaries in the art of plain but fascinating journalism. We have such a course at Syracuse University, where missionaries and nationals are being taught.

We need a thorough two-year course for the real experts. Then we must have shorter courses in writing for every missionary and for many nationals. It seems an impossible task, but when we get Christians thoroughly aroused we shall have more than enough writers.

Britain is much more aroused about the literature problem than we are in America. Britain and America together have far and away the longest list of writers in all history. We have the experience, the presses, the paper, the brains, the money—more than half the world's wealth. We ought to hang our heads in shame if we permit the Communists to capture with ink the world from under our noses. There would be only one reason for it. They would be on the job while we remain half awake to this opportunity.

This is the time to wake up. I urge every church board to train the largest possible number of its missionaries each year, in clear, simple writing as well as reading. I plead that missionary schools, every one of them, institute these courses.

Then we must plan to send presses, to send thousands of tons of paper, to subsidize our books, to organize for distribution. This is going to cost us much more money than we now spend. How much?

If every Christian would add 50 cents a year to his benevolence budget for teaching people to read and for literature for the new literates, it would pay for the increased cost. This practical program should enlarge the interest and the giving of the Church. If world-minded Christian philanthropists realized the opportunity we have of teaching Christian democracy around the world, we should not lack funds to keep the process going. It is the greatest highway for the Church. It is also the most effective defense program against the desperate misery which endangers the peace of the world.

There is now a new reason why the churches should plunge into teaching and writing like giants and not like pygmies. We come now to the third fact. The United Nations on November 16, 1949, voted to send thousands of men and women with technical skills to needy areas. If the Church is there teaching the illiterates and furnishing simple literature, there will be a foundation for the new U.N. program. Our writers will be ready to rewrite the difficult textbooks of the agricultural experts and doctors and home-economics experts in the language of the masses. We shall have the presses there ready to publish the useful literature. We shall have bookstores there ready to sell it. All of it can be permeated by the Christian spirit.

Education helps bad men do more harm. Knowledge will not save the world. Only God can do that. So the very success of this tremendous effort to lift the world depends on sending out men with the love of Jesus Christ in their hearts. Hunt up Christian technicians, train them, offer them! If we do that, then literacy and simple literature and technical aid will all work hand in hand in one powerful force to save the world.

It is being said that this decade can be the greatest in history.

I believe that. What Christians decide is more fateful than the acts of the United Nations. It will be the greatest decade in history only if our world program has Christian character.

Nothing stands in our way save the lack of vision and consecration of our churches. Military preparations are not saving us because our real enemy is misery, hate and despair; guns only make these things worse. People want a program which can lead them to peace and freedom from fear. They are praying for leadership. We have it in us to decide issues which will reverberate for a thousand years.

God has thrown open a great door of opportunity. He calls Christians to dare like those at the first Pentecost. He calls Christians to bold, strong strides, to enormous new advance. He asks Christians to go forth to tell *good news* to all people of the world. He calls us to awaken and convert and educate our churches. We can have such a spiritual revival as never was seen in all history. No use saying "Never yet has it been that way." This is the century of the "never-yet." We never before had radios, airplanes, television, electric lights or atomic bombs. In the realm of science the impossible is happening. Frightened scientists are urging us to catch up spiritually with their awful inventions before we destroy ourselves. We too can have miracles of the "never-yet" if we are big enough, inspired enough, if we have faith like the men who founded the Church. We shall hear, not just 50,000 on New Guinea, but 1,000,000,000 illiterate non-Christians of Asia and Africa say, "We want Christ."

I speak for 1,000,000,000 illiterates who need our help. I am not afraid of the Communists. I'm afraid of nominal Christians who have neither fire nor vision—men who begin to see why this might be hard, or unprecedented, or premature if not properly surveyed, or too informal, or too big. The put-on-the-brakes type, the go-slow type alone can ruin the Christian program. O ye of little faith, keep your feet off the brake. We have nothing to fear but fear.

I tell you what we need to fear : *fear the way we are now,* for we aren't good enough, daring enough, far-visioned enough for this great hour.

With the atomic bomb hanging over our heads, millions want

to repent—are eager for something Christian to do for the world besides wringing their hands in helpless frustration. People are ready to follow courageous Christian leadership. The illiterate billion waits for them. It is the call of God!

The Decisive Encounter

By Norman Goodall

THE present generation is at one of the decisive turning points of history. True, it is always easy to use superlatives about one's own period. History tells of innumerable crises and revolutions which, seen in clearer perspective, have proved less crucial than their participants thought. But even if the long drama of our human story has more critical episodes to unfold than those in which our generation is involved, the significance of the present moment in history can scarcely be exaggerated.

There are two factors in the present situation which intensify this crisis character of our age. One lies in what might be called the power-consciousness of the generation. The other is to be seen in the revolutionary temper of the masses, especially those hitherto known as subject peoples. Out of either or both of these factors it is possible for events to happen which will mark the end of an age with a decisiveness not belonging to any previous transitions from one epoch to another. On the one hand, something as disastrous as annihilation is conceivable. On the other, there may follow transformations in the patterns of society and in ways of living which will constitute an entirely new era.

The two factors which we have named as intensifying the crisis in which we are involved are of peculiar concern to Christians. We have spoken of the power-consciousness of this generation. Of all religions, Christianity is the religion of power. Its "good news" includes such trumpet tones as "Ye shall receive power" . . . "It is your Father's good pleasure to give you the Kingdom" . . . "Knock, and it shall be opened unto you" . . . "Nothing shall be impossible unto you" . . . "All things are possible to him that believeth." Now there is a fundamental difference between the standpoint from which these invigorating notes proceed and the assumptions which lie behind much of the power-consciousness of our generation. On this crucial difference something more must be said later in this chapter. But there is at least one thing in common between the prevailing mood of our power-conscious generation and the emancipating force of Christian faith. It is the conviction that life is dynamic, not static; that events are malleable, not fate-bound; that we are meant to live creatively, not mechanically or stagnantly. In this conviction Christians have reason to feel deeply at home. To such a situation they have a word to say which contains more encouragement than rebuke, more confidence than despair.

Again, in the revolutionary mood of the masses today—whatever else may be contributing to it—there lies a conviction which belongs very closely to Christianity. It is that of the worth of the ordinary man—the peasant, the toiler, the serf—even though this ordinary man may have belonged immemorially to a subject people or a slave population. Running through all the earth today is a dangerous but exciting awareness of the creative possibilities that lie before the ordinary man in a universe which offers him power.

Of course these dynamic notions by no means express the whole of Christianity. Separated from the rest of the Christian religion they may, indeed, constitute a new and more disastrous paganism. On them may be erected a new idolatry with consequences which may plunge the whole world into darkness and savagery. Yet these same ideas—plus much else—belong essentially to Christian faith, and the fact that they have got abroad in the world today, in more widespread fashion than ever before, cannot be dissociated from what Christians have been saying and doing during the last few generations. There are three instruments, in particular, through which Christian agencies have contributed to the spread of these dynamic notions. It is worth recalling them and recognizing their potency.

The first is the instrument of Christian education, initiated and developed on an enormous scale through the world operations of the Christian Church. This is a day in which a good many fundamental questions are being raised about the methods and objectives of education, and for a long time these questions have been applied very searchingly to the educational activity of the Church. It is possible to argue at length about the content of the education which has been given, or about its appropriateness to the environment and surrounding culture. Challenging questions may even be asked about its continuing fidelity to the Christian presuppositions on which it is based. Yet none of these discussions alters the fact that the great instrument of education, launched in country after country by Christian forces, was fashioned in obedience to the Christian conviction that emancipation from ignorance, access to the means of enlightenment and self-development, were in Christ's name due to all sorts and conditions of men.

The second instrument is that of Christian medicine. "Medical missions" are commonly accepted as the most serviceable and least disputable activity of the Christian movement. Those Christians who are not yet awake to the deeper significance of the world Christian mission will give to "medical missions" their encouragement and support. Non-Christians who take exception to other aspects of the missionary enterprise will speak well of this service not only because of its humanitarian value but on the ground that it need not be confused with any dogmatic or ideological features of Christianity. But such an attitude is really too naïve. "Medical missions" constitute one of the most revolutionary instruments of Christianity in action. Christian medicine is a science built on an enormous religious presupposition, namely, that however degraded a human being may be, whatever the apparent value of some tiny, maimed bit of humanity, in Christ's name he deserves everything that knowledge and skill can bestow upon him for his good. Now this is not a presupposition which has lain behind all systems of healing, nor does it necessarily belong to modern medicine considered as a purely scientific exercise. As a matter of fact, in non-Christian lands where modern scientific methods are being increasingly acquired, there is often to be seen a fundamental difference in aim and even in method between those who engage in the work of healing on the basis of Christian convictions and those who do not. Seriously to contend that any poor specimen of humanity in any part of the world has a right, with divine sanction behind it, to the best service which the whole paraphernalia of modern scientific medicine can provide is to make a claim of enormous and revolutionary significance.

In a place called Bethel, near Bielefeldt in Westphalia, is a famous Colony of Mercy associated with the name of Friedrich von Bodelschwingh. Growing out of a powerful missionary vocation has been built up there through the years a remarkable network of educational and medical institutions directed to the care of epileptics and mentally deficients. In some ways the heart of the colony is best seen in a hospital set apart for babies and young children. At the entrance is a beautifully carved figure of the Good Shepherd carrying a lamb in His arms, and within the wards lie the most pitiful collection of little lambs imaginable. Some years ago a potential benefactor was being shown round the colony and, like all other visitors, he was chiefly moved by what he saw in the children's wards. A little later, having recovered emotionally, he said to the superintendent, "Tell me, how many of these children become sufficiently well to live a normal life?"

"About one in a hundred."

The visitor broke out impatiently: "It isn't worth it!"

"But," asked the superintendent, "suppose that one were your son?"

It is on this conception of sonship—but sonship of a heavenly Father—that the ministry of Christian medicine rests. To have let this notion loose in the earth is to have planted a revolutionary idea in the minds of the masses.

The third instrument is that of Christian preaching. Not a very revolutionary weapon, some would say. But what is here intended is not harmless exhortation or moralizing on themes which have lost their startling character through familiarity. We are thinking of preaching as proclamation—proclamation of the stupendous fact that the ordinary man matters so much to God that He would die for him. And we are recalling the effect of such proclamation on those whose ears have not become dulled by familiarity or a sense of unreality. Now it is true that in authentic Christian preaching the main emphasis is on the nature of the God who sets this value on man. Its center of gravity does not lie in some natural right of man to be so regarded. But this stooping of God toward man is man's uplifting. It is the beginning of his most powerful liberation. And some of the most potent movements in the world today have their origin in this revelation, whatever secondary factors and mundane agencies have since intervened. Christian revelation is the most dynamic starting point for social revolution. In this matter the world Christian mission has more to answer for and to follow up than is sometimes realized.

We have contended that three of the most powerful instruments of Christianity's outreach into the world have inevitably fostered a disturbing notion about the nature of man—especially about the creative possibilities of the ordinary man in a universe which offers him power. Here it has at once to be recognized that around a creative and redemptive idea which is fundamentally Christian, selfish and materialistic ambitions have gathered. In many of the revolutionary movements of today men are claiming rights regardless of duties. They are pursuing ends without reference to means. They are clamoring for a Kingdom, not that within it they may serve their rightful King, but on the assumption that they may enthrone themselves and do what they like with the resources of the Kingdom. If this course continues nothing but disaster can fall on us all. But it is possible to look on the most dangerously critical period in history with very different eyes if we know that the most dynamic idea within the ferment of our time is good, not bad, and that it is inseparable from the God who sent His Son into the world not to condemn the world but that the world through Him might be saved.

From this standpoint Christians today have a better reason than any atheistic revolutionaries for calling men to work and sacrifice as those who stand at the dawn of a new day. The prevailing tendency of the champions of Western Christendom to adopt a somber, defensive attitude, as those who, with the approach of nightfall, will maintain a grim loyalty to an age that is dying, is all wrong. Christians have greater authority than any others to be the heralds of a new age. They have the authentic word of encouragement and hope to share with the adolescent revolutionaries of the East. That word will carry its own searching correctives, but its keynote is "Lift up your heads, for your redemption draweth nigh!"

We have urged that the key to some of the most disturbing features of our time lies in the Christian conception of God and man. Christians can therefore approach one of the most decisive turning points in history with more confidence than fear; in hope, not in despair. It would, nevertheless, be a mistake to conclude from this that the course before us is easy, and that all that is required in our common Christian strategy is a more confident proclamation of a Gospel to which men will readily respond. Christian history and Christian experience warn us that the course of true love—even the love of God—never runs as smooth as this. Therefore, there is our further contention, namely, that at this present decisive turning point in history the battle is joined on the grand scale between Good and Evil, between the Christian revolution and all revolutionary forces whose basis is ultimately pagan. In order to realize how far-reaching and deep-seated this decisive encounter is, it will be well to recall a powerful element in the Christian Gospel which has its own searching significance for our day.

It is commonly assumed that the presence of Jesus brought the best out of men. It is less frequently remembered that His presence also brought the worst out of them. In the most glaring New Testament instances of this, what happened is to some extent disguised from modern readers because the encounter is presented in terms of demon possession and exorcism. When we read of demons reacting violently to Jesus, protesting against His presence or fuming at Him, we tend to dissociate the demons from the human being with whom Jesus was dealing. But, of course, in these instances Jesus was not confronted by a human being plus a crowd of demons. He was dealing with one man or one woman. We may call them split personalities, dual personalities, or individuals lacking integration; but the central, human feature of the situation consisted just of Jesus and another person. And—for the time being, at all events—that person was worse rather than better because Jesus was there. He really was bringing the worst out of them.

If it were proper to use the word science in reference to an age in which most of the word's modern connotations were unknown, we could say that this language about demons was the scientific terminology of the day. It was the explanation offered for maladjustment and consequent violent behavior. No doubt it was a consolation to all concerned—patients and relatives—that this sort of language lightened the burden of responsibility. The poor patient was not to be blamed. So today we explain some antisocial behavior by shifting responsibility onto a repressive father, a possessive mother, a strait-laced aunt, a careless nursemaid or a faithless lover. Or if the malady is not an individual one but a social phenomenon troubling the body politic, we trace its essential source to economic injustice, to capitalistic society, to imperialistic domination or to "the psychology of a suppressed people." We are not here making light of these explanations. There was a lot of truth in the old demon-possession theories; there may be more in our psychological and neurological explanations. And a Christian critique of society may convince us that the wholeness of corporate humanity cannot be achieved without radical economic and political reformation. Further, there is a point in all this kind of diagnosis where the theories which try to lift the burden of responsibility from the man or community that is acting demonically are trying to do something valid and wise. Nevertheless, there is also something in this attempt which springs from human weakness and has its dangers. We may recall how Shakespeare poured scorn on this tendency in *King Lear:*

> This is the excellent foppery of the world, that when we are sick in fortune—often the surfeit of our own behavior—we make guilty of our disasters the sun, the moon and the stars; as if we were villains by necessity, fools by heavenly compulsion; knaves, thieves and treachers, by spherical predominance; drunkards, liars and adulterers, by an enforced obedience of planetary influence; and all that we are evil in, by a divine thrusting on; an admirable evasion of whoremaster man, to lay his goatish disposition to the charge of a star!

In Shakespeare's day the astrologers were helping men to shift responsibility to the stars, just as they do today in India and other parts of the East, or among certain newspaper readers of the West whose sophistication has gone full circle and landed them in the primitive again.

The point is that whether the current terminology be that of demon possession, astrology, anthropology, psychology or sociology, there is a root of rebellion and violence in man which will make him less than amenable to rational counsel or even to good news addressed to his natural goodness. In fact, in some circumstances, to confront him with reasons or even with a demonstration of what is his good, will—for the time being at all events—

have far from good effect. In other words, as of old the presence of Jesus will bring the worst out of him.

The fact that the most vivid New Testament illustrations of this phenomenon belong to the pathological cases should not cause us to overlook the operation of the same tendency in much more "normal" people. It may be seen, for example, in the influence of Jesus on the most religious people of His time—or those commonly regarded as the most religious—the priests, the scribes and pharisees. It is not for us to write these off as humbugs. The tradition in which they stood was a very great tradition and the personal standards and achievements of many of them were exceedingly high. They represented the church before *the Church*—that Jewish church which antedates the Christian Church and which, though very different from it, was its genuine precursor. It is, of course, obvious from the Gospels that the presence of Jesus brought the very worst out of these men. In some ways it was a more awful worst than a poor maniac's foaming at the mouth. It was the perversion of something good; the more terrible because it left the victim tenaciously sure that he was right. At the most critical point of the encounter these men had no sense of need, no grace to ask deliverance from whatever was possessing them. With few exceptions they became more stubbornly and defiantly sure of themselves. And, again, this attitude was aggravated by the presence of Jesus.

The Gospels show us still another plane on which the same sort of thing happened. Here its implications are even more serious for those who have "accepted" Christ and are professing discipleship. At a critical moment in the fulfillment of His own mission on earth Jesus disclosed to His closest friends new depths in His own humility. He set His face toward a more costly selflessness and demonstrated His divinity by a more lowly acceptance of suffering. Yet in that moment the disciples began to dispute among themselves which of them was greatest. Just when Christ makes most clear His own repudiation of prestige and fame His most intimate friends display that self-seeking and jealousy which constitute the most unchristian blot on the fellowship of believers. A fresh disclosure of holiness provokes a virulent uprush of evil. Perhaps the final tragedy of Judas illustrates the same thing. At the decisive moment Jesus offered him the most unmistakable gesture of friendship. "And when He had dipped the sop He gave it to Judas Iscariot." This was a customary token of intimate trust and affection. Holiness made its final appeal to friendship. But Judas, "having received the sop, went immediately out; and it was night."

We have expounded at some length one of the profoundest and most persistent elements in the Gospels. If we overlook it, whether in our personal apprehension of Christianity or in our common Christian strategy, we are likely to go astray in our measure of the decisive encounter in which we are now involved. But if we remember it, we can look on the present situation—and especially the events of the last decade or so—with deeper spiritual discernment. We have been living through an era in which demonic forces have been surging up in country after country. Up to a point it has been possible to give a rational account of what has brought the most tumultuous events to pass. There was a time when liberally minded, sympathetic folk could understand and explain Hitlerism. They recalled the mood of Versailles; they remembered Germany's national bankruptcy and despair, and the rallying cry which spoke to this condition. But none of this liberal, sympathetic reasoning touched the real explanation of the vile thing which finally appeared. With even more sympathetic understanding we may look on many of the nationalist movements today. We can think of dispossessed masses justifiably clamoring for their rights. We can realize what it must mean to subject peoples to be coming into their own. As the first part of the chapter contends, we can even see in the ferment of which these movements are an expression the consequences of the dynamic ideas which have their origin in the Christian Gospel. Yet all this leaves unexplained the frenzy and violence which keep characterizing the movements.

The same must be said of that most formidable symptom of the revolutionary era—Communism. There is much in its origin and aims which calls for sympathy. Some people have even described it as a Christian heresy. (Though surely it is a little difficult to see how an ideology which disavows any belief in God can be a Christian something, even a heresy—except from the excessively tolerant standpoint of the schoolgirl who wrote that "the Devil in any other walk of life would have been a good man.") Yet not even the most rational and sympathetic interpretation of Communism gets anywhere near the meaning of that sinister, savage core in the movement which is a threat to the very ideals which have been incorporated in it.

Now the era which has been characterized by this kind of virulence is not one in which Christianity has been little known or even little practiced. It is one in which the Gospel has been more widely known than ever and its precepts more faithfully obeyed and by larger numbers of people than at any previous time in history. In parts of the world where the churches locally are troubled about declining numbers it is sometimes forgotten that, with the world taken as a whole, there are far more Christians and far more full churches than hitherto. Further—although no Christian can be complacent about this or fail to admit that much more ought to have been done—Christian principles have been applied to more fields of human endeavor than in earlier ages. Much of the world's impatience with the rate of social progress is itself a direct result of Christian teaching and Christian insights.

We are, therefore, confronted with this paradox. On the one hand, Christ has been more widely proclaimed and known than heretofore and His precepts have commanded increasing obedience. Yet, on the other hand, there has been a savage uprush of demonic forces just at those points where Christian insights have been most clear or the Christian heritage—as in prewar Europe—most rich. It is my contention that this paradox arises from the presence of Christ, not His absence. What we are witnessing—what we are involved in (for we cannot be merely onlookers)—is not an epoch in which Christianity is dead and done with, a paper thing of the past. It is one in which the decisive encounter is on between God as He is in Christ and the radical core of evil in man. To revert to the terminology of the New Testament, the demons have recognized Him and are making their frenzied protest: "What have we to do with thee, thou Jesus of Nazareth? Art thou come to destroy us? I know thee who thou art, the Holy One of God." The battle is joined. Here is a war even more significant than the first, second, or a threatened third World War. It is the decisive battle of the ages.

Now ultimately there can be only one outcome to this encounter.

To put it colloquially, Christ has been in this sort of situation before. God in Christ has already shown where the victory lies. Neither the violence of the demons, nor the stubborn self-righteousness of the scribes and Pharisees, nor the spiritual collapse of the first disciples, resulted in the defeat of God. These things led— shame on human nature!—to the Crucifixion of Christ, but there is no more victorious sign in the world than the Cross of Christ. Because of the victory already accomplished on Calvary a day will come when the kingdoms of this world shall become the Kingdom of our God and of His Christ. Whether God brings this conquest to its consummation in some swift climax of history and the end of the world, or whether He chooses to use this world order as the setting for successive epochs in His Kingdom, the issue is clear. In Christ He brings out the worst in order to deal with it for good and all, and this is what He will do with the worst that our generation is experiencing and perpetrating.

This does not mean, however, that we may adopt the attitude that all is well; this thing will work itself out; we can let the conflict pass us by while we quietly get on with our personal affairs. To begin with, Christians must take specially to heart the New Testament reminder that this stirring up of evil by the holiness of God occurs within religious as well as secular societies. One of the battlefields is in the hearts of the religiously minded. Professing Christians are not immune from the critical encounter. We must be on our guard lest, at such a time in history, the goodness of good men become cold and hard and Pharisaic. We must beware lest the Church lose its passion for the lives of men by becoming absorbed in ecclesiasticism. We must watch lest as Christians we grow grudging, churlish and self-righteous, adopting the attitude that all the wickedness lies in somebody else. Those whom Christ has blessed with His intimacy must shun dispute about status and prestige, even though the dispute be dignified by ecclesiastical or theological terms. For all these things were the sins which occasioned the Crucifixion and if they are committed again at such a time as this we shall be as culpable as our religious counterparts of old. Because the decisive encounter is on, all who profess and call themselves Christians must the more tremblingly and urgently watch and pray lest they enter into temptation. All other Christian

obedience starts at this lowly place. No other tactics will avail if
we fail here.

Secondly, it is imperative that all who have been given insight
into the nature of the battle now joined should regard themselves
as under orders. Primarily this is a very personal and individual
matter. The Christian movement cannot move except through persons who know themselves to be under orders from Christ and
whose character and service are subject daily to the discipline and
purification of His spirit. In the Christian warfare there is no escape from this most personal of all obligations and callings. "What
the Church should do" . . . "What Christianity has to offer" . . .
"What Christendom stands for"—all these things turn on there
being a church or an embodied Christianity operating through
countless individual loyalties. To stress this elementary fact is not
to retreat into an individualistic pietism. It is to get to the simple
and inescapable basis of every great movement which aims at enduring achievement. Sooner or later this test has to be met: Are
the aims, ideals, promises and professions of this movement being
vindicated at the point of local and individual fidelity? The more
revolutionary the movement, the more remorseless ultimately is
this test. In how many young movements today are the seeds of
decay already apparent at this point? How many brave new worlds
have collapsed because of this? For a single Christian to fail here
is to imperil the whole cause at the height of the decisive encounter between good and evil. There can be no larger Christian strategy without this as the sure foundation of all its operations.

In the third place, there is needed in this critical encounter such
a deployment of the Christian forces as will make possible, under
God, the concentration of the right kind of power at the most
strategic points. When we use such a word as "strategy" in relation to Christian service it must always be remembered that the
supreme command of the Christian forces lies in other than human
hands. The total situation is one that can be apprehended by God
alone, and through the operation of His spirit there is a wiser than
human direction of the manifold agencies of His purpose. Further,
Christian strategy does not imply that God has developed His
directive responsibility on a single authoritative center within
His visible Church. Nor is it held to be desirable or possible for a

high command composed of church statesmen to determine the course which the Christian movement should follow. "Where the Spirit of the Lord is, there is liberty." "There are diversities of gifts . . . there are differences of administrations." "It is God which worketh in you both to will and to do of his good pleasure." But within the fellowship and freedom of Christian faith a common sense of direction is obtainable. Common convictions can be reached as to the points of greatest need and opportunity; common concerns can find expression and lead to co-ordinated action. Among the various instruments through which this unity of purpose is becoming apparent are the International Missionary Council and the World Council of Churches. Through the period which has brought these agencies into existence there has been a deepening consensus of judgment among Christian leaders throughout the world as to priorities in planning and action, and it is against the background of this experience that we speak of the strategic deployment of the Christian forces in the present decisive encounter.

From this standpoint there is manifest need for a concentration of Christian resources at the points where the revolutionary ferment of our time is most in evidence. We have already contended that the world Christian mission has been instrumental, however indirectly, in disseminating that dynamic idea of which many of the revolutionary movements of today are a partial, if sometimes distorted, expression. This means that within the Christian movement there is a special capacity for understanding why men are clamoring for freedom and opportunity and to what end Christ would make them free. It means also that in Christian agencies there lies particular responsibility for not leaving their own creative but disturbing work unfinished. There is a wise prayer which petitions God "for the completion of our conversion." This may be applicable to a good many situations, but to none does it belong more seriously than to our adolescent apprehension of Christian freedom and our perception of the fullness of life for which God has made and redeemed us. Not to go on from this eager perception to a mature—and finally more satisfying—experience of the relation of responsibility to freedom, of integrity to independence and of self-sacrifice to fulfillment, is to suffer arrested development. This is the spiritual peril today which attends many of the surging aspirations of the East or of Africa—even those aspirations which are in part an expression of a genuinely Christian insight. It is far from easy to proclaim and impart these things to people in a revolutionary mood, to embody them in wise educational policies and to draw out their implications for social and personal behavior. But the task of helping men, in the light of such insights, to understand the times in which they live and to act on the basis of a distinctively Christian judgment within their revolutionary ferment is one of the foremost tasks within our common Christian strategy today.

Happily this task has not to be regarded solely in terms of a responsibility of the West toward the East. To do this would be to ignore one of the greatest factors in the Christian scene today—the existence of the so-called younger churches. (The term is becoming increasingly inappropriate for Christian communities that have been, or are being, matured through testing and persecution.) This attitude would also imply oversimplification of the nature of our contemporary revolution, for although the ferment is most in evidence in the reawakening East or in the restlessness of subject peoples, the West is no less the arena in which traditional patterns of society and traditional standards of behavior are being challenged and subject to reformation. At the meeting of the International Missionary Council at Whitby, Canada, in 1947 the phrase "Partners in Obedience" was coined to describe the relations between younger and older churches, and it is on this basis that the strategy of concentration on the most critical areas in the world needs to be worked out, as has been indicated in previous chapters.

In the concentration of resources at points of special need there are certain constantly reiterated calls which lay a special obligation on the West. A major one concerns the provision of more adequate theological equipment for Christian leadership. It has long been recognized that in this there has been a lamentable failure in the Christian strategy of the past. The meeting of the International Missionary Council at Madras in 1938 reported that "almost all the younger churches are dissatisfied with the present system of training for the ministry and with its results" : and this world meeting formally declared that "the present condition of theological education is one of the greatest weaknesses of the whole Christian enterprise." Something has been done since 1938 (within the very severe limits imposed by a period including the second World War), but progress is not sufficient to call for a variation of the 1938 verdict. In 1949 representatives of the churches of East Asia, assembled in Bangkok, and those of Latin America in Buenos Aires set forth some of the more urgent tasks which lie before them. While the main emphasis of the conferences was on the evangelistic calling of the Church, it is impressive to note how often attention was drawn to the need for that fundamental Christian thinking which it is the task of theological colleges to stimulate and nurture. If the younger churches are to outthink Communism and other dynamic anti-Christian forces and to rethink the meaning of their own cultural heritage, such thinking must be on the basis of a sound grasp of the essential content of Christian faith. Both the front-line task of evangelism and the continuous pastoral service of the Church depend ultimately on a ministry well nurtured theologically. To go on leaving the younger churches impoverished in this vital particular is a strategic failure of the first order. A little reflection on the number of theological teachers engaged in training the whole-time ministry for the churches of the United States or Great Britain will disclose an enormous disparity between the wealth of the West and the poverty of the East, the South and other areas. Most urgent strategic considerations demand a redeployment of these resources.

This pressing need calling for a strategic concentration of resources could be multiplied almost indefinitely. There is the crucial need for literacy among millions. There is dire need for Christian literature, including much more adequate distribution of that charter of Christian faith—the Bible. It is a sobering fact that even the basic textbook of Christians is inaccessible to millions of those who most need it. A year or two ago it was discovered, even in such a country as Ceylon, that a group of young church members had been waiting for four years to secure copies of the Bible in their own vernacular; it had gone out of print during the war and was not yet in circulation again. More recently a visitor to New Guinea was about to address a congregation of Papuans through an interpreter. Before the service he was asked what Scripture reading he would like and he chose the second chapter of Ephesians. "I'm sorry," said the interpreter, "I can't read that to the congregation. The

Epistle to the Ephesians hasn't yet been translated into the language of this tribe." It is worth dwelling on what a deprivation of this sort must mean to a young Christian community. Soon after the war it was estimated that the demand for copies of the Scriptures—those already translated—exceeded the supply by some 10,-000,000. The United Bible Societies are vigorously endeavoring to meet the situation, but they are still awaiting adequate resources to supply the total need.

There is also the vital business of training lay leadership—a necessity everywhere but a matter of life-and-death urgency to the churches in most of Asia and Africa, where it is impossible to envisage a day when a whole-time paid ministry for every local congregation will be economically possible. (To this consideration there is now added the fact that in the new pattern of society being shaped in China it may be legally and socially impossible for a whole-time "professional" ministry to receive support from the community. Whether this special factor operates for a long or short period, the fact that it has now to be reckoned with only intensifies a need which has long been recognized as urgent on other grounds.) Again, there is the need to develop special techniques for presenting the Christian faith to particular groups or situations —for example, in the mass societies of the great urban centers or in the vast rural areas which still constitute the foundation of Asiatic civilization. On all these and other allied questions there is a growing understanding on the part of the churches of the West of the broad lines of policy which should be pursued.

This understanding has been reached and is being furthered through the closest possible consultation with the younger churches. At a number of points these broad agreements are being implemented in united action, so that the gifts and resources of one part of the Church may be given maximum effect within the whole range of the Church's ministry. As already emphasized, this process is not regarded within the non-Roman churches as one which should—or could, with real effectiveness—be ordered or carried out through a highly centralized organization. A common strategy can only be the result of voluntary agreement based on mutual confidence. It has to grow out of convictions arrived at within the free association of all the churches concerned. But although much more has to be achieved along this line, there is taking place more united action based on a commonly agreed strategy than is generally realized. The major weakness is in the matter of *tempo*. United Christian action in such matters as we have illustrated has not yet shown itself capable of outstripping the speed at which other forces are moving. The new impetus will come only when there is better knowledge and deeper conviction about the nature of the Church's world mission today.

There are two needs which spring from something deeper than any strategic considerations.

The first is the need for greater boldness in experiment in what may be called "frontier service." By this we mean service at the point where the margin between things Christian and non-Christian is most clearly in evidence. It is service at the point of difference between the Church and the world; it is outthrusting service into any unchristian situation. In the pioneer days of the world Christian mission—days not yet ended or even begun, still, in some parts of the world—this "frontier service" possessed the clear and vivid characteristic of being service across a geographical boundary. The missionary very definitely *went out* from a church, a culture, a way of life which in general possessed certain characteristically Christian features and *went into* a non-Christian society, culture and way of life. There, with infinite patience as well as boldness, he lived experimentally and with some measure of creative ingenuity. In varying degrees these "ambassadors" were conscious that they were not merely single units operating apart from the total movement which had sent them forth. There were the churches and the total life of Christendom behind them; but, in the nature of the case, these missionaries were compelled—as individuals or as a group—to think afresh, to take risks and fashion for themselves those ways of creative ministry which would best make clear the meaning of the Christian faith in a particular, local situation. The great impetus which the modern missionary movement assumed in the nineteenth century found its instrument through thousands of ordinary men and women who, conscious of this thrusting forth of the Spirit, lived boldly and experimentally on the "frontiers."

Although the "mission fields," in the traditional use of the term, are still the scene of this kind of frontier service, great changes have, of course, taken place in the total situation. The success of the Christian movement has resulted in those younger churches which now need, from their Western "partners," much service of a kind which no longer possesses the more vivid and obvious "frontier" characteristics. The service is not, on this account, any less important or imperative. From within the younger churches themselves there is need for a new dynamic by those who will break new ground and take new initiatives in thought and action. At the same time it has become abundantly clear of late years that the critical "frontiers" between the Church and the world, between the Kingdom of God and the unredeemed life of man, cannot be charted in geographical terms only. They cut across life in the West as well as the East. They run across all areas of the world and all sections of society. They run into the life of the Church itself. What is needed is a new movement of "frontiersmen" who, from older and younger churches alike, will make their creative impact in the "mission fields" of industry and economics, politics and the arts, and in every area of human relationships. Such a movement can scarcely be organized, though as it comes to birth it will create its own instruments for ordered action—as it did in certain Christian resistance movements during the war and as it is beginning to do in various community experiments or in new types of Christian ministry today. The essential need is for Christian men and women who, with the Christian faith and the Christian fellowship as the point from which they go forth, will enter all occupations, trades, professions and vocations, determined by the grace of God to make known in word and service the saving power of God.

The other and final need of which we speak is one which underlies everything else that has been said in this book and especially the central argument of this chapter. The decisive encounter which is now upon us is no local skirmish between human forces. Its nature is not to be seen even in that larger alignment of visible forces which is now taking place and which may sooner or later precipitate another world war. The encounter is deeper and even more serious than this. As we have already described it, it is the decisive encounter between God as He is in Christ and the radical core of evil in man. If we choose to replace the New Testament language about demons and the need for their exorcism by new categories, we shall be heading for disaster if we behave as though the essential issue has become less serious than it was in New Testament times. One and all, we are caught up into a spiritual encounter and we can become participants in the victory of God only through the forces of the Spirit. No massing of brute force—even with the aid of the vastest possible stockpile of atomic weapons— will cope finally with the problem of human violence. Demons, however their name is paraphrased, cannot be dealt with by reason, even the reason that is embodied in legislation and international agreements. The self-righteousness which resists Christ's most searching demands cannot be argued into goodness. There is no medicine for frenzy save love. And by love we mean not a sentimental notion or an amiable disposition but a spiritual quality that is of the essence of God Himself, the power that controls the stars in their courses and holds within itself the meaning and purpose of all other power. Every phase of our Christian calling and obedience turns on our receptivity to this, the ultimate power, made accessible to us by Jesus Christ.

During the early months of the war a visitor to the South Seas found himself the guest of a small island community. Although not the scene of that unqualified, idyllic happiness which romanticists —including Christian ones—enjoy describing, the life of the whole community bore authentic marks of Christian achievement and the Church was central to the interests of the people. It happened that, at the time, the head chief of the island was ill, so the visitor called on him to offer greetings from the churches of the West. He began by commiserating with the chief in his sickness, but the tables were soon turned when the patient offered his condolences in the malady which had befallen Europe. He recalled how, not more than 50 years earlier, his island had been a scene of paganism, discords and often savage strife from which Christian faith had since brought redemption. "Do you think it would now help," the head chief added, "if we sent a mission to Europe?"

The question may have been a little naïve. It may have ignored the complexities of history, oversimplified the situation in the West, and to some extent idealized what had been accomplished in the South Seas. Nevertheless the shaft went home. It was a reminder of those tragic ironies of history which spring from the tragic sinfulness of man. It pointed to a reality and a need in regard to the Christian mission which are becoming increasingly clear—that the Christian movement is not primarily a movement from continent to continent; it is the outreaching and going forth of Christian men and women, from within the fellowship of the Ecumenical Church, into every unredeemed situation. And, most of all, the Christian movement comprises proclamation and testimony concerning the power of God which can change situations and even the hearts of men. The Christian Church proclaims a Gospel of power. It testifies to the forces of the Spirit. It summons men to those obediences through which God will again make Himself known in Spirit and in power.

The Church calls men and women to no more urgent obedience than worship. It can frame no wiser or more assuredly victorious strategy than prayer. No man-made restrictions or man-devised punishments can hinder this. No iron, bamboo or any other curtain can divide from one another those who pray. At the last, it will be through the obedience of the Church, the fellowship of the Spirit, that God's way will be known in the earth, His saving health among all nations.

THE
AUTHORS

CHARLES TUDOR LEBER   ROSWELL P. BARNES

W. A. VISSER 't HOOFT   GLORA M. WYSNER

EMORY ROSS

CHARLES W. RANSON

THODORE F. ROMIG

TAMAKI UEMURA

RAJAH B. MANIKAM   W. STANLEY RYCROFT

FRANK C. LAUBACH   NORMAN GOODALL

The Authors

Charles Tudor Leber is a secretary of the Board of Foreign Missions of the Presbyterian Church in the U.S.A. and chairman of its Administrative Committee. He is Chairman of the Executive Board of the Division of Foreign Missions of the National Council of the Churches of Christ in the U.S.A. By virtue of his position with the Division of Foreign Missions, he is a vice-president of the National Council. He is a member of the Department of International Justice and Goodwill, of the Department of Church World Service and chairman of the World Literacy and Christian Literature Committee of the National Council. He is a member of the Ad-Interim Committee of the International Missionary Council. Dr. Leber was born in Baltimore in 1898. Graduated from Johns Hopkins University in 1920 and Princeton Theological Seminary in 1923, he held pastorates in Trenton, Baltimore and Scranton. He received the degree of Doctor of Divinity from Washington and Jefferson College. Entering the general work of the Church in 1936, he has since traveled in some 60 countries of the world in behalf of the Christian world mission and overseas interchurch service. Dr. Leber is author of *The Unconquerable; The Church Must Win; Is God in There?*

Roswell P. Barnes is secretary of the Division of Christian Life and Work of the National Council of Churches. For ten years he was associate general secretary of the Federal Council of Churches, having joined its staff in 1936 as associate secretary of the Department of International Justice and Goodwill. Born in 1901 at Council Bluffs, Iowa, he was graduated in 1924 from Lafayette College, after which he took graduate work at Columbia University and Union Theological Seminary in New York. After teaching at Blair Academy and Macalister College, he became minister of the University Heights Presbyterian Church in New York. World War II found Dr. Barnes actively engaged as a member of the Ecumenical Commission for Chaplaincy Service to Prisoners of

War and as secretary of the Commission on Aliens and Prisoners of War. He was a member of the Church Committee for Overseas Relief and Reconstruction, the Commission on a Just and Durable Peace, the Christian Commission for Camp and Defense Communities, and the Religious Advisory Section of the Joint Army and Navy Committee on Health, Welfare and Recreation. In 1949 Dr. Barnes went to Germany as visiting expert to the Secretary of the Army to study the program of education and cultural relations of the Office of Military Government. He surveyed the effects of the military-government program on the political and social attitudes of the German people and the needs of refugees. He has been active in the World Council of Churches. Dr. Barnes is the author of *A Christian Imperative*. He is a member of Phi Beta Kappa. Lafayette College awarded him the degree of Master of Arts in 1926 and the degree of Doctor of Divinity in 1942.

Willem Adolf Visser 't Hooft is general secretary of the World Council of Churches. From 1931 to 1938 he was general secretary of the World's Student Christian Federation; prior to that, for seven years he was secretary of the World's Alliance of Young Men's Christian Associations. He was ordained to the ministry of the Reformed Church, Geneva, in 1936 and admitted to the pastorate of the Netherlands Reformed Church in 1949. In 1928 he received the theological doctorate from Leyden University. In 1939 he was recipient of the degree of Doctor of Divinity from Aberdeen University, Scotland. The Theological Faculty of Budapest, Hungary, made him Honorary Professor in 1946 and Princeton University honored him with the degree of Doctor of Divinity in 1950. Dr. Visser 't Hooft is an honorary member of the British and Foreign Bible Society and of the American Bible Society. He has been awarded the Medal of Gratitude by the Netherlands Government and is a Knight in the Order of the Dutch Lion. He has attended practically every ecumenical meeting since 1925 and has traveled all over the world many times. He is author of *The Background of the Social Gospel in America; Anglocatholicism and Orthodoxy; None Other Gods; The Church and Its Function in Society; The Wretchedness and Greatness of the Church; The Struggle of the Dutch Church; The World Council of Churches,*

Its Nature and Its Limits; Rembrandt et la Bible; The Kingship of Christ. Dr. Visser 't Hooft is editor of *The Ecumenical Review.*

Glora M. Wysner is a secretary of the International Missionary Council, to which post, in the New York office, she was appointed in 1949, having served since 1942 as a secretary of the Foreign Missions Conference of North America. She was born in Anderson, Indiana. After four years as a teacher in the public schools of Mt. Vernon, Ohio, and three years as a social worker in Cleveland, Ohio, from 1927 to 1939, she served as a missionary of the American Methodist Church in Algeria. She holds the degree of Bachelor of Arts from Ohio University and Master of Social Science from Western Reserve University. In 1942 she received the degree of Doctor of Philosophy from the Hartford Seminary Foundation. Dr. Wysner was ordained a minister of the Methodist Church in 1935. As a secretary of the International Missionary Council, and previously as a secretary of the Foreign Missions Conference, Dr. Wysner has surveyed and counseled in the work of churches and missions through extensive travel in Algeria, Tunisia, Egypt, Syria, Lebanon, Iraq, Turkey, North Sudan, Kuwait, Bahrain, Iran, Hashimite Kingdom of Jordan and Palestine. She attended the Near East Christian Council meeting in 1949 in Beirut, Lebanon, and the World Council of Churches Commission on the Life and Work of Women in the Church in Geneva, Switzerland, as consultant from the International Missionary Council, in 1950. She is the author of *The Kabyle People* and *Near East Panorama.*

Emory Ross is secretary of the Africa Committee of the Division of Foreign Missions of the National Council of Churches. Previously he served as general secretary of the American Leprosy Missions, Inc., and later as executive secretary of the Foreign Missions Conference of North America. Before that, for 20 years he was a missionary to Africa under the Disciples of Christ, at posts in Liberia and the Congo. He was born in Kendallville, Indiana, in 1887. He received his Bachelor of Arts degree and later the degree of Doctor of Divinity from Eureka College. He did graduate work at the University of Chicago and the University of Wisconsin. Dr. Ross has traveled extensively and often in Britain, Portugal, Belgium and France in conferences on African matters, religious liberty and other questions connected with the world mission of the Church. He is a life fellow of the Royal Geographical Society and a life member of the Royal African Society, both of London; and a fellow of the American Geographical Society, New York. He was awarded the Chevalier de l'Ordre du Lion by the Belgian government. More recently he was elected president of the American Leprosy Missions, Inc., trustee of the Liberian Foundation; member of the International Institute of Political and Social Science, Brussels; president of the Board of Trustees of the Phelps-Stokes Fund; member of the Executive Council of the International African Institute, London; Director of the Liberia Company. Dr. Ross is author of *Out of Africa*.

Charles W. Ranson is general secretary of the International Missionary Council, of which, for a brief period, he was research secretary, having come to the Council in 1946 from missionary service in India. In 1929, under the Methodist Missionary Society of London, Mr. Ranson was appointed to South India, where he served until 1943 in educational and evangelistic work in Madras. In 1942 he held the posts of chaplain jointly to St. Marks Church, Simla, and St. Andrews (Church of Scotland), Simla, and Acting Chaplain to His Excellency the Marquis of Linlithgow, Viceroy and Governor-General of India. From 1943 to 1945 Mr. Ranson was a secretary of the National Christian Council of India, Burma and Ceylon. He was born in Ballyclare, Ireland, in 1903. He attended Methodist College, Belfast; Oriel College, Oxford (Frere Exhibitioner, Oxford University); Edgehill Theological College, Belfast. He attained Bachelor of Letters (Oxford University). Mr. Ranson is a fellow of the Royal Economic Society, London; member of the Royal Institute of International Affairs, London; a member of the Church's Commission on International Affairs. He visited Germany in 1936 with a group of churchmen and scholars from Great Britain, brought together by Archbishop Temple and Lord Lindsay for conversations with leading representatives of the National Socialistic Party. He attended the Amsterdam Assembly of the World Council of Churches and the meeting of the Central Committee of the World Council of Churches at Chichester, 1949, and

Toronto, 1950. In 1949-1950 Mr. Ranson made a journey around the world in connection with his attendance at the Eastern Asia Christian Conference at Bangkok. He is the author of *A City in Transition; The Things that Abide; The Christian Minister in India; Renewal and Advance.*

Theodore F. Romig is associate professor of Christian Missions at McCormick Seminary in Chicago, to which post he was appointed in 1950. Previously Mr. Romig served as a missionary of the Presbyterian Church, U.S.A., in China, where he was born of missionary parents in 1909. After graduating from the College of Wooster in 1931 and from McCormick Seminary in 1934, Mr. Romig returned to China that same year. He was stationed at Hengyang, Hunan Province, where his field included seven counties with an area of 10,000 square miles and a population of 4,000,-000 people. During the war years he traveled 8,000 miles through the interior of China, escorting medical and personal supplies for the hospitals and missionaries in Hunan Province. After service in Communist China in 1945 Mr. Romig returned to the United States to become visiting professor of missions at McCormick Seminary. He went back to China in 1947 and was stationed in Nanking. After his return to the United States in 1949 he was assigned to special services with the International Missionary Council. Mr. Romig is author of *What of the Church in China?*

Tamaki Uemura is minister of the Kashiwagi Church of Tokyo, president of the Japanese National Y.W.C.A. and a National Public Safety Commissioner of Japan. She is also vice-president of the World Y.W.C.A. She was born in Tokyo in 1890. After attending Joshi Gakuin in Tokyo, she studied abroad at Wellesley College (U.S.A.), New College (Edinburgh) and Divinity Hall of Edinburgh University. From Wellesley she received her Bachelor of Arts degree in 1915, from Edinburgh in 1929 her Bachelor of Divinity, and in 1947 the College of Wooster (Ohio) gave her the honorary degree of Doctor of Laws. Dr. Uemura is an ordained minister of the Nippon Christo Kyokwai and founded the Kashiwagi Church, of which she is now minister. In addition to her church work she is a much sought-after public speaker and lecturer and influential Japanese national-affairs leader, as well as a world traveler who has attended many significant ecumenical gatherings. She was the first Japanese civilian to enter the United States following World War II. She is the editor of three symposia: *Why I Believe in God; What I Think of Christ; Christianity and Society.*

Rajah B. Manikam is joint secretary for East Asia of the International Missionary Council and the World Council of Churches, having come to this newly created office from the secretaryship of the National Christian Council of India. He was born in India in 1897. He is a graduate of Madras Christian College. Later he studied in America at the Mount Airy Seminary, Philadelphia, and Teachers College, Columbia University. He holds the degrees of Doctor of Philosophy from Columbia University and Doctor of Divinity from Knox College, Toronto University. Dr. Manikam was for a time vice-principal of Andhra Christian College, Guntur, India. He attended the Madras meeting of the International Missionary Council in 1938, was a delegate to the Whitby Conference of the International Missionary Council in 1947, the Amsterdam Assembly of the World Council of Churches in 1948 and the Toronto-Whitby meetings of these councils in July 1950. He was chairman of the Joint Commission on Eastern Asia of the International Missionary Council and the World Council of Churches and served as chairman of the Eastern Asia Christian Conference in Bangkok, December 1949. In October 1950 Dr. Manikam was ordained into the ministry of the Tamil Evangelical Lutheran Church at an impressive ecumenical service held at All Saints Cathedral, Nagpur.

W. Stanley Rycroft is a secretary of the Board of Foreign Missions of the Presbyterian Church in the U.S.A. with the portfolio for Latin America. He came to this post in 1950, after serving for ten years as executive of the Committee on Co-operation in Latin America now of the National Council of Churches, being now chairman. He was born in Formby, England, in 1899. He was an officer pilot in the Royal Air Force during World War I, twice shot down in action. He is the recipient of the degree of Bachelor of Commercial Science from Liverpool University, the

THE AUTHORS 329

Licentiate degree from the London College of Preceptors, and the degrees of Bachelor of Arts and Doctor of Philosophy from San Marcos University in Lima, Peru. He served in Peru as an educational missionary under the Free Church of Scotland and as vice-principal of the Anglo-Peruvian College in Lima. He has traveled through Europe and India and repeatedly and extensively in Latin America. He was a delegate to the International Missionary Conference at Madras and the Latin American Evangelical Conference in Buenos Aires, and was a consultant on Latin America at the Amsterdam Assembly of the World Council of Churches. He is the author of *On This Foundation* and editor and co-author of *Indians of the High Andes.*

Frank C. Laubach is consultant and special representative of the World Literacy and Christian Literature Committee of the Division of Foreign Missions of the National Council of Churches. In this capacity he has served for 15 years, after 20 years in the Philippines as a missionary of the Congregational Church of the United States. Born in Benton, Pennsylvania, in 1884, he received his higher education at Princeton and Columbia universities, receiving the degree of Doctor of Philosophy at the former. Dr. Laubach is internationally known as "The Apostle of Literacy." He has helped governments and Christian missions in 61 countries to set up campaigns against illiteracy. By his literary method and modifications influenced by his method it is estimated that approximately 50,000,000 people have learned to read in 206 of the world's languages. In 1946 he assisted the United Nations Educational, Cultural and Scientific Organization to prepare recommendations for a world plan of fundamental education. Dr. Laubach is the author of *Toward a Literate World; The Silent Billion Speak; Teaching the World to Read; The Streamlined English Series,* including the widely read *The Story of Jesus.*

Norman Goodall is a secretary of the International Missionary Council. He was appointed to this post, in the London office, in 1944 after eight years of service as secretary of the London Missionary Society for India and the South Pacific. He was born in Birmingham, England, in 1896. After business, military and government experience, in 1919 he entered Mansfield College, Oxford, from which he holds the degrees of Master of Arts and Doctor of Philosophy. In 1922 he was ordained into the Congregational ministry and from then until 1936 served Congregational churches in London and Herts. Dr. Goodall is a member of the Council of Mansfield College, Oxford; sometime chairman of the India Committee, Conference of British Missionary Societies; he was chairman of the West Central Africa Conference at Leopoldville in 1946. He has traveled widely in India, Burma, Ceylon, Malaya, New Guinea, Australia, New Zealand, the Middle East, Africa, South America and North America. He is author of *Exploring the Library; With All Thy Mind; Pacific Pilgrimage; One Man's Testimony*. He is editor of the *International Review of Missions*.

Bibliography

WE PLACE here a covering ecumenical booklist. Obviously it is suggestive rather than comprehensive. For most readers a modern library is available covering all areas mentioned in this volume. For those who need access to a library which specializes in the field of the world Christian movement the Missionary Research Library, conducted jointly by the Division of Foreign Missions of the National Council of Churches and Union Theological Seminary located at Union Seminary, 3041 Broadway, New York 27, N.Y., is ready to be of service by mail or on your personal visit. R. Pierce Beaver, Ph.D., is librarian. He has been of major assistance in the preparation of this list. We believe the following books and periodicals, which may be borrowed from the Missionary Research Library or purchased elsewhere, will be of particular interest to those who desire to proceed further with this story of world Christian faith.

Books by the contributors are indicated at the close of each biographical sketch in *The Authors* section.

Chapter I: *What Too Many People Don't Know*
Anderson, W. K., ed. *Christian World Mission*. Nashville, Commission on Ministerial Training of the Methodist Church, 1946. (A good symposium on the historical background and panorama after World War II.)
Bates, M. S. *Religious Liberty: An Inquiry*. New York, International Missionary Council, 1945. (A masterly survey of an important issue.)
Davis, J. M. *New Buildings on Old Foundations*. New York, International Missionary Council, 1946. (An important study of the cultural and economic base of the younger churches.)
Fleming, D. J. *Bringing Our World Together*. New York, Charles Scribner's Sons, 1945. (The Christian contribution to world community.)
Grubb, K. G., and E. J. Bingle, eds. *World Christian Handbook*. London, World Dominion Press, 1949. (The most recent survey volume on the Protestant world mission; includes survey articles on regions and countries; statistics for 1949 on the Christian community and staff; and a directory of missionary and ecumenical agencies.)
Hume, E. H. *Doctors Courageous*. New York, Harper & Brothers, 1950. (The story of the contribution of medical missionary work.)

Latourette, K. S. *A History of the Expansion of Christianity*, Volumes I-VII. New York, Harper & Brothers, 1937-1945. (A carefully documented, comprehensive survey of the spread of the Christian movement from the first century through 1944.)

———. *The Emergence of World Christian Community*. New Haven, Yale University Press, 1949. (Progress in world-wide Christian unity.)

Parker, J. I., ed. *Interpretative Statistical Survey of the World Mission of the Christian Church*. New York, International Missionary Council, 1938. (The latest comprehensive statistical survey of the Protestant world mission; the figures of 1936, assembled 1937; still extremely useful; includes interpretative chapters.)

Phillips, G. E. *The Gospel in the World*. London, Gerald Duckworth & Co., 1939. (An excellent introduction to the principles of the world Christian mission.)

Soper, E. D. *Philosophy of the Christian World Mission*. New York, Abingdon-Cokesbury Press, 1943. (A good general introduction.)

Van Dusen, H. P. *World Christianity*. New York, Abingdon-Cokesbury Press, 1947. (The rise of the ecumenical movement broadly interpreted.)

Wiser, W. H. and C. V. *For All of Life*. New York, Friendship Press, 1943. (The impact of Christianity through modern missionary ministry upon individual and communal life.)

The World Mission of the Church. New York, International Missionary Council, 1939. (The Report of the Madras Conference in 1938.)

Chapter II: *The Strength of the Nation*

Blanshard, Paul. *American Freedom and Catholic Power*. Boston, Beacon Press, 1949. (A study in freedom and power.)

Bower, W. C., and P. R. Hayward. *Protestantism Faces Its Educational Task Together*. Appleton, Wisconsin, C. C. Nelson, 1949. (The story of 25 years of achievement through the program of the International Council of Religious Education.)

For a Christian World. New York, Home Missions Council of North America, 1950. (The findings and seminar papers of the National Congress on Home Missions, Columbus, Ohio, January 24-27, 1950; the home-missions agencies consider their total evangelistic task.)

Hall, C. P. *The Churches Deal with Economics*. New York, Department of the Churches and Economic Life of the Federal Council of Churches, n.d. (A pamphlet introduction.)

Hutchison, J. A. *We Are Not Divided*. New York, Round Table, 1941. (The story of the Federal Council of Churches.)

Latourette, K. S. *Missions and the American Mind*. Indianapolis, National Foundation Press, 1949. (The importance of the missionary factor in shaping the American outlook.)

Morse, H. N. *Again Pioneers.* New York, Friendship Press, 1949.
(A program and strategy to achieve a Christian nation.)
One World in Christ: A Program of Advance in Foreign Missions.
New York, Foreign Missions Conference of North America, 1948.
(A large pamphlet presented to the Foreign Missions Assembly
at Columbus, Ohio, October 6-8, 1948; setting forth a co-ordi-
nated plan of advance for co-operating missions and representing
"North America's share in a world enterprise.")
Van Kirk, W. W. *A Christian Global Strategy.* New York, Willett,
Clark & Company, 1945. (A clear look at the place and oppor-
tunities of the Christian Church.)

Chapter III : *Europe—Survival or Renewal?*
Beloff, Max. *The Foreign Policy of Soviet Russia, 1929-1941.* New
York, Oxford University Press, 1949. (An adequate outline.)
Bennett, J. C. *Christianity and Communism.* New York, Association
Press, 1948. (An admirable introduction to the decisive issues in
the conflict between Christianity and Communism.)
Carr, E. H. *The Soviet Impact on the Western World.* New York,
The Macmillan Company, 1947. (A useful guide to Russian-
Western relations.)
Dean, V. M. *The United States and Russia.* Cambridge, Harvard
University Press, 1948. (An analysis of the history, present and
prospects of U.S.A.-U.S.S.R. relations.)
Smith, H. K. *The State of Europe.* New York, Alfred A. Knopf,
1949. (A keen analysis of the present situation.)
Smith, W. B. *My Three Years in Moscow.* Philadelphia, J. B. Lip-
pincott Company, 1950. (One of the better of numerous books
which give information about, and insight into, the East-West
struggle from the Western point of view.)

Chapter IV : *Faith and Fear in the Near East*
Addison, J. T. *The Christian Approach to the Moslem.* New York,
Columbia University Press, 1942. (A historical survey of Chris-
tian contacts with Islam.)
Christian Sects of the Near East. New York, American Near East
Association, 1949. (A brief pamphlet guide to the Christian and
Moslem groups in the area.)
Gibb, H. A. R. *Mohammedanism.* New York, Oxford University
Press, 1949.
———. *Modern Trends in Islam.* Chicago, Chicago University Press,
1947. (Two reliable introductions to the subject.)
Hourani, A. H. *Minorities in the Arab World.* London, Oxford
University Press, 1949. (A good introduction to the minority
groups within the Near Eastern countries.)
Islamic Sects of the Near East. (A companion pamphlet to *Christian
Sects of the Near East* listed above.)
Levonian, Lutfi. *Moslem Mentality.* London, George Allen and Un-

win, 1928. (A discussion of the presentation of Christianity to
Moslems.)

The Middle East: A Political and Economic Survey. London, Royal
Institute of International Affairs, 1950. (A handbook on the
current situation in the area.)

The Middle East Journal, a quarterly. Washington, Middle East Institute. (An excellent source for current information and significant articles on all aspects of Near Eastern affairs.)

Speiser, E. A. *The United States and the Near East.* Cambridge,
Harvard University Press, 1950 (revised edition). (Historical
background and detailed survey of the major factors in the current situation in the Near East.)

Wilson, J. C. *The Christian Message to Islam.* New York, Fleming
H. Revell Company, 1950. (The problem of evangelism in Moslem lands.)

Zwemer, S. M. *A Factual Survey of the Moslem.* New York,
Fleming H. Revell Company, 1946. (A thoughtful presentation
of an important subject.)

Chapter V: *Africa in Revolution*

Abundant Life in Changing Africa. New York, Foreign Missions
Conference, Africa Committee, 1946. (Report and papers pre-
sented at the West-Central Africa Regional Conference held at
Leopoldville, July 1946.)

African Affairs, a quarterly. London, Royal African Society. (A
journal of information and a wide variety of articles on African
affairs.)

Hailey, M. H. *An African Survey: A Study of Problems Arising in
Africa South of the Sahara.* 2nd ed. New York, Oxford University Press, 1945. (An important reference work on African affairs.)

Sundkler, Bengt. *Bantu Prophets in South Africa.* London, Lutter-
worth Press, 1948. (The rise of indigenous sects, in part a product
of the interracial situation.)

Chapter VI: *There Are Many Christians in Asia*

Bernstein, David. *The Philippine Story.* New York, Farrar, Straus
& Co., 1947. (An analysis of the background of Philippine independence.)

The Christian Prospect in Eastern Asia. New York, International
Missionary Council, 1950. (Report of the East Asia Conference
held at Bangkok in December 1949 under the joint auspices of
the International Missionary Council and the World Council of
Churches. It faces realistically the present situation and the task
of the Church.)

Foster, John. *Then and Now.* New York, Harper & Brothers, 1942.
(The historic church and the younger churches.)

Furnival, J. S. *Colonial Policy and Practice.* Cambridge, Harvard

University Press, 1948. (A comparative study of Burma and Indonesia.)

Landon, K. P. *Southeast Asia: Crossroad of Religions.* Chicago, University of Chicago Press, 1949. (Cultural transition in an area where religion has molded culture.)

McCune, G. M., and A. L. Grey. *Korea Today.* Cambridge, Harvard University Press, 1950. (Helpful for an understanding of the situation in Korea on the eve of the invasion of South Korea in 1950.)

Mills, L. A., and associates. *The New World of Southeast Asia.* Minneapolis, University of Minnesota Press, 1949. (A group of experts present information on various aspects of the region.)

Chapter VII: *The Agony of China*
Bodde, Derk. *Peking Diary: A Year of Revolution.* New York, Henry Schuman, 1950. (An American expert on China gives firsthand reports of events in Peking during the first year of the new regime.)

Dallin, D. J. *The Rise of Russia in Asia.* New Haven, Yale University Press, 1949.

———. *Soviet Russia and the Far East.* New Haven, Yale University Press, 1948. (This and the preceding title provide an adequate treatment of Russian influence in China and neighboring areas.)

Fairbank, J. K. *The United States and China.* Cambridge, Harvard University Press, 1948. (A reliable description of the general background of the current situation in China.)

——— and others. *Next Step in Asia.* Cambridge, Harvard University Press, 1949. (A sequel to the previous title.)

Winfield, G. F. *China: The Land and the People.* New York, William Sloane, Associates, 1948. (An excellent general introduction to China.)

Chapter VIII: *A Japanese Story*
Aoyoshi, Katsuhisa. *Dr. Masahisa Uemura, A Christian Leader.* Tokyo, Maruzen, n.d. (A biography of Mrs. Uemura's father.)

Kawai, Michi. *My Lantern.* Tokyo, Kyo Bunkwan, 1939. (The autobiography of a Christian leader.)

Kerr, W. C. *Japan Begins Again.* New York, Friendship Press, 1949. (The Christian Church in postwar Japan.)

Reischauer, E. O. *Japan, Past and Present.* New York, Alfred A. Knopf, 1947. (An excellent brief survey.)

———. *The United States and Japan.* Cambridge, Harvard University Press, 1950. (A reliable guide to an understanding of the current situation.)

Sugimoto, E. I. *A Daughter of the Samurai.* Garden City, Doubleday, Page and Company, 1925. (The education and life story of a Christian woman.)

Chapter IX : *India and Pakistan—The Price of Their Freedom*

Nehru, Jawaharlal. *Independence and After: A Collection of Speeches, 1946-1949.* New York, John Day Co., 1950. (The transition from colonial status to independence as reflected in the public addresses of India's political leader.)

————. *Toward Freedom: An Autobiography.* New York, John Day Co., 1941. (Glimpses of world history.)

Philips, C. H. *India.* London, Hutchinson's University Library, 1948. (A brief guide to Indian history.)

Rosinger, L. K. *India and the United States: Political and Economic Relations.* New York, The Macmillan Company, 1950. (An introduction to the relations between India and the United States.)

Spear, T. G. P. *India, Pakistan and the West.* New York, Oxford University Press, 1949. (A useful guide to the present situation.)

Symonds, Richard. *The Making of Pakistan.* London, Faber & Faber, 1950. (The growth of Pakistan from early Moslem settlements to the present Dominion status.)

Chapter X : *Latin America Tomorrow*

Davis, J. M. *The Cuban Church in a Sugar Economy,* 1942. *The Economic Basis of the Evangelical Church in Mexico,* 1941. *The Evangelical Church in the River Plate Republics,* 1943. *How the Church Grows in Brazil,* 1943.
All New York, International Missionary Council. (Studies in the growth and the social and economic adjustment of the Protestant churches in these several regions.)

Herring, H. C. *Good Neighbors.* New Haven, Yale University Press, 1941. (Toward an understanding of the lands and peoples of Latin America.)

Howard, G. P. *Religious Liberty in Latin America?* Philadelphia, Westminster Press, 1944. (Pressure on Protestantism in Latin America.)

Mackay, J. A. *The Other Spanish Christ.* New York, The Macmillan Company, 1933. (A Protestant appraises the religious life and teaching prevalent in Latin America.)

Quintanilla, Luis. *A Latin American Speaks.* New York, The Macmillan Company, 1943. (A comprehensive story of inside Latin America.)

Whitaker, A. P. *The United States and South America.* Cambridge, Harvard University Press, 1948. (A good introduction to the Latin countries and their problems, including their relations with the United States.)

Chapter XI : *Literacy—The Problem and Its Challenge*

Buck, Pearl. *Tell the People.* New York, John Day Co., 1945. (Mass literacy education in China under James Yen.)

Fundamental Education, edited by UNESCO. New York, The Macmillan Company. (The need of illiterates throughout the world.)

Nida, Eugene. *Learning a Foreign Language.* New York, Committee Missionary Personnel of the Foreign Missions Conference of North America, 1950.

North, E. M. *The Book of a Thousand Tongues.* New York, Harper & Brothers, 1939. (The thrilling story of Bible translation and publishing.)

Ure, Ruth. *The Highway of Print.* New York, Friendship Press, 1946. (The program of Christian literature production.)

Chapter XII: *The Decisive Encounter*

Latourette, K. S. *The Christian Outlook.* New York, Harper & Brothers, 1948. (A historian predicts the future course of Christian development.)

———— and W. H. Hogg. *Tomorrow Is Here. New York,* Friendship Press, 1948. (An interpretation of the Whitby Conference of 1947.)

Mackay, J. A. *Christianity on the Frontier.* New York, The Macmillan Company, 1950. (Essays on Christian issues in our time.)

Man's Disorder and God's Design. The First Assembly of the World Council of Churches. New York, Harper & Brothers, 1948. (The Amsterdam Assembly series in one volume.)

Poling, P. N., ed. *God and the Nations.* Garden City, Doubleday & Company, 1950. (Essential factors in the current struggle for the souls of men, interpreted by Vera M. Dean, Harry R. Rudin, Pitirim A. Sorokin, Walter W. Van Kirk and James P. Warburg.)

Stowe, Leland. *While Time Remains.* New York, Alfred A. Knopf, 1946. (An appraisal of the factors responsible for the present situation.)

Warren, M. A. C. *The Truth of the Vision.* London, Canterbury Press, 1948. (A thought-provoking book on the Christian hope.)

Periodicals

Christianity and Crisis
A biweekly journal of Christian opinion, New York. (Excellent reporting and comment on events and trends in Europe and other regions with especial attention to Christian factors.)

The Ecumenical Review
A quarterly, Geneva, published by the World Council of Churches. (A journal interpreting the ecumenical movement.)

The International Review of Missions
A quarterly, Edinburgh, published by the International Missionary Council. (The ecumenical journal of the co-operative missionary enterprise.)

Religion in Life
A Christian quarterly, New York, published by Abingdon-Cokesbury Press.

Theology Today
A quarterly, Princeton, N.J. (The life of man in the light of God.)
World Dominion and the World Today
A bimonthly, London. (An international review of Christian progress.)

Index

Emperor of Japan, 227, 230, 232
Empress of Japan, 238
Europe, Christian vocation in various
occupations, 83; Eastern Churches
have renewed vitality, 89, 90; industrial workers must be reached,
87, 88; interchurch relations, 93, 94;
reconstruction and relief, 85, 86;
refugee problem, 86; survival or renewal, 73-96; theological renewal, 80,
81
Evil, stirred up by holiness, 313
Existentialism, 82

Fairview Evangelical and Reformed
Church of Dayton, Ohio, 51
Faith shared with neighbors, 50, 51
Fascism, 32-35
Federal Council of Churches, 44, 51,
52
Ferris Seminary, 204
Formosa, 223
Fosdick, Harry Emerson, 53
Freedom, proceeds from God's revolu-
tion, 202
Frontier Service, 319

Gandhi, prophet of religious universal-
ism, 249
Goethe, 132
Gold Coast, approaching self-govern-
ment, 133
Goodall, Norman, biographical sketch,
329-330
Good and Evil, the decisive encounter,
308-311
Gospel, power, 278
Granada, Leonardo Dia y, 24
Greece, forces of renewal, 92
Greenfield, Mrs. Constance, 218
Greenfield, Helen, 222
Grew, Joseph, 237, 238
Groundnut scheme, East Africa, 139,
140
Guatemala, see Latin America

Hail, J. B., 204, 205
Hartford Theological Seminary, 207
Hepburn, James C., 205

Hewat, Elizabeth, 222
Hikaru, Shizue, 226
Hinduism, 249, 250
Hiroshima, 230
Holiness, stirs up evil, 313
Home churches, China, 198, 199
Horton, Douglas, 232
Hromadka, Joseph, 24
Hsiang, Foh-Mei, 236
Human personality, mystery, 193
Human rights, United Nations Cove-
nant, 104
Hungary, 17
Hung Hsiu Ch'uen, 179
Hu Shih, 187

Iglehart, Charles, 233
Ilano, Josefa, 236
Illiteracy, statistics, 286, 287; the problem, 286, 287
Imperial University, Japan, 211
India, Brito, 251; Christian education,
253, 254; Christianity's message for
Moslems and Sikhs, 261; Christian
medicine, 254, 255; Christians, 251,
252; Church of South India, 256;
College of Social Service, 255; Communism, 248, 249; early Christianity,
142; education, 245-247; financial condition, 243, 244; government support
of literacy program, 295; Hinduism,
249, 250; industrial progress, 243;
Mahatma Gandhi, 249; Moslems,
250, 251; Mount Kanchenjunga comparable to Mount Sinai, 222; Mudaliar Lakshmanaswami, 254; partition
of, 241; predominantly Hindu, 241;
public health, 245; religious freedom,
247, 252; religious universalism, 249;
Robert de Nobili, 251; Saint Francis
Xavier, 251; Saint Thomas; Sarvepalli Radhakrishnan, 249; Sikhs, 251;
social progress, 242; summary, 262;
the price of freedom, 240-262
Individual responsibility, 314
Indonesia, 163-165; Advanced Theological School in Djakarta, 164; predominantly Moslem, 164
"In God We Trust," 42